NEW CALIFORNIA WRITING

2011

NEW CALIFORNIA WRITING

2011

Edited by Gayle Wattawa

Introduction by Malcolm Margolin

HEYDAY, BERKELEY, CALIFORNIA

This book was made possible in part by generous support from the California Council for the Humanities and the Bay Tree Fund.

Library of Congress Cataloging-in-Publication Data

New California writing 2011 / edited by Gayle Wattawa; introduction by Malcolm Margolin.
p. cm. — (New California writing)
ISBN 978-1-59714-156-7 (pbk. : alk. paper)
1. California—Literary collections. 2. American literature—California. 3. American literature—21st century. I. Wattawa, Gayle.
PS571.C2N48 2011
810.8'09794—dc22 2010051151

Cover Design: Lorraine Rath
Interior Design/Typesetting: Leigh McLellan Design
Printing and Binding: Thomson-Shore, Dexter, MI

Orders, inquiries, and correspondence should be addressed to:

Heyday
P.O. Box 9145, Berkeley, CA 94709
(510) 549-3564, Fax (510) 549-1889
www.heydaybooks.com

10 9 8 7 6 5 4 3 2 1

green press INITIATIVE

Heyday is committed to preserving ancient forests and natural resources. We elected to print this title on 30% post consumer recycled paper, processed chlorine free. As a result, for this printing, we have saved:

22 Trees (40' tall and 6-8" diameter)
7 Million BTUs of Total Energy
2,106 Pounds of Greenhouse Gases
10,145 Gallons of Wastewater
616 Pounds of Solid Waste

Heyday made this paper choice because our printer, Thomson-Shore, Inc., is a member of Green Press Initiative, a nonprofit program dedicated to supporting authors, publishers, and suppliers in their efforts to reduce their use of fiber obtained from endangered forests.

For more information, visit www.greenpressinitiative.org

Environmental impact estimates were made using the Environmental Defense Paper Calculator. For more information visit: www.papercalculator.org.

CONTENTS

ACKNOWLEDGMENTS

MY THANKS TO the California Council for the Humanities for their generous support of this collection. To all of the authors who sent their writing for consideration: my deepest appreciation. This collection could easily have been twice as long, and I hope that everyone will continue to submit material for future editions. For their helpful and generous advice, suggestions, support, and feedback, I am particularly grateful to William Deverell, Nancy Hom, David Isaacson, Susan Ives, William Justice, Bruce Kelley, Andrew Lam, Ralph Lewin, David Loeb, Malcolm Margolin, Michael Murphy, Richard Rodriguez, Andrew Tonkovich, and George Young.

INTRODUCTION

Malcolm Margolin

CALIFORNIA WAS INVENTED on a sunny fall day in 1849. A hastily assembled group of men, delegates to the state's first constitutional convention, crowded into the second floor of a two-story stone building in Monterey. They unrolled maps on a large wooden table and went to work setting the boundaries of the state-to-be. They drew lines, redrew lines, adjusted the lines they'd redrawn, then readjusted those lines. They argued with increasing passion, unfazed by the fact that they were fighting over areas none of them had ever visited. In a moment of premature decisiveness the Boundary Committee, with assertive strokes of the pen, positioned California's eastern boundary in what is now New Mexico. What a great idea! A reporter described what followed: "A dozen members jumped up, speaking and shouting in the most confused and disorderly manner. Some rushed out of the room; others moved an adjournment; others again protested they would sign no constitution embodying such a provision." In response to what the reporter characterized as "tumult," new lines were drawn, closer to the east slope of the Sierra. Voilà! California had now settled into the shape we all know so well. But do these boundaries make any sense whatsoever? Do they encompass a definable ecological or cultural area? Of course not, but who cares? The delegation had crossed "set the boundaries" off their to-do list and moved on to another momentous matter of governance: the design of the "Great Seal of the State."

California is a construct of the human imagination. Without an inherent physical or cultural coherence to define it, it has long served as the world's largest Rorschach test. Before statehood there were

Spanish explorers in caravels seeking the fabled land of El Dorado, Franciscan monks driven by dreams of service to God and the joys of martyrdom, and of course that unprecedented rush of gold seekers whose greed impelled them across the Sierra in Conestoga wagons or up the coast in whatever excuse for a boat would carry them. In later years, Asian immigrants crowded onto steamships to search out Gold Mountain, Midwesterners boarded trains for the land of orange groves, Okies piled into jalopies, hippies wafted here in VW buses, Latinos crossed the border legally or illegally. From everywhere people came to a California whose only boundaries were the human imagination.

In 2011 California is still a land of myth, but in these difficult times the myth has soured. What we hear (and indeed feel) today goes something like this. California is a fallen Eden. Where there were once paradise and self-fulfilling optimism, today we have dysfunction and despair. California can't do anything right anymore. The land of innovation can't pass a budget, keep its parks open, educate its young, provide families with homes, take care of its sick and elderly, or keep its young out of jail. "Paradise Lost" shows up repeatedly as a headline for articles in the national press. Schadenfreude has become California's biggest export.

Sadly, the current myth seems to have more than a kernel of truth. While the image of California's past as paradise is debatable—ask an Indian, a farmworker, a Japanese American who was interned during the war, or an inner city African American what their experiences in "paradise" have been—there is no doubt that California is in deep trouble. We see ourselves as living in an era of decay, and the land of tomorrow has now become the land of yesterday. Although new for California, this attitude is hardly new in the world at large. There have been other periods in history when people saw their world unraveling.

"Times are bad," wrote the Roman statesman Cicero, and as evidence of how bad things were, he added "and everyone is writing a book."

Is it my imagination, or do bad times produce great writing? In an era such as this, the self-justifying clichés and smug certainties that characterize periods of prosperity ring hollow. One senses, at least among thoughtful people, a willingness to question, to probe, to invent new ways of seeing things, to revisit the past with fresh eyes, to create new dreams. We are indeed, in the words of the purported Chinese curse, living in interesting times; let us turn our attention to one of the few benefits that "interesting times" bestow on us, the emergence of a probing, funny, thought-provoking, and courageous body of literature.

The assembling, winnowing, selection, and arrangement of material for *New California Writing 2011* took more time and involved more thought than the creation of California itself. The idea originated with George Young, Heyday's resident sage, who for years has urged us to collect writings about California for an annual anthology along the lines of Houghton Mifflin's Best American series or Algonquin's New Stories from the South. Gayle Wattawa, Heyday's acquisitions editor, took on the project and in addition to searching for material herself, she put out a call to Heyday's friends, colleagues, and authors for suggestions. Material came pouring in, and as characterizes our era, it came from a number of sources: small literary magazines, some long established and others brand new; book publishers large and small, corporate and independent; blogs; big-city newspapers and online journals; even a commencement speech. It came from writers all over the state, established and emerging, old and young, of differing ethnicities and writing in various genres. Over many months stories, essays, and poems arranged themselves in ever-shifting, carefully labeled stacks on Gayle's desk. After much reading and rereading, sorting and resorting, a final selection was made—each piece in genuine, emotional dialogue with tough questions, each piece pulsating with literary energy, the whole even greater than the sum of its parts.

Everyone at Heyday is thrilled with this book. I find myself reading passages aloud to visitors who range from heads of cultural institutions to the UPS driver. I hope you enjoy the selection, and I hope it introduces you to writers and publishers you never heard of but would like to know better. This is great literature, and great literature, in the words of Shelley, "lifts the veil from the hidden beauty of the world." The world is certainly more alive, intense, and interesting when seen through the eyes of these writers, but that's not the only veil this collection lifts. It also exposes the beauty (too often hidden) of the human imagination—our capacity to challenge demons, confront evil, wonder at miracles, laugh at tragedy, to clown and to mourn, to sing in celebration and shout in outrage. California, in the often quoted words of Wallace Stegner, is like America, only more so. After you read this collection I hope you will conclude that the best of California literature is like the best of American literature, only more so.

NORMAL TIME

Michael Chabon

WE'VE HAD A run of crazy stuff going on around here lately, culminating (for the moment) with global economic collapse and my mother-in-law's suffering an injury that looks as if it may permanently alter the contour and quality of her life, as well as the whole family's—a pair of calamities that followed on a series of unpleasant surprises, diagnoses, minor crises, the dog undergoing a "spinal stroke," professional setbacks, sorrows in the second grade, the loss or destruction of many objects of value, a brutal twenty-month-long presidential campaign, and all the usual, unusual alarums and disruptions that result when six people and a Bernese mountain dog, requiring various mental, emotional, and physical accommodations, therapies, and treatments, conduct an ongoing experiment in measuring mutual interference in one another's reality distortion fields by sharing a house in Berkeley, California, a place that may, at any moment—which will, given the way things have been going lately—be destroyed by a massive once-a-millennium earthquake, or by a raging October wildfire, or by the fire that immediately follows the earthquake. And when I say *lately*, I'm using the term very loosely. This shit has been going on around here for years.

The thing is, we are six lucky people (and a dog), and all our needs and desires are amply met. We have set up the household to run smoothly when possible and to recover quickly when smooth is not an option. The children do their chores and their homework, the adults our work as spouses, parents, and writers, and if you took a sample of any random hour any day, if you employed some human calculus to arrest our progress, to ascertain our state at any given instant, you would find contentment with one another's company, love and respect, a fruitful exchange of ideas, compulsive storytelling, joking around, even the odd outbreak of peace and quiet. But since this thing with my poor mother-in-law (broken femur, shattered wrist), I've been sitting here trying to figure out how long it has been since the days around here have been normal. Steady. Routine. Productive. Neither beset nor fraught nor teetering on some brink of disaster, free of emergency and crisis. I spend a lot of time thinking about, wishing for, working to arrange and to render inevitable, the return to our lives of Normal Time. And yet in trying to work my way back to the last golden era, I find myself casting my memory so far that the exercise begins to call into the question the very idea—an idea, by the way, that forms the basis of my understanding of our family life, here on our notional seam between the fault line and the burn zone—that there has ever been such a time. It turns out that the whole thing may be a delusion.

Like everyone—I hope—I suffer from a number of delusions, many of them apparently ineradicable. There are the geographical delusions. When I am in Pittsburgh or Paris, for example, I can never prevent myself from thinking of the point where the Allegheny, Monongahela, and Ohio conjoin as facing eastward, or of the Left Bank as extending to the north of Notre-Dame. Most of my delusions of longest standing have to do (such is my legacy as a human being) with the acuity of my judgment, of my memory, and of my insight into the hearts of others. But the worst and most wondrous of the delusions that plague me tend to take the form, like this idea of Normal Time, of vague but unquestioned certainties about the nature and course of my life.

Here's an example: I am forty-five years old. By even the most conservative estimate, it has been nearly a quarter of a century since I climbed eagerly aboard this one-way rocket to Death in Adulthood and left the planet of my childhood forever in my starry wake. I know this. My grandparents, my boyhood bedroom furniture, a miniature schnauzer of admirable character named Fritz, the dazed and goofy splendor of bicentennial America: I will never see any of those or a million other things again. And yet always lurking somewhere in the back of my mind is the unshakable, even foundational knowledge—for which *certainty* is too conscious a term—that at some unspecified future date, by unspecified means, I will return to those people and to those locales. That I am going back.

No, that's false. The delusion is not really that I believe or trust that I will be returning one day to the planet of childhood; it's that the world I left behind so long ago is still there, somewhere, to be returned to; that it continues to exist, sideburns, Evel Knievel, Spiro T. Agnew, and all, like some alternate time line Krypton that never exploded, just on the other side of the phantom-zone barrier that any determined superman would know how to pierce. When I watch a film or a television show from the period and see again the workingmen wearing short-sleeved shirts with neckties, or the great wide slabs of Detroit automobiles, or the blue mailboxes with the red tops, or when I happen to hear from some random radio the DeFranco Family singing "Heartbeat (It's a Love Beat)," I do not think merely, *Oh, that's right, I remember that* or the more pathetic *I wish I could go back there again.* What I feel is something more like gratitude, a sense of relief, the way you feel when you wake from a dream in which your beloved has died, and the world is grief and winter, and then you find her warm and snoring in the bed beside you.

But even that delusion pales beside this mad hankering, this utopian or millenarian yearning for the coming days of Normal Time, of time to spare, of time in plenty. Time not just for work and reflection and unhurried lovemaking but for all kinds of fine and tiny things. Time to learn German. Time to print out the digital photos and reorganize the albums. Time to lavish on my younger children as I seem to have lavished it on their older siblings (though back then I thought there was never enough time for anything). Time for regular lunches with my mother. Time to get deep into a baseball season again, to linger over the box scores in the morning, to watch a meaningless game between teams I don't care about, just out of fondness for the game. Time to write the short stories I used to fling like Frisbees out into the blue, the libretto for an opera of *The Long Goodbye*, an annotated version of my failed, never-completed novel *Fountain City*. Time simply to stretch out, to play with, to dandle and dilate and waste with my children and my wife.

Instead it's just, as Arnold Toynbee or Henry Ford or Dr. McCoy used to say of history, one damn thing after another, and often several damn things at the same time, overlapping swaths of color on the digital calendar, conflicts and cancellations, two tasks half-done badly where one might have been pulled off in style. There is never, in the words of Irish poet Tom Paulin, any "long lulled pause / before history happens." Only days after my wife and I guided our last baby into kindergarten, we began preparing in earnest to send our half-grown woman off to high school next fall; in the interval, the stock market crashed and my mother-in-law fell down a flight of stairs. There is no Normal Time, or rather, this is it, with all its accidents and discontinuities. With a breathtaking sequence, your last child leaves home, gets married, has children, and then you fall and break your leg, and the next thing you know, you're approaching the point at which space curves back on itself or doesn't. The end, unless the end, too, is a delusion. After that, either way, there is no time at all, and you're never going back again.

FATHER CLOSE, FATHER FAR

Dagoberto Gilb

THE ONLY MEMORY I have of my father in what was my home was him leaving it. I remember the event not by its amount of time—I don't know whether it took five minutes or some hours—and not by some emotional, psychologically clichéd effect. It imprinted because I knew I was supposed to care, and I didn't. I realized that he was saying goodbye, that he was leaving the house. What was strange for me was that he was there at all. His presence in the house was where my attention focused, because up to that moment, I wasn't even aware of his existence. I can say, chemically testing the memory now, that I even grasped then the sentimental importance of it. That might only be because my mother was hovering anxiously and I picked up on it. He said something. I doubt it was much. I'm sure it was something reassuring in some gruff sort of way—though "gruff" might be superimposing now. I do remember it was supposed to mean something, I could tell. It just didn't to me. I don't know if that says he hadn't yet lodged himself in some deep psychic part of my life, or ever would, whether he should have, or could have, whether anyone my age then would have acted better or worse or the same, whether it reflects more what is my own nature. But there it is, primally established. I couldn't have been much past three years old, tops.

My father became a distant mythical figure, more force than man. Though nothing Old Testament, he was what my mother would use as a threat of wrath and punishment. Not that it had altered any wildness I was being criticized for, and in a short time I would learn this was only a feint, easily dismissed. He was a little old-style to me—I would make visits like on three days a year, which were really only a few hours to have to tolerate—but that could easily have been only in contrast to my mother, who was congenitally young in fashion and behavior. I did know a couple of things about him that made him uniquely strong and tough to me: one, that he'd been a Marine sergeant in World War II, a scout in the Pacific Islands advanced out to locate Japanese camps, and, two, that he'd quit going to school at thirteen to work and, except for the time in the military, he'd never stopped. That became forty-nine years of employment, from 5:30 a.m. to 5:30 p.m., six days a week, until he was laid off.

Where he worked was at an industrial laundry—what he called "the plant"—in downtown Los Angeles, near the corner of Washington and Vermont. My mother had grown up next door to it with her mother, my grandmother, who died when my mom was a teenager; they lived in what in Spanish would be considered *la casa chica* of one of the two owners of the laundry where my father worked. That is to say, my grandmother was his mistress and not his wife.

I was thirteen the summer I started working there too. I was excited about it because I wanted to have money, even if I was scared and intimidated the first days I was there. I had to be moving fast by six in the morning, and I had to work beside full-grown men. I was also getting paid the same as them, and though my father didn't say much to me, he told me to never tell them what I made, never show anyone my paycheck. There were basically five large areas to work: sorting, washing, folding, sewing, and loading. I was put in the sorting room in the beginning, where cloth sacks of soiled laundry would be dumped on the cement floor, gathered around, and sorted out into wooden bins with wheels. If it was from a hotel, it was sheets and pillowcases. Restaurants had napkins and tablecloths and grease rags and aprons. The big jobs were hospitals, with sheets, pillowcases, and surgical greens of all kinds, often caked or gelatined with blood. My first days I learned where maggots grew and how to get used to the hot stink of all classes of rot. Most of the sorting-room men—there were no women on this floor, and no white people whatsoever—were from Mexico, but also a few from Central American countries, and a third were black dudes, a couple of whom at first scared the shit out of me—one by his massive size, the other his konked, do-ragged hair—but who I came to like, just as I grew to not be the least uncomfortable around the most flamboyant gay Mexican I've never seen the likes of since. When he walked from one end of the room to, say, the toilet, the whole crew, plus or minus thirty men, whistled and hooted as he swished with such fun, calypso exaggeration, grinning like he was on his own runway, modeling the tightest pedal pushers.

There were eight hours a day, six days a week, for loud talk and loud laughter, crazy stories of petty and felony crime, jail and prison, scams and deals, virility and fertility, stupors and raging highs, gossip and slanders, and sometimes there'd even be singing, solos and group harmonies. And so the day would pass, not much like how people talk the bad of having to have a fucking job, once you overlook the part that it was minimum wage, until a guy near one of the garage-size doorways would make those Mexican chirps to warn us *he* was nearby or coming through: *he* being the boss, the floor super, that is, my dad. Then it would get quiet and go all business. He would enter, a fast and muscular walk, through one doorway and follow a looping path to the other doorway, eyes like a reptile, and be gone. Maybe a couple of times he stopped and talked to a foreman. You didn't even hear his voice, and you knew it was nothing but business. And so, at the job, what I knew of him was still as a mythical creature, more force than human being, the one who brought the checks on Thursday, who once in a while would bring a second, last check on Friday if he wasn't happy about some employee whose time had come. Though I was sure the men thought otherwise, I knew as little about him, personally or otherwise, as they did. It's true that before the morning whistle and after the end-of-the-day one, if I wanted to, I could go behind the metal countertop that divided the path—with the time clock and the slotted racks on either side—to the plant's interior, and I could even sit in the wooden swivel chairs by the rolltop desk. I had seen things he did that the others couldn't—watching the unemployed coming in asking for work, him telling most of them *no hay nada hoy* or the like, except the rare time when, for reasons mysterious and random to me, he'd have a job not moments after he'd said no to someone else, telling this man or that woman to be there in the morning. He was the boss.

I loved that I had my own money, and I worked my two summers of junior high until, in high school, after I quit football and track (could not bear the coaches yelling), I also started working four hours after school and all day on Saturday, taking a bus until I could drive myself. I lived with my mom and all her melodramas, while my father I only knew bossing at the plant. I'd been moved from the sorting room to the [illegible] bigger floor, where all the mangles steamed, dried, and pressed the sheets and tablecloths and napkins, where mostly women, around seventy-five of them, worked. Hot as it was all the time, I liked it there. One woman, Felipa, had been at the plant a few years longer than my dad, and her partner, María, only a few years less, and they, like many, even knew my mom. People always saved me the best tacos ever made, which, rolled up and wrapped in foil, they'd heat up near the gas flames at the back of the giant industrial dryers. I was almost seventeen when, one day, my father came up to me and pulled me aside and suggested my hair was too long. I felt like I was against a wall. Up to that point, we'd never had one intimate conversation, disagreeable or pleasant, not even when I had to visit him at his home one of those nights a year I was expected to. Nothing much more than please pass the mustard, and I like the Dodgers. All else, if anything, was listening, tolerating, waiting to go home. I did not think my hair was too long, and really it wasn't, and what did it have to do with him, anyway? But I didn't say so. I nodded my head, and we went back to our work. A day or two later I called in, lied and told him I found a new job, closer to home, and said thanks.

I really didn't see my father much from then, even began disregarding the assumed obligatories (Christmas Eve, his birthday), until many years later. I'd moved north of L.A. for college and moved to El Paso and then back again, and eventually had my own family: I thought it would be good for my sons to meet these grandparents too—I myself hadn't known any. In my non-adult years, I believed I had descended from a rich man. That was only because when I visited him those days,

I surmised that, not just for occasions but every single day, his wife and their daughter and he ate at a dinner table, and there might even be bowls with vegetables, like peas and green beans and carrots, even if they did come out of a can—I considered this the praxis of the rich. Also, he always drove a Cadillac, which maybe he got new, I didn't know. I bought into that image like all dumb people who don't know better. It was his pretense, what he wanted projected. Rich people did drive Cadillacs, in fact, and from the streets, nobody really could know otherwise, especially workers at the laundry, who, like me, saw him with wheels like the owners. They drove Cadillacs too, though maybe they were Lincolns, until finally they rolled in a Mercedes.

When he died, I didn't expect anything. Aside from the fact that he didn't really know me or particularly like me or how I lived or turned out, or that we weren't close whatsoever, even if there was something of his I should have had, a memento say, I didn't think of that, and even now wouldn't think it was necessary. I mean that in the kindest way, too. I understood the relationship. Besides, he had a wife. When he married her, she was around twenty-three, and he was almost fifty. She'd come to L.A. from Memphis, was even a second cousin to Elvis Presley (her mom a Presley). Twenty-five years later she was much the same as she was then, with ridiculously long red polished fingernails, which paralleled the thin, fragile tall she was. She was always drinking a Coke with a bendable straw, smoking Virginia Slims, digesting prescription pain pills—while at the wheel she tore it up, every ride a race she won. What she drove just before his death was an older Datsun sedan. After he'd been laid off, my father studied for and earned a commercial real estate agent's license. But over the next ten years he'd only sold one significant piece of property, and with his cut, probably expecting more to come, he went in all cash for a new Eldorado, banking maybe $2000 that remained. Nothing more came.

Now his wife had the very low-mileage Cadillac, and she was selling the Datsun. Our best car was a Chevy Nova near its end. As unimpressive as her Datsun was, it was much better than it. I have to admit that the word *family* occurred to me then, though more like a card played in a board game. Like an earnest word they used on TV shows. It was a word that I only applied to my own wife and children, nothing beyond. If I had family like others talked about it, this was maybe my mom, and she was married to someone, and even that was, to me, about her life. I'd never asked for anything from my father ever. Not a loan, nothing. I wouldn't have considered him if I'd ever thought I needed one—not to mention that the answer would've been no. Besides, I didn't even know parents were expected to help, for example, with college. I didn't know some did until I transferred to a university as a junior and learned it was common. I was used to finding jobs and working, making my own money. But I saw this as a unique circumstance. My father's wife was going to sell the Datsun, and it wasn't worth so much. I sincerely don't know why, but it strained me to ask. I was a father with two young sons, working construction, and I had sinful pride, but we could use a small break. That she hesitated caught me unexpectedly. It was that somebody else wanted to buy it from her. I told her I'd pay whatever the best offer was. Seemed fair, I meant it, so how could she say no to that? It was, after all, because she was now a widow with a shiny Eldorado, and a house I think was all mortgage free, and everything else, from him. And I'd pay her exactly the same amount as anybody would, right?

I didn't like it very much when she didn't sell it to me, though I didn't make a point of telling her. I also didn't like my brief flu of bitterness. Not shaking it off meant I wanted what I never felt offered, never really saw except as a pretense on a Christmas Eve or a birthday dinner over some overcooked hamburgers. What it confirmed was what I already believed from the beginning—it was the inheritance from my father I'd grown up with. So I came around to seeing how her selling it to a boy across the street from her was the right ending. She wanted to help him out because he was going to UCLA soon, and he needed the car. And what he would do in return was drag out to the curb her one or two plastic trash cans every week. Because she did not like to do that. It was, probably, something my father'd always done. And from then on, it was this neighbor boy, every week, for many years too, which was particularly valuable as she herself got too frail, so it really worked out for her, I bet more than she could've expected.

I could never imagine growing up in a house with a man like my father, his culture, his world. Never, and never one moment wanted to. Could not for the life of me see how he and my mother would have survived two dates. But I am so grateful that he gave me a job when I was thirteen. That was it. It's who I am still, so I do think of him, and I do say thank you to him for that, even if it doesn't seem much like what you're supposed to be saying.

After I drunkenly crashed my marriage into a tree, there were several years of recovery time when I didn't know if I would receive, least of all deserve, the forgiveness of my sons. I wanted them to support their mom at whatever trade-off cost to me, and, willed by me and or slammed into me, I accepted its price. Though I clung to a hope, I feared I would forever lose not just the future with them, but that they'd tear up our memories like photos from a family album. The most happiness I had ever known were in these years of my life with my wife, my boys, us—our family, and my only family ever. I was so close to my sons. What I had loved about their mom more than all else about her was that from the moment of each of their births, I was less important to her than they were. Second place to one and to both. And that was not just right to me, but good, as in Right and Good, as in what nature commands instinctually. I too loved them, a love that fumbles around for words. More love, I would pronounce, than Abraham's, because I would have defied God's request to sacrifice Isaac if he were one of my boys. Again, I don't know how much that is my own psychic essence or is a consequence of my own childhood experience, if it is cultural or a creation, how specific or common. They were my favorite toys and pets and games, shows and sports, my best friends and my little brothers but best of all my sons. We watched TV when or if we wanted to, like sneaking, and threw tennis balls against the living room walls in the house to play keep-away, moving furniture to make space. Outdoors I hit baseballs to them and bounce-passed for them to drive to the hoop. I coached teams for nine years until I had to watch them from the stands. I bought them books they read and wouldn't ever and forced them into museums they yawned in, and their childhood was like having mine beside theirs and nothing whatever like what I'd known at their age.

When my oldest son graduated from the University of Texas, his first job with his new bachelor's degree in journalism was a paid internship for a newspaper in Jackson, Tennessee. I was proud of him, of course, but I was thrilled like a girl getting her first date when he asked me to drive there with him for his move. And I played it cool like a girl on a date, too. As soon as we were in his old Honda together, it was unavoidably more than only an adventure for me. Even though we happened to live near one another in Austin, where I was now employed, those were his college years, and, though worried all the time like any parent, I tried to let him have his father-free college years. Now the car seats were way too close together, and neither of us had traveled this kind of driving trip to The South, and we had all the usual route conversations about maps and gas and road food. We tried to keep pace with the clutter of what seemed like the no speed limit of I-35, until we skirted the even more crazed Dallas traffic, and cruise-controlled I-30 with its trailers and rigs and satellite dishes and real thing country kitchens, passing the cities and streets that were Springs and Dales. We side-tracked to Hope, Arkansas. I liked President Clinton. My son was obsessed with Bill Clinton the way others might be with Elvis. His birth home was much more modest than you would expect, even painted and cleaned up as it obviously was. With its new roof and new siding, it still wouldn't be one of the most desired houses in the definitely not rich neighborhood, since it was right against the railroad tracks too. And nobody but us was there to see it. My son wanted pictures and smiled as if he'd found gold. Soon we were in Little Rock and did a repeat at the Arkansas State Capitol and then the Governor's Mansion. We were alone there too. I took photos of him at the back gates, the ones where patrolmen were said to drive scandalous women in to visit our future president, or back from, whatever that bad was. My son laughed like he was thirteen again, but when I took the photo, he was back on board, his pose as adult as a cabinet appointment.

Memphis's Pyramid in sight, we crossed the Mississippi and not a few hours later we were in Jackson and eating at the restaurant of Carl Perkins, singer-songwriter of "Blue Suede Shoes," where I put it together that my son was a little nervous. I'd been nervous too, bitchy particularly along the way about him driving I-40 with one hand and casually wanting to change lanes in front of tightly spaced caravans of gleaming eighteen-wheelers passing us like they were on the German autobahn. That is, in a foreign country. Which we were, which is where he was going to be living for a while. This was not like our homeland in El Paso, wouldn't seem to be a Mexican or Chicano or a word like it and had never been. They even had gravy that was white. I remembered being his age—I'd never done or had the qualifications for anything close to this. I remembered how thrilled I was that he'd wanted me along. We visited his new job and we got a motel room and, when he wanted to go off alone, that seemed understandable. Probably it was my forehead that scrolled a *drive carefully!* message, because when he came back, apologizing for smashing into the back of a car at an odd intersection, it was as much him pre-emptively owning up to some shitty *I told you so*. No, I said, it happens, and to anyone, and no biggie if the other car was fine. No damage there, and the Honda lost some meaningless trim, and we got to shop for a new headlight at the Walmart and install that.

Realizing that it was through these incidents that you learn a town, it occurred to me that we should get a map. It was a small town, and why not see as much of it as we could before he started? Lay it out, learn a few streets so on assignments he'd feel less lost. He liked this as a practical idea, as a smart, educated guy, not as a son agreeing with a father. And that's when I had a moment: like when he was born, my first, it was my own rite of passage, a move from one stage of life to another. Looking over the map, the big streets, the main drags, it was as though I was examining a metaphorical X-ray. No matter what I could guess, there was too much more I would never know as well as he would very soon. As to Jackson, we figured it was roughly five long north-souths and three long east-wests, and we drove them: here's the industrial area, here's the poorest and black, here's only rural, while this over here it's middle class, and up there's probably rich, here's the old center, here's where all the chain stores are. It was a good day, and the next I was getting on a bus, leaving him there a grown young man, my son who I knew could take care of himself. How do you describe this saddest happiness of feeling your baby boy hug you goodbye as a grown man?

Several years later it was a drive with my younger son, who had graduated from Stanford. We came out of El Paso and through the southern New Mexico desert, the mountain silhouettes of dead Indians, the mystical glyph of electrical poles, the train hauntingly silent at the near distance beside us, the peels of dead tires on the highway, the sky as blue as the best jewel. We bogged down in the construction that is the expanding Tucson and headed north at Phoenix, stopping for some luxury Thai noodles in the high-end theme shopping mall that is Sedona, and to stare into the stunning pit of the Grand Canyon until we finally took aim: this son was wanting to go to Los Angeles. He wanted to see, taking notes and photos, where he had lived his first three years and where I grew up too.

Where he was born there was only change for the better—the Silverlake area was even hipper than when we lived there, even if the weirdo On Club was gone (it'd been gone since before we left, transformed into a transvestite hang, and that was gone too). The Cuban coffee joint was still there, and Los Globos nightclub too. The duplex we rented from his conception to his birth, the one overlooking Sunset Boulevard, was more tropically lush than when we were there, palm leaves shading the windows and doors. The cracks in the walkways of the apartment building in East Hollywood, where he lived next, were no longer where parsley was cultivated by the elderly Armenian couple, but the neutered ceramic boy in the dry fountain had passed the days like he was in Rome. We went to where I grew up, where Los Angeles Southwest College is now, on the land we called The Dips and where I once found a dead body and knifed a boy. Drove him to the shopping mall on Crenshaw where that dumpy market now there was once called Food Giant and where that shabby drugstore really had the best scoops of ice cream. Showed him a bicycle route up Imperial that took us to the Watts Towers. We cruised over to Long Beach Boulevard, which has almost gone completely Sinoloa, and on Tweedy, the street that used to be for jacked-up Chevys or lowered Plymouths, we stopped for the best caldos de pollo and mariscos you could find on this side of the border—at least, the biggest bowls.

It was time past in time now. Just the other day, a few years ago, in the past when my mother was young and too alive, wasn't dead, when I was younger than him, all this invisibly alive still in what is me. My son clicking photos, hearing the stories, seeing what I saw—this seeing, a mind-altering inhalation of father and son musks, actual or psychic, as much me as my memory of him is still as the smallest smiling baby, the memory not real and more than real, in a haze of symbol and myth, all the bright colors to faded inevitable death, memory even when it's right there in front of you—in front of him. A son, precocious here too, who wants to know, who is taking notes to crack what is to all of us the source of this secret, the ontological paradox, we all have to live.

But here was a mystery that was revealed: I took him to that industrial laundry, the brick-veneered building my dad called the plant. Still so much as it was in my time and I think in my father's too—not only memory. Sure, an older doorway, its old paint shedding, might be sealed and padlocked, and a window is now plywooded over, near the large work table where all the prettiest women once folded special orders. But there still is that business sign, painted in black-and-white on the red brick in the Forties or Fifties, maybe even the Thirties, too high up, though faded some, no reason to sandblast off. My son and I stopped and looked inside because the aluminum roll-up door was half open to let some of the hot air out, the cooler outside air in. The laundry carts with wheels were still around; the cloth bags of laundry now hung by hooks to automated guided tracks on the ceiling that eliminated probably ninety percent of those long-ago jobs, including my dad's. We walked that same old cement sidewalk outside and came to the wide-open gate where the delivery trucks were parked and loaded. New trucks, new colors, new company name. There was a company uniformed man standing in the yard by a truck backed into the loading dock. I started talking to him from a distance, going toward him, my son following. He was Mexican, in his thirties. In Spanish, I told him how my father used to be the floor boss, the super, for forty-nine years. I told him how when he worked here, when I worked here too, the truck drivers were always white guys, and the Mexicanos were hidden inside. Everybody here's Mexican now, he laughed.

I looked inside the warehouse, and then back at my son. All they could do was kick us out. We went in. Through the stockroom of orders not yet in the trucks, the reserve racks of towels and linen, past that and up the ramp to the folding room, where I'd worked years until I didn't. I'd remembered it as you would your first bedroom, as huge, even if it were really the width of a closet. Not a closet: it was at least half the size of what my memory preserved it as—big, spacious. And there were those mangles. The very ones, not replaced in all these years. They looked old when I was young. Since my first visits, they had been the most impressive machines on the floor, steam wafting off their column-sized rollers. It was always so hard to explain what they were to anyone. To my son. Only now he was standing there, seeing what I'd seen since as far back as my memory could take me, even taking pictures. These were the machines that Felipa and María fed sheets forty hours and a half day on Saturday for double the years I'd been alive, each. There were three other mangles in the space, cooking the room more, raising the heat to at least twenty degrees more than whatever was outside. One always had a line of women in front of a trough of napkins feeding damp towels. The others were pillowcases, and tablecloths, all these items that had to be pressed and dried. And, from the other side, folded, and stacked, and bundled. More women on the other side, lots more women then. But that no more. Instead, it was a feeding machine, and in front of it, another machine that fed the feeding one. And behind, machines that took the still-hot, ironed piece, another that folded it, and then, finally, a woman who put it on the stack.

Some things aren't understood well enough through words. Like most of the young in these United States now, my son had never been inside a factory. Intellectually, I knew that. But seeing that machine, operating, pushing out its hot, pressed product, was like...seeing that very machine. Knowing exactly what it was in its actual existence. So much that can be related can only be pointed to from a distance. An edge of it maybe, a corner. Its front. Like a memory, like a metaphor, the hope is that by glimpsing a part, a surface, the whole can be intuited. It just isn't always enough, and sometimes there has to be all of something, an entirety, to let through what time and space make impossible.

Maybe twenty-five feet from the door to the office, which would be the entrance and exit path to and from the time-clock, hung a wooden-handled chain, painted black, that reached to whatever was way higher up above. That whistle was what made my father the most powerful man on the job. He pulled it in the morning, breaks, lunch, and longest, I'm pretty sure, for quitting time. Nothing I can remember him doing seemed to exercise more his job's authority and the pleasure that came with it. One time, I cannot even guess how old I might have been, he held me in the air. And I pulled it.

BOY CLEANING TROUT

Albert Garcia

HIS FATHER taught him
the belly, the only white part,
should give with the tip of his knife,
so he keeps pushing until its soft flesh splits
and the blade slides easily
up between fins to the head.

Just down riffle, his father watches
the boy spreading it open. The meat
should be his first concern: orange-red
it's native, white
it's fed in a hatchery—no taste.
He looks for its sex,
a pearly skein of roe the color of cantaloupe
or a thin thread of sperm
tucked back against its spine.

He works his fingers
under the cool entrails, pulls hard,
tosses all but the white tube,
the gut, into the stream. This
he squeezes between finger and thumb
to see a gray mash,
the fish's last meal of mayflies.

His knuckles white-red with cold, he rubs
the cavity thoroughly, rinses, then hooks
the burgundy feathers hidden
under shining flaps of its head.
His father taught him long ago
that these take oxygen from water,
that all living things need oxygen
He notices the little cloud escaping his lips
and remembers the fish's mouth
opening and closing, gills
lifting in what looked like exhaustion
but could have been pain.

FROM *BLOOD STRANGERS*

Katherine A. Briccetti

BLUEPRINTS

I AM DRAWN TO fathers and sons because my two boys were conceived with the sperm of a stranger. When people refer to Benjamin and Daniel's "father," I correct them. "The donor," I say, not meaning to be rude, but needing to make the distinction. "No dad in this family."

In the spring of 2005, my younger son Daniel and I waited in the San Francisco airport to board a plane to Kentucky to visit my own father, a man I hardly knew, a man whom I had lost and then found again. Now we visited every few years, trying to make up for lost time, trying to settle into our adult relationship, a relationship that defied easy definition.

Standing at the gate with my ten-year-old, I found myself staring at a teenage boy and a man ahead of us, the boy hunched over an electronic game, the father resting his arm across his son's shoulder, fingers grazing his neck. Not taking my eyes off the teenager, I smoothed my boy's silky hair, watching the future my sons would not have. The future I once believed I had stolen from them.

When the boy looked up from the game, his father turned the caress into a playful squeeze, a jostle almost, as if remembering how men are supposed to show their affection for one another. Sometimes when my sons brush away my embraces, when they think they're too big for them, like a halfback I charge them and grab them in a quick, rough hug, pretending it's nothing more than a tackle. Absurd as it may sound, I even find myself grunting when I accost them, my voice deepening in my imitation of a male-bonding ritual.

Waiting in line to board the plane, I remembered a conversation I'd had with Daniel on a walk home from kindergarten years before.

"Hey," I'd said, as we turned the corner on our block in Berkeley. "How do you feel about not having a dad?" I wanted to keep it light, not project my anxiety onto him, make it sound like, "Did you feed the dog this morning?"

"Um..." Daniel paused. "Sometimes good and sometimes bad."

Uh-oh. Here we go. In preschool, having two moms had made Daniel an object of envy, but maybe by kindergarten two moms were no longer enough to make up for the absence of a father.

"Okay," I said, preparing myself. "What's the bad thing about not having a dad?"

"The bad is because you can climb up on a dad and he can lift you really high."

I stifled a laugh. "You mean like Uncle Mike does?"

"Yeah. I can touch the ceiling when he lifts me."

"All right." I prepared for the rest. "What else?"

"That's all."

That was all? The only bad thing about not having a dad was not having someone to climb on? I wanted to believe him, desperately wanted this to be true, but I feared he was old enough to know what might hurt my feelings. He might have been holding back, protecting me.

"What about the good?" I asked as we neared our house. Instead of looking over at him, I stared at the jacaranda I'd planted next to the sidewalk the year before, noted its growth. "What's good about not having a dad?"

"It's good because they're meaner. Jack told me his dad is meaner than his mom."

All right. Score another for two moms.

"You're like the dad."

I felt as if I might stumble on the sidewalk. "I'm like the dad?"

"Yeah, you're meaner than Mama."

I smiled, but something stung inside my chest. I knew he meant "stricter" when he said "meaner," and he had me pegged. I am the heavy, the alpha female in our pack. I holler more, and louder, than Pam does. Too often I overrule her, and then she and I argue over how to share authority.

"But you know I love you, right?" I asked Daniel. It was lame, but I was desperate. I wanted to be known as the mom who let him wrap his arms and legs around her like a koala cub and who kissed the warm spot in the soft hollow of his neck. The mom who played basketball in the driveway and pitched baseballs at the park. I needed to be acknowledged as a Good Mom. Did he appreciate any of this?

"Yeah, I know, Mommy," he said, glancing up and grinning. "You love me."

I was saved.

"But you're still meaner."

I sometimes wonder whether my family's legacy, what feels like an invisible blueprint, has influenced my choices, however unconsciously, and led me to create two children who will not grow up with the man whose genes they share. Their relationship with their biological father—if they ever meet him—will mirror my relationship with mine: lost opportunity for anything deeper than simple acquaintance.

My children are the third generation in our family to be adopted in some fashion and the third generation to grow up without their father. These repetitions fascinate me. I'm attracted by the pattern: the thirty-year spread between each of these events—from the nineteen thirties to the sixties to the nineties—the numbers suggesting a type of balance, or symmetry, like a repeating design in a quilt. Granted, the three adoptions were of different types—traditional, step-parent, and second-parent—but the threads of father absence woven throughout bind us together.

It wasn't until the man in the airport smiled at his son that I could see their resemblance. The father was balding, and his eyes were rounder than his son's, but when they smiled at each other, there was no questioning their kinship. Their lips and the creases in their chins were identical. I'd have been embarrassed if they'd turned and found me intruding on this intimate moment, but I was riveted.

Around that time, whenever I caught my reflection in store windows, I saw my mother. Although she was dark-haired and I was blonde, I had her plank-like body and eyes that disappeared when I smiled, and at forty-seven, my face was becoming hers. Our lips—reedy lines when we concentrated—were the same. More and more often now, usually when I'm being silly with my boys, I catch myself saying something in exactly the tone my mother would use. Even though she's still enjoying her earthly incarnation, I feel as if I'm channeling her spirit. If women turn into their mothers at a certain stage, do men turn into their fathers? My sons share many of my family's physical characteristics, but they must also resemble the donor, whose photograph we've never seen. Both boys inherited my fair skin and blonde hair, and Daniel got my mother's wide, round eyes, but I don't recognize my eldest's steeply vaulted Mr. Spock eyebrows. These may have come from his biological father. The need for my sons to compare themselves to this man, the need to see themselves reflected in him, might become important when they reach adolescence—when they try to figure out who they are, where they belong, which man they came from.

I'm beginning to understand how repeating ruptures across generations have affected me and my children as well as to recognize the ways we've broken free of the blueprint. And I'm realizing something else: how losing, in different ways, both my father and my stepfather has shaped me, perhaps made me tougher, more resilient, dogged in my pursuits. I better understand now my continuing drive toward reunions—beginning with a Greyhound bus trip at sixteen to meet my father again. It's the mélange of my genetic make-up and early experiences that propelled me toward years of detective work, drove the decade-long search for my father's birth mother, and impelled me to travel from my Berkeley home to Texas and Missouri to meet missing kin. During those journeys, I would uncover the secret my mystery grandfather took to his grave, and I would finally find the grandmother I never knew.

A woman behind the teenage boy in line shifted her weight. The boy's father spoke to her, and she handed him a boarding pass. It took me a moment to realize that she was the mother; she had been invisible to me, standing in line behind them. I realized that this could be me in a few years: redundant, unnecessary when the need for Mommy is less passionate, when I'm no longer the center of my sons' universe, when my sons might turn their attention to the missing man. Perhaps there will be one more search that will take place in this family; perhaps my sons will set off on their own quests to find their father.

Once, running errands on Solano Avenue in Berkeley when Benjamin was about five, we passed the donor on the sidewalk—or a man who could have been the donor. According to the file from the sperm bank, he was the right height and body type, and something about his eyes made me inhale sharply. I don't remember if it was the hue of blue, matching Ben's perfectly, or if it was their almond shape and particular slope, but I felt for a second as if I was looking into my son's eyes. The man's glance at Benjamin lingered a beat too long, and I tightened my grip on my boy's hand. I didn't want to meet the donor—for I was convinced in that instant that it was him—yet. I turned my back on the man, hurried Benjamin to the car, and nudged him into his car seat.

If, when they turn eighteen, my sons decide to locate the man who helped us make two marvelous boys, if they feel they lack a piece of their identity, or if they just want to know what he looks like, the sperm bank will release his name, and they can go looking for him. I have mixed feelings about this possibility. I don't want to find him if he's an out-of-work, four-times-divorced, drug-addicted deadbeat dad who'll show up at our house every Friday night wanting to hang out for the weekend. I don't want to be disappointed by him, and I don't want my boys to wish they'd never looked for him.

On the other hand, because we can tell from the notes in his file that more than likely he's a decent guy, I hope they do find our donor, so we can get a look at him, so we can study photos of him as a boy, which I'd like to place side by side with those of my sons at parallel ages. And I want to find him so that I can wrap my arms around him, the man who gave us the gift of our children, and ask him just one question. How can I ever thank you?

Since each donor is allowed ten offspring, my sons could have eight half-siblings scattered around the country, girls and boys sharing half of their genes. Someday I'd love to see what these kids look like, what characteristics they share, as well as how each is unique. Sometimes I imagine an odd gathering in a park in the hills east of San Francisco: tofu hotdogs grilling on a barbeque, badminton players' shouts ricocheting off eucalyptus trees, and all the kids and adults in red T-shirts with the inscription *Family Reunion of Donor 042-75.*

At the airport, a voice through the speaker called our row. I lifted my carry-on bag and slung it over my shoulder. Daniel picked up his backpack, slipped his hand in mine, and together we boarded the plane.

CARRYING ON

During my first pregnancy, I had fretted about what would happen if I had a boy. Who would show him how to pee standing up and how to shave? I worried that other families would shun us in the park because we were a two-mom family and that kids at school would say cruel things to him because he didn't have a father.

Peeing turned out to be the easy part. One day, as Benjamin sat on the toilet with his feet on the toddler step stool, I said, "You know, men usually stand up to pee and you will, too, someday." The next day, as I walked by the bathroom, I saw him standing with his legs pressed against the toilet bowl, leaning over it, his face straining with the effort of concentration. A couple of years later, Daniel simply copied his big brother, and thus the skill of peeing standing up was mastered in our house.

Other tasks—like explaining our family to the boys' friends as they got older—were more challenging. One day as I drove Ben and his friend Abe from kindergarten to their afternoon childcare, my thoughts were interrupted by Abe's voice from the back seat.

"Who is Benjamin's real mom?"

I hesitated. "Both of us are," I said, using a singsong voice to hide my unease. "He has two moms."

He pondered this for a few seconds. "No, I mean who gave birth with him?"

"Oh, I see what you're asking. I did. I gave birth to him."

"So how did he get his other mom?"

We pulled up to the after-school program. "His other mom and I made him and Daniel. Do you know how babies are made?" I unbuckled my seatbelt and opened my door.

He giggled. "No."

"Don't forget to take your lunch box with you," I said.

Benjamin joined in. "Is it like how kitties are made?"

"Yes, all mammals are made the same way."

"Is it like how monkeys are made?"

"Yes."

Abe's turn. "Snakes?"

"Turtles?" asked Ben.

"No, those are reptiles; they lay eggs outside their bodies."

Laughing, the two boys ran to the locked redwood gate and waited for me to catch up.

A week later, Ben and I walked onto the school playground just before the bell and met up with Abe and his father, Nick, who was dressed in a suit and carrying a worn daypack. Next to the play structure, Abe stopped.

"I know how you got Benjamin and Daniel!" he shouted. "You married a man and had them, and then you got a divorce, and that's how you and Pam got them." He was a precocious child, much more verbal than Ben. At that moment I wished he wasn't so damn smart.

I knelt next to him and Nick leaned over him, resting his arm on his son's shoulder. "They had a little help from a doctor," Nick started.

"Actually, a man gave us his sperm," I said, looking into Abe's face. "Like a present. And I put it inside of me and that's how we made Benjamin and Daniel."

I glanced over at Nick to make sure I hadn't gone too far. He was nodding.

"What do you think about that?" I asked Abe.

"That's *weird*!"

The word was a punch to my solar plexus. I glanced at Ben standing beside me. His head was tipped back in laughter, as if Abe had said a bathroom word. Did he really think Abe was funny or was he covering up embarrassment? Did this hurt him as much as it hurt me?

"No, it's *different*," I said.

"Yeah, it's different, not weird," Nick said. "Benjamin and Daniel are beautiful boys." He sounded flustered.

Abe picked up his backpack and ran to his classroom line. I kissed Ben on the top of his head and watched him catch up with Abe. Nick gave me an apologetic look. "Oh well, at least it's a start."

"A good start," I said, and we parted ways at the schoolyard gate.

AN ORDINARY LIFE

I held up a T-shirt imprinted with a photo of my two blond children on the front, and the sales clerk glanced back and forth between me and four-year-old Daniel, who was doing chin-ups to peer over the counter. She smiled and raised her eyebrows at him.

"He looks just like you," she said, meeting my eyes. "Is your husband tall, too?"

I glanced down at Daniel while running through possible answers in my head. I still changed the subject when strangers asked about my husband. Often I nodded or said "umm-hmm" and prayed that we'd move on to something else. But at the shop on University Avenue, for the first time in front of a group of strangers, I did something different.

"I don't have a husband," I said softly, turning my gaze to my checkbook. "My partner is a woman, and we used the sperm bank to get pregnant." I said this in a clarion voice in front of Daniel and the other customers, and the clerk didn't slam shut the cash register drawer and refuse to serve me. No one even looked my way. Emboldened, I tore out my check and handed it to her. Daniel rested his chin on the counter and peered up at the clerk.

"We know the donor is a little taller than me and has brown hair," I said, even though she hadn't asked about his hair color. With what I hoped was an air of nonchalance, I spoke as if I had this conversation every other day, but blood banged against my eardrums, and my neck and face turned warm. It was the first time I had come out like this, in front of a half-dozen strangers. I waited for a sharp intake of air from someone in the store, or an awkward silence. But before I could continue, the woman beside me, rummaging through a bin of shirts, looked my way.

"I have a friend in the same situation, but she's having a hard time deciding whether or not to use the sperm bank." I couldn't place this woman's accent. I guessed Russian and pegged her as a grad student at Cal.

I nodded. "Yeah," I said. "It's a hard choice, whether to use the sperm bank or ask a friend for a really big favor."

She nodded.

The sales clerk, an Asian American woman who looked about my age, jumped into the conversation. "I have friends who used the sperm bank and they have a beautiful boy. I think he has some Asian in him."

A man in his twenties with a beard and a long braid down his back approached the counter and nodded. "Cool."

Never before had I spoken so freely about this with strangers. Pam, the boys, and I belonged to a social group of one hundred gay families who got together at the children's museum, zoo, and holiday parties, and at these gatherings we shared stories about ovulation predictor kits, co-parenting, and domestic versus foreign adoption. We occasionally signed petitions and drafted letters to the editor about gay marriage. But most often we just sat back, watching our kids swing, slide, and run across the grass at the park, while we parents talked about toilet training, ear infections, and starting kindergarten.

My family and friends knew the details of my donor inseminations and pregnancies and had accepted my partnership with a woman. But out in public, in the grocery store and the library, I'd been too afraid to speak freely. I didn't know who would cluck their tongues and mutter something like, "Goes against nature," and who would smile and say, "What beautiful children they are!"

But with the clerk and customers in the store, it was as if we were discussing whether the rain would keep up for the rest of the day or quit soon. It was a perfectly acceptable exchange, sharing stories—a little unusual or special, but perfectly acceptable.

I felt a loosening of tension around my rib cage I hadn't realized had been there. To have my life accepted as just another ordinary life, to have it viewed as common and regular, was a singular moment. I couldn't wait to tell Pam. She, too, had not yet spoken with strangers about our family. When Ben was a toddler, a woman passing on the sidewalk told Pam he looked just like her. Recently, more than once strangers had assumed she was the boys' grandmother. Pam usually just nodded. But now that the kids were getting older, we needed to be more direct, more honest. I wanted to tell her how well this had gone so she could try it, too.

Except for the time I told my story to the woman at Totland Park, I'd been silent about my family in public since Ben was born almost seven years before. But something in me changed that day at the T-shirt shop. I had risked the truth and survived. The next time someone asked about my husband, I would try the same response again. "Nope, I don't have a husband," I'd start, looking them directly in the eye.

As I took Daniel's hand and we walked to the door, I glanced back at the clerk and the customer, their heads bowed together like confidants picking through the sale bin.

"See you later," I said with a little wave.

"Bye," the clerk said. "Hope that rain stays away for the rest of the day."

DEAR MR. ATENDE

Susan Straight

Dear Mr. Atende,

I AM WRITING to let you know the rocket is not going to fly today. My son Reynaldo Antoine and I spent all weekend working on the rocket, and it will not fly high enough for you. I am saying this up front. You will see it today in the classroom. This morning, Reynaldo almost cried. I thought he might not even go to your class today, since you said those things to him last week, but I know he wants to prove you wrong.

But not with the rocket. We used three balloons. But the rocket hovers in the air for two seconds and then goes sideways and down. We did it twelve times before Reynaldo got mad and went to play the piano instead. You didn't know that he plays the piano.

It will not make it past the line my son said you drew on the wall. Three feet of travel and ten seconds aloft for a grade. Aloft is a strange word. At Back to School night last week you sounded English. And then you told us you were born in Nigeria and went to live in London when you were twelve. You told us you went to France this summer to work on a science grant.

Reynaldo is thirteen. He was born at Rio Seco General Hospital, right around the corner from your school. So was I. So was his father. We don't go anywhere. My son told me what you said to him in the parking lot last week. You said, "Boys like you are a particular disappointment to someone like me."

For the rocket, your note said: Use items from your own home. You should not have to make an excursion to the store, and your parents should not have to help you.

Like we all have balloons in our own homes. We had tape, and a Dixie cup, and string. I had the fifteen pennies to put in the cup. I always have pennies. But who has balloons like that now? If somebody has a birthday, you get those foil balloons with birthday greetings. Or graduation.

Reynaldo graduated from sixth grade in June, and he got you last week. He has a balloon in his room flat as some alien pancake. Helium. I know what helium is. When my son brought home the periodic table last week, I loved seeing all those elements and gases. Before you think you know what you know about my son and me, let me tell you I got an A in Biology and an A in Chemistry. I went to Linda Vista High. You're sending your students there. But the kind of balloon you need to make a rocket? Who blows up balloons for anything anymore? No one.

Just because you don't see me in the parking lot or at the school doesn't mean I don't take care of my son. I work. Not every mother can be at the school to check on every balloon.

Reynaldo told me he asked another boy in class. Jeremiah. Jeremiah's father went halfway to L.A. and found a four-foot long balloon at some craft store. I don't have the gas or the time to drive around looking for balloons. I work all day and it feels like I do laundry and dishes all night.

And you said no excursions. Like parents do not help. Like this weekend project wasn't about parents.

Jeremiah's father runs some website about parenting and the Christian lifestyle. He works at home. My son told me. Jeremiah's father is at the school all the time volunteering. I am a customer service representative in the circulation and subscription department of the *Rio Seco Daily News*. I am not working from home. I work in Pomona. In September people call for vacation stops and starts. Our call volume is extremely high.

That father has probably made rockets before. You have made rockets before. I have not. I can do many things you cannot. I know you are from Nigeria, Mr. Atende. You have told the students about twenty times and then you told them about how important science is—Reynaldo wrote down principles and laws and reasoning, and you told them that American students are falling behind because of their lack of interest in science and their own laziness. You told them that your upbringing was difficult and your education rigorous—I remember because Reynaldo asked me about rigor mortis. You looked right at Reynaldo and his friend LaCurtis when you said lazy. He told me.

I know your mother didn't make rockets. I'm not talking about your mama. You also told the students you are not married. My son says you always stare at them when you talk about responsibility. If you are not married, you are definitely not making rockets with your kid at ten p.m. on a Sunday night.

Sweet. That's what Reynaldo and his friends say when Kobe dunks, too. And that's about the likelihood of me helping make a rocket fly. I hear them say "Sweet" and it means "So cool" and I'm getting none of that. It means they're observing. Like "observation record" on your chart at the bottom of the rocket project. Record the height and duration of the flight. Then add pennies to the cup and record the effects of increased weight.

But starting out with fifteen pennies? Did you make this rocket project when you were in school in Nigeria, Mr. Atende? Because fifteen pennies is heavy when you hold them in your hand. And ain't no four-foot balloons in no store around my house. Not at Rite Aid. Or 7-Eleven. We have birthday balloons, and we used three. One on the bottom, we thought, to lift up the cup. Taped the string to the other two on top. Three balloons and I'm tired from helping him blow them up and when we untwisted the twist ties and let the air out, the rocket sat there in the air for about one second and then raced around on the floor like Cinderella's damn carriage pulled by pink rats.

They only had pink balloons. Reynaldo couldn't believe it. And I couldn't be running all over Rio Seco 'cause I have a seven year old and he had a dentist appointment and I had groceries to buy and laundry and you sent that project home Friday afternoon saying it had to be done on Monday.

My weekend isn't like yours. That's a damn scientific fact. You put together all those compounds I loved studying in Chemistry, and mine looks like H2ONACLAmmoniaBleach and whatever the hell oven cleaner's made of. And fruit snacks and chicken and rice. Rice is hard as hell and then softens up when you cook it. We lived on rice when I was small.

I don't make rockets. And my husband doesn't live with us anymore, so you think you know all about me, but he didn't make rockets either. He does drywall and plaster and dominoes and Hennessy. So now you made Reynaldo feel like shit. 'Cause he couldn't ask his father, like in your perfect mind in your perfect compound world. But you don't even know half those kids can't ask their fathers. Because Mr. Atende, I don't know what the hell you think about the black kids, but I know you don't even have a clue that a lot of the white fathers are gone, too. Cody and Cheyenne—their dad is gone. Kids talk. Reese's dad is gay. In Florida, with his partner now. Billy's dad died in a motorcycle accident when he was five. His mom works in the cafeteria, but you never see her. And Madison's father left his family for a student. He was a professor. His mom is a rich white woman with a Mercedes and big diamond earrings, but one day she told me all about it in the parking lot. I don't know what possessed her to talk to me, but she did.

I don't make rockets, but I have ears.

I do things you will never be able to do. I make teacakes from scratch. Not from a tube. My grandmother made teacakes in Louisiana. I know how to clean a kitchen. I don't mean wash the dishes. I mean scrub the sink white and make the faucets shine and the stove burners and even the tile behind the stove. I mean clean the grout on the counter with a toothbrush. My grandmother taught me to clean a kitchen. Take a razor blade to the hard water stains on the porcelain.

You probably pay someone to clean your kitchen.

What do you think I am teaching Reynaldo? He plays the piano. He doesn't like math. Did you know that? He's way lighter than you, Mr. Atende. You think he doesn't know that? It's science. Genetics.

So Mr. Atende, you think he's a spoiled light-skinned African American who had life easy all this time. Up 'til now. When you decided to teach him and all these other kids a lesson about rigorous. And you think he's a ghetto fool because he was laughing one day in the parking lot with the other boys from the Westside, even though he doesn't walk home with them and we live on the other side of the school. I have been in the parking lot of the junior high. I have seen where the kids stand and how they walk. The first day I went to work late so I could watch how they went.

I am typing this on the computer at my job. My supervisor is talking on the phone to his girlfriend. He is married, and his girlfriend calls here every day. I can see him through his window. He watches us in our cubicles. That's one big table divided into five pie slices by plywood. Perfectly even. A pie chart. My piece of pie faces his office. I can see him turn and hunch over like he does and he's talking to his girlfriend. So I am typing. I have fifteen minutes. It is eleven-ten here. That's when the phone calls about service slack off from the morning people. They complain about where the carrier threw the paper. But it's September now. Old people are going on vacation. They will call about their vacation stops around lunchtime. While they sit around the table and look at brochures for cruises.

We did not go on vacation. I am fully aware that you, Mr. Atende, went to France and Italy, that you had a grant to study at a major university for the summer. Reynaldo told me. He told me that you are amazing. He told me that you look at him like he's 50 Cent Junior, or maybe because he's light skinned, like he's an embarrassment to blackness.

He's light because his great-great-grandmother was raped in Louisiana. She came over on the boat from Senegal. Then her daughter was raped, too. Get over it. We did.

We didn't travel this summer because Reynaldo took summer school. Not because he failed something, like you asked him that first day when they said what they did in summer. He took band. He is in the jazz band. I thought you might like to know that. He plays the piano. The band teacher loves him. She wants him to play percussion. Drum line. Mr. Atende, you can be from Africa all you want, but you don't know drum line. I know you don't.

So his rocket doesn't fly here at home. It will not fly in your classroom today, and if you make my son feel bad about that, you will have to deal with me. In the parking lot. I don't mean in the office, with the principal. I mean in the parking lot. I'll take off work early if you make Reynaldo cry. I'm not playing.

That's how we say it here in California. We don't play.

And next weekend, I heard you are sending home a project again. Make a car. I don't make cars. Reynaldo already told me about it. Jeremiah's father has already got what he needs. The wheels are push-pops. Nobody eats push pops any more, but I will buy some. The body is manila folders and Popsicle sticks and tape, and the car is supposed to be powered by a balloon and a straw.

Reynaldo's father and his cousins make cars on the weekend. They make lowriders painted candyflake purple and gold. They put in exhaust systems and all that crap. But they don't make wheels from push pops. I will do the best I can, but I want you to have this letter tomorrow. I have seen your classroom. Your desk is a rectangle, high up off the floor, and the floor is that crappy school linoleum, and my son is sitting there watching you. He is watching you watch him.

Sincerely,
Cerise Antoine

GEORGE BLANDA ATE MY HOMEWORK

Brad Schreiber

Dear Miss Christopher:

As you know, I have never turned in an assignment late. So it is with great regret that I report to you that I do not have my homework completed at this time. While I know that you never, ever accept late papers, the reason I have not completed my essay is not due to laziness or some other lame excuse that you have undoubtedly heard before, like "I was sleeping outside in the backyard and a gust of wind blew my paper into a tree where a blue jay ate it."

Perhaps I should say that I do have an essay but it is not in the form you expected. The reason for this is simple: It's due to George Blanda, the backup quarterback for the Oakland Raiders. I was quite prepared to discuss, as you requested, how Ernest Hemingway's *The Old Man and the Sea* speaks to our society's attitudes about aging and death. Sunday was the day I had set aside to write my paper. I was flipping through the book, taking additional notes, with my TV quietly on in the background. I assure you it was not distracting me. And then, around one o'clock, I could not help but notice that the Oakland Raiders were playing the San Diego Chargers. And then, to my great surprise and relief, I found that the central character in Hemingway's novel and the second string quarterback of the Oakland Raiders have quite a lot in common.

Miss Christopher, I am assuming that you are not a fan of the National Football League. If you are, great. But if not, let me suggest why an appreciation of the NFL can give new insights into Hemingway's work. You see, George Blanda is not only a quarterback, he is a field goal kicker. That's pretty rare. And he was released by the Raiders in the pre-season because he is forty-two years old which, according to the standards of the NFL, is one step away from being in a wheelchair in a retirement village like my Uncle Dave in Cocoa Beach, Florida. And yet he—Blanda, not Uncle Dave—was brought back, despite this being his twenty-first year in the league, and he has stepped in to replace the regular quarterback, Daryle Lamonica, who was injured.

In essence, while I watched the opening of the first quarter, I had the stunning realization that George Blanda is totally analogous to Santiago, the old fisherman, in Hemingway's work. Santiago has gone eighty-four days without catching a fish. Blanda has gone over two decades without winning a championship.

Normally I would say any student trying to dissuade you from giving him or her an F for non-delivery of a standard essay by melding a discussion of a great work of fiction with a three-hour telecast of a football game is not deserving of your respect. But what happened yesterday in the Oakland Coliseum capped off an extraordinary string of circumstances, one that might be unrivaled in the history of sports, if not human endeavor. And human endeavor certainly includes the act of fishing.

You see, Miss Christopher, five weeks ago Blanda came in for Lamonica and threw three touchdowns to beat the Pittsburgh Steelers, 31-14. The next week he kicked a forty-eight-yard field goal with a mere three seconds left to garner a 17-17 tie with the Raiders' AFC West rivals, the Kansas City Chiefs. None of this might inspire awe on your part, I realize, but it was very crucial if Oakland is to win its division over the Chiefs. OK, so the third week Blanda comes in with a paltry one minute and thirty-four seconds left to throw a touchdown pass and tie the Cleveland Browns. And now, Miss Christopher, the truly eerie moment in this seemingly random series of events occurs, because again, with three seconds on the clock, Blanda kicks another game-winning field goal. Raiders 23, Browns 20.

Now, if we stopped there, even someone like you, Miss Christopher—and I do not write this in any way patronizingly—might say,

"OK, George has had a run of good luck, especially for the oldest guy in the NFL. But this kind of thing must go the way of all flesh." But it doesn't. It should have ended there: Lamonica got healthy and, as first string QB, he started the next game against the Denver Broncos. And yet, strangely enough, he was relatively ineffective. It was almost like the Raiders and all the fans in the Bay Area could no longer accept him as their leader. It did not feel like a defection. It was more like Blanda, in his swan song to the game he loved for so long, was saying to those who needed to believe in him, "If I am going to leave you, I want you to bask in the most resplendent memory possible." It was Groege Blanda not just trying to play with every remaining fiber of his strained, bruised and sagging middle-aged body but trying to say thank you to the organization that gave him one last fleeting chance at a little glory.

And so help me God, Miss Christopher, my breath left my body when, with a miniscule 2:28 left in the fourth quarter (that's the final quarter, in case you are not familiar with the rules), Blanda connected with Fred Biletnikoff for a touchdown pass to defeat the Broncos 24-19. Everyone was stunned, especially considering that Biletnikoff is really kind of small, does not have blazing speed, the strength of a tight end or the leaping ability of a Lance Alworth, and is an unlikely candidate for a wide receiver. A lot of people claim Biletnikoff, though widely respected, uses too much Stickum in order to catch passes.

So I hope that you now understand, even if you cannot fully accept, that yesterday I had to see if Blanda played again. And you know what, Miss Christopher? He did. Lamonica, the young generation, the equivalent of Santiago's boy assistant Manolin, took the snap from center and set the ball down, laces out, as Blanda, elderly but experienced, with hands sore from the fishing line of life ripping across his skin, kicked the ball with seven seconds left from the sixteen-yard line.

The crowd fell silent, but only for a moment. A great seismic roar shook the Oakland Coliseum as if it was on the San Andreas Fault during April of 1906. The ball sailed through the uprights. The announcer, Bill King, shouted to be heard above the din: "This man may have tied the entire Bay Area into a knot from which it may never extricate itself again." It was one of the greatest calls in sports history, commemorating Blanda's fifth straight miracle in a row. Raiders 20, Chargers 17.

I was so overcome with emotion, Miss Christopher, that I started thinking, if this amazing 1970 season is Blanda's last, perhaps he can find some solace in it. Perhaps he will find some way to soothe the bitterness of being called an "NFL reject" when he joined the Houston Oilers. In *The Old Man and the Sea*, Santiago catches the biggest fish he has ever seen. Blanda has the most amazing string of last-minute heroics in football history. Tragically, Santiago has the sharks eat away the magnificent marlin he has caught, until there is nothing but the skeleton. Blanda was a has-been, a washed-up, the Ancient Mariner of the League. And yet Santiago shall fish again, although he has come home to his Cuban village with nothing to show for his efforts; and Blanda will kick and pass again surely, even if he is a mere sub for Lamonica, who has been utterly inconsistent this year when he wasn't injured. Santiago and Blanda have both tasted the sweet, sustaining fruit of victory, and in the twilight of their lives they simply want to hold tight to whatever tattered wisp of dignity can be mustered.

In the end, the old man Santiago dreams his usual dream of lions at play on the beaches of Africa. Blanda, near the end, dreams of starting in a Super Bowl near the beaches of Miami. Ernest Hemingway said, "Bullfighters live their lives all the way up." So do decrepit but brave fishermen and aging quarterback–place kickers.

Brad

Dear Brad:

I am not clear from the above why you were unable to write a more cogent essay. I am very disappointed. However, I will accept this as your assignment and give it a D, with the following proviso: You make more time for future assignments. And, at least in this class, you will never, ever make any kind of allusion to sports again.

Miss Christopher

THE MOTHERHOOD POEMS

Beth Alvarado

ON THE BIRTH OF MY FIRST GRANDCHILD

THE BABY WAS born early. Eight weeks early to be exact. They now count gestation in weeks not months. I stood in the hall and heard his first cry. Like a kitten, small and mewing. He was small. Four pounds, three ounces.

For six weeks the baby will be in neonatal ICU, which they say like this: Nick-U, as if it is a small university. There are monitors and feeding tubes and other tiny babies in their incubators. People look sad when they see the pictures of the baby but he is our baby and we are not sad. Smaller babies are born every day.

Has the baby gone home? Has the baby gone home? Has the baby gone home?

The baby has a name, a long name. A first name, a middle name, a last name, but no nickname. To pick one would be presumptuous—on the part of me, the grandmother. The baby has a small neck but a strong one. He stretches it so he can look at the window. His eyes are sometimes open. His hands are big for such a small baby.

The baby has his father's dimples. We can see them now that he has gained weight. We can see them when he smiles. For those of you who do not know, his father can hold two quarters in each dimple, for a total of a whole dollar on his face.

I guess we should say the baby has his own dimples. He has his own thin fingers and long feet, his own double chin and tiny penis. And, yes, we know: when the baby smiles, it's just gas.

Has the baby gone home yet? Has he been strapped into the car seat in the back seat of the small car and hurtled down the L.A. freeways between SUVs and eighteen-wheelers? Have you carried him up the cement stairs? Did you cradle him in your arms? Did you hold on to the railing? You do know, don't you, that the rails of escalators in department stores are contaminated with germs, with yeast, with vaginal yeast, as in from the vaginas of strangers.

You will need to remember to wash your hands now. Please. You cannot wear flip-flops when carrying the tiny baby, not up and down cement stairs. Tell me you did not talk on the phone while driving.

ON GIVING BIRTH

The mother of the baby, my daughter-in-law, lay on the bed in the hospital for four days, trying *not* to have the baby. Magnesium dripped into her blood to stop the contractions, she had to lie on the bed in such a way that she didn't disturb the fetal monitor and its faithful record, the thump thump thump of the baby's heart.

On those limbo days, my son was so tall and his hair seemed especially black and shiny. He was utterly calm when he was with his wife but when we left the hospital and he and I were alone, he zoomed into hyperactivity—talking to me and on the cell phone at the same time, walking fast, worrying. He said, "love ya, bro" at the end of conversations with his friends. In California, everyone says "I love you" to everyone all the time. Is it a symptom of anxiety, an awareness of the tentative nature of life, or a habit? When you live in L.A., one of my students said, you know each day could be the one you die.

Outside the hospital window, Wilshire Boulevard stretched sixteen blocks to the Pacific Ocean where the homeless men camped out on the grassy bluff above the beach and the Mexican peddlers sold them lone pieces of fruit and little bags of peanuts. Inside the room, my son and daughter-in-law were Ohming and breathing. Sometimes her voice was strong, sometimes ragged with pain. To weep, to flee the scene, those were my strongest impulses, but I had promised my son I would stand in the hall. My job: to be the Center of the Earth.

Why was I so frightened for my daughter-in-law? Is Death always among the attending? Hospitals are surreal capsules out of time and place. Britney Spears was down the hall having a caesarian. Men with thick necks stalked Labor and Delivery. Our baby was in distress. Paparazzi camped out front. The doctor, a tall British woman with long black hair, was firm. One more push would do it. One. More. Push. The baby cried, such a small cry, but he was a tough cookie, our baby. He could breathe.

When my son went to Nick-U with the baby, I was to stand next to his wife. They had to surgically remove the placenta, which had secured itself with scar tissue to the wall of her uterus. I threw myself over her and started weeping. I stroked her forehead furiously. You can have painkillers now, I told her, Demerol. Ask for Demerol. Please. This is no time to be brave.

ON BREASTFEEDING

When you are the grandmother, the baby is not your responsibility. Oh, you might get to sit on the couch and hold it occasionally, but it's not your fault if the baby is not getting enough to eat and it certainly is not your fault if the lactation expert said to feed it with a syringe. No more supplemental bottles, she said. We want to avoid nipple confusion.

Your son calls you. Don't worry, he says, his voice full of worry, the baby's fontanel isn't depressed. No signs of dehydration yet. Your daughter-in-law, you can hear the weeping in her voice even though she isn't weeping. A syringe? you ask politely. Instead of the supplemental bottle? (You must excise from your voice any trace of alarm. You must be calm, reassuring. You are the grandmother, the paternal grandmother, a whole different set of eggshells.) You go to Travelocity. You click "Anytime." You scroll for flights. (Syringe feeding? Who ever heard of syringe feeding?) Tomorrow, you tell her, I'll be there tomorrow.

Oh, but you know how hard it is. The tiny baby has to open his mouth so wide. Almost like a snake, he must unhinge his jaw—for the breast, even the smallest breast, is larger than his head. He must take the whole nipple into his mouth and when the milk rushes down, warm and sweet, it must flood his mouth and his throat. He gulps. His eyes are round and, as yet, unfocused. Is it an adoring gaze or panic? Is he afraid he will drown?

His tiny nostrils are pressed against the flesh and you remember, with his father, pressing your finger, just there, so he could breathe. All this: his fuzzy head, the pulsing soft spot, his round eyes and wild gulping, his grunting against your bare neck as you hold him, waiting for the blesséd burp, his limp body when he falls into sleep, all this you remember. Baby against your heart.

And all this: the doubt, the loneliness, the fear no one can assuage, not even your mother for you are the mother now and even though you might want to hide in the closet, 24/7, crying, you cannot. Someone needs you, a someone you don't even know. Look into his eyes, he is a mystery. Face it. That's why his name doesn't fit him, and why no name would. Who is he? And he gazes at you with unfocused eyes. He does not know you, except by the smell of your skin, the sound of your voice. He cannot see you and, because you are his mother, he may never be able to see you, not clearly. Your beginnings are too close, skin against skin, this is a love affair, admit it. You will never recover.

ON THE NATURE OF BABIES

Does the baby want to be swaddled? Maybe he wants to lie face down on your forearm. Maybe he wants you to walk him up and down the hallway, your bare feet on the worn carpeting. Maybe he wants you to sway back and forth as you hold the pacifier in his mouth and watch television. Maybe he wants you to turn the television off. Maybe he wants you to sing little songs about his short life. This is what you did with his aunt, your daughter, who had colic and ear infections. (Oh, the drawing up of the knees, the jutting out of the bottom lip in pain, these are all so familiar.) Maybe he wants you to sing songs like those you sang to your babies: House of the Rising Sun, Down in the Valley, Mercedes Benz. Prison songs, drinking songs, down-on-your-luck songs, songs—it occurs to you now—that might be inappropriate for a baby.

Although, you must admit, this baby lives in a neighborhood where crime is common. His father, your son, was caught in the crossfire between the Armenian and Russian mafias. A bullet left a hole in his car. The clerks at 7/11 praised Allah for his deliverance. Which, while we're on the subject: when will the owner of your son's apartment complex ever realize he is a slum-lord? When will he replace the carpeting? Fix the leaky gas stove? Repair the crumbling plaster under the window? Before the baby starts to crawl, please, and can ingest lead paint.

Oh, these babies, they are like tiny birds. Voracious. They need milk, time, patience, jump seats, car seats, strollers, cribs, co-sleepers, changing tables, diapers, fire-escape ladders, gender appropriate onesies, nightgowns, jumpsuits, coats, hats and booties. They need bathtubs and baby wipes and baby wipe warmers. Plus receiving blankets, don't forget receiving blankets, you can never have enough receiving blankets. You fold the corner down, just so, to swaddle the baby. You put him to sleep on his back? Not his tummy!? The world has changed, your son tells you. (As if, at fifty-one, you are senile.)

There is a book about mothers and babies you are supposed to follow but you haven't read it. The words swim on the page like the baby swam in the womb. When your daughter was little, you pushed her underwater to the swimming teacher and instead of going to him, she turned, her eyes open in water, and swam back to you. She was swimming without breath, back to you. She would drown to get back to you. There was the way the book said it was supposed to be and the way it was. This is what your daughter taught you: each baby sets the world spinning on a new axis.

Your husband dreams he is holding the baby. The baby is so strong, he jerks back, pushes with his legs, and your husband drops him. Well, he almost drops him. It's a dream and so the moment of dropping is the moment of not-dropping. In dreams, life can correct itself automatically. So he doesn't drop him and when the baby is cradled in his arms again, the baby says, I still love you. Meaning, we guess, "even though you almost dropped me." This is a dream about listening. The baby is trying to tell us something. But what? We don't know. Maybe he wants more to eat, your husband says. Maybe he wants us to visit.

If it were my dream, which it is not, the baby would be telling me: I am strong. It is okay for you to love me, Nana. Don't be afraid. No one will take me away from you. This is the fear and the baby knows it. He knows that his absence would be unbearable. He knows he has already taken root. He knows this. When I hold him and I stop singing, he cries. Soon, he will sing back to me. Oooo-oo, oooo-oo, he will sing, his voice against my neck breathy and demanding.

JOHN WAYNE LOVES GRANDMA DOT

Victoria Patterson

JOHN WAYNE wandered Newport Beach at night. An observer watching him drift through the streets might think his wanderings were random and thoughtless, but John Wayne had his own logic and pattern. He believed in things unseen. He walked slowly past certain homes, skateboard at his side, sensing possibilities, as though the homes were showing him: see, this is how it can be.

He saw the glow from inside a window, sensed the way the kids felt toward the parents, or how the parents loved each other, or even how the dog liked the way he got fed every night and rubbed on his belly. John Wayne lingered, careful not to be noticed. He didn't want to scare anyone; he just wanted to feel.

Most homes reminded him of basements or art galleries: coldness hung around them, a hint of darkness, maybe even abuse. He set his skateboard down and flew past, noticing the flickering lights of a television. His gut reaction might be wrong, but he didn't want to find out. He wanted no part. The gravelly sound of his wheels on the sidewalk calmed him.

His skateboard jumped curbs, flipped down cement steps. Darkness, shadows, moonlight, stars, the constant noise of the ocean, and no one to tell him what to do. He fell, but that was part of the adventure: scrapes and bruises, once a broken arm. A stranger drove him to the hospital. The nurse injected him and told him to count backwards from ten. He tried, but he couldn't remember what came next—ten, nine—that was it. The nurse gave him a troubled look, and he wanted to explain, "Don't worry. I had a drug overdose. I hurt my head," but his mouth wouldn't open. He went under the anesthesia, and he died for a little while. When he woke up, there was a cast on his arm and his head hurt. The dying wasn't so bad. He knew that it was a different kind of sleep, another type of waking.

After the drug overdose, his mother continued to do his laundry and set the baskets by the back door of their house, along with bags of food, but otherwise his family fired him like a bad employee. His brother and sister avoided him. His mom looked at him and sobbed. They called it tough love, but it wasn't about love: John Wayne was an embarrassment.

Although people pitied him (he could see pity in their faces), he didn't think the way he lived was such a bad way to go. He smoked marijuana, even when he took showers, his head far enough from the spray to keep it lit, and an ashtray on the toilet seat for when he washed his hair. He no longer used cocaine and heroin, and although he somehow knew that this was connected to his brain damage, it was a relief. Money was a problem insofar as he had to *do* things to get it. The men took him in their cars, but it was over fast, not so bad when it was quick, and sometimes tender. Unless they got angry and violent and pushed him down. He knew how to fight back, but he hated to hurt anyone; that's why he left home the first time. Once, he stabbed his stepfather's arm with scissors, but it was in self-defense. He had cried for a week. He let the men do what they needed just so long as he could get his money and keep floating through the streets.

Sometimes he slept at the Newport Inn, a run-down hotel on the fringe of Costa Mesa near the freeway. Henry Wilson paid his bill each month in full. John Wayne met him every Wednesday at midnight, Wilson's black Mercedes idling in the dark, the back door ajar. The hotel sign was lit up with blinking red and blue palm trees. He didn't like the loud, drunken fights and the cop cars.

Otherwise, he slept under a bridge. He dug a burrow in the dirt and covered it with cardboard. The sounds of the trucks and cars driving over the bridge was better than the screams, loud music, and sirens at the hotel, but it was cold and there was no bathroom. He used the liquor store bathroom on the other side of Pacific Coast Highway, but the owner hated him ever since he'd caught him stealing a twelve-pack of Coors. John Wayne ran across the highway, twelve-pack under his arm, and ducked under the bridge, the man yelling, "You little fucker! Try that again and I'll shoot your fucking head off!"

John Wayne went to AA and NA meetings. He sat on the raggedy couch, bummed cigarettes, and listened to the people talk. There were free doughnuts, cookies, cakes, and coffee. Once in a while, he raised his hand, made everyone in the room laugh, announcing, "Hello, my name is John Wayne, and I'm a drug addict." That was all he ever said. The people welcomed him, patted his back, and treated him kindly, and he went for the company, safety, food, coffee, and cigarettes—not to stop using drugs.

He was sorry for his parents and his twin siblings, with their tight faces and tight hearts. They didn't know what it was like to let the ocean come inside you. He felt it course through his veins, a charging through his heart, letting him know that he was nothing but it didn't matter, it was okay to be nothing, because nothing was everywhere: wind, palm trees, even the expensive cars and clothes. How could he explain that it was okay to be nothing? His stepfather called him weak and stupid. When his stepfather yelled at him, he let the words hang over his head like butterflies.

He missed his mom. Sometimes he imagined it was her hot breath whispering in his ear, "You're so beautiful," not Henry Wilson.

John Wayne knew that Rosie watched him from her bedroom deck. His life changed when she gave him the key to Uncle Stan's apartment over the garage of her grandparents' house, where no one went upstairs, except for her.

She didn't make John Wayne do anything. Sometimes, she looked at him like she was sorry for him, but most of the time she just looked at him. People liked to look at him, and he learned not to talk, since that was when people got upset, their eyes changing from pleased to disturbed.

He took long hot showers and left the red light on. There was grace in the walls, the clothes left in the closet and dresser, and the blue bong.

It was as if the clothes and bong were waiting for him. The clothes fit him and he liked the tie-dyed shirts and frayed Levi's. He wore Uncle Stan's necklace with the tooth pendant, stroking it for comfort. It was like a slender bone.

From the apartment window, he watched Rosie's grandparents engrossed in their rituals in the house below. There's Grandpa and Grandma, he thought. Watching them made him feel safe, he didn't know why. They sat on their barstools, eating their meals, a dependability. Grandma Dot had silvery white hair. Grandpa was tanned and there was a patch of white hair on either side of his head in a U shape. The skin between the hair reminded him of a bull's-eye. Their meals were poked and prodded, they took small bites. Grandpa drank vodka martinis with speared olives while Grandma Dot drank Schlitz straight from the can. She was petite, always dressed with care, so the sight of her tipping a can to her coral lips was dramatic. She sat on the barstool with her legs crossed like an aged movie star.

Grandma Dot sensed a presence in her son's apartment above the garage. At first she believed it was poor, troubled, eccentric Rosie. She began leaving two crisp twenty-dollar bills every week (and sometimes three twenty-dollar bills) in one of Grandpa's martini glasses with Spending Money written on a piece of paper and taped to it. She left the glass at the foot of the stairs, and whoever the person was accepted the money, leaving the empty glass for her. She became convinced that it wasn't Rosie. When her Schlitz started disappearing from the garage refrigerator, she bought twelve-packs of Coors and left a note explaining that Schlitz was rather difficult to come by.

John Wayne continued to sneak into the garage and steal the Coors, and although he didn't read a note that was left there, crumpling it into a ball and chucking it in the trash, he understood that he should not touch Grandma Dot's stash.

Grandma Dot was a serious insomniac, her large booze intake also an attempt to lose consciousness. Secretly, when her mind was inebriated enough, she pretended that her son still lived upstairs, that he hadn't left her, and this allowed her to avoid the reality. She saw a red glow from the apartment every night, and the light didn't go off until she herself had abandoned the barstool for bed. She liked the attention.

John Wayne watched Grandma Dot through the kitchen window below while she played Solitaire, sitting on a barstool in the kitchen, on the counter beside her cards, her beer sweating on a napkin, her ashtray stockpiled with stubs, her pack of Merits, and her lighter. Once, late at night, she slipped fluidly off the barstool. He was ready to run down the steps and save her, so sure that she had hurt herself, but she picked herself up and sat herself right back on the barstool. Then she slowly, dramatically, drunkenly lit herself another cigarette.

He saw the hallway light through a bulbous plastic window in the ceiling of the house. It looked like a lit-up blister. He began waiting for the light to go off, and then he would go downstairs; she would leave the front door open for him.

The kitchen counter would be set up for their breakfasts with two green cloth tablemats and a bottle of fake sugar. Their grapefruit spoons lay upon green-checkered napkins, and he would rub his thumb along the sharp ridges, amused that a spoon had this jagged feature. The wooden salt and pepper shakers were between the mats. Inside the refrigerator, he found grapefruit halves, wrapped in cellophane with half cherries bleeding in their centers.

It smelled like Grandma Dot. He loved the smell: part perfume, cigarettes, and something sweet and stale, something purely Grandma Dot. His meal she left for him near a warming oven, covered with tin foil like a Christmas present. He ate at her barstool, as close to her leftover spirit as he could get, careful not to disrupt their morning setups. He became well acquainted with Grandma Dot's taco special, her meatloaf, and her pork chops. He felt privileged, and he loved the meals, as much as he imagined anyone would ever love Grandma Dot's food. There was always a cold beer in the refrigerator. He knew it was his because it was the only bottle of Coors, just one, every time, in a sea of Schlitz.

Grandma Dot's stack of cards sat beside a glass ashtray and a cheap plastic Bic lighter near the telephone. He respected these objects, passing his fingers lightly, reverentially over them. Her cigarette stubs had her bright lipstick prints, like flowers of pink and coral.

Afterwards, he left his plate and his utensils by the sink, where she washed them properly in the morning.

Once in a while, John Wayne would sleep in the small twin bed in The Daisy Room near the hallway, even closer to Grandma Dot. A light sleeper, he left the glass sliding door cracked open so that he could hear the bay. He named every room. The Green Room had wallpaper in the bathroom with green fish on it. The Daisy Room had large daisies across the wallpaper and a magnetic plastic daisy plant where the magnets held the daisies' heads.

He would leave long before the grandparents woke and go back to Uncle Stan's apartment, after making the bed, but leaving the pillow above the bedspread, a signal to Grandma Dot that not only had he eaten her meal, he had slept downstairs. He would lock the front door behind him.

One morning, waking from a deep and safe sleep, he didn't make it back to the apartment before the grandparents woke. He listened patiently to their morning ritual. Grandpa made coughing noises; the newspaper rustled. They never spoke, not even a good morning or goodbye or have a good day. There wasn't hostility; John Wayne would have left. He was done with that. It was as if talking were unnecessary.

The back door slammed. The house shuddered when the garage door opened and shuddered again when it closed. John Wayne and Grandma Dot were alone.

He sneaked back to Uncle Stan's apartment while she washed the dishes, and it was as if she took her time with the dishes, giving him the leeway. She turned off the faucet, hands sudsy with dish soap. He saw her listening for the *tip tap* of his feet.

SAN CLEMENTE

Carol Muske-Dukes

SHAME & SHAME! sound of neap tide,
Pull & surge, watery law partners—

Surfers ride out, then
Zigzag back inside crest, falling crest—

Then bars—Beachcomber Pier, its rickety
Path over waves. Sun/moon, blue neon
Martini glass, white neon stars—

Staunch Republican white stone benches
Along the promenade. Carved, under bird-
Splat: Everything in Moderation & Memories
Eternal as the Sea. Where's the thirty-seventh

President, soul of checks & balances betrayed?
Ghost surfer, he's home & away, shame & shame.
Continent's stop here, south of the floating oil-rigs—
This heavenly sweep of pitiless sea. Dolphins,

Our leaping geniuses, are here now to save us—
Help us be kind. We are not. The tide checks itself,
Balances, as the sea rolls over in the salt plain.
A criminal mind, uncaught, rolls jack-flat & over

Everything in Moderation. How poems depend on
"Fugitive causes." Fugitive, here is your sanctuary:
Memories Eternal as the Sea. I stood once with my love
On this coast on a cliff near the old Del Coronado—

Watching hang-gliders suspended in the sky over blue,
Neon dragon-flies—they grow old along this sea-walk.
Joggers & shoppers ascend & descend. Look, says a lovely
Old woman: The idea for escalators came from the waves.

FIRE, STORM, OATH, APOCALYPSE

Kenneth Brower

In my mid-teens, when I first showed an interest in writing, and later, in my twenties, when I actually took up the craft, my mother would occasionally recommend two novels by George R. Stewart, one called *Fire* and the other *Storm*. In either book, she said, elemental nature was the protagonist and human beings were secondary. She thought I might be capable of producing books like that. It was her somewhat jaundiced view that my priorities were skewed already in that direction: that I was starting out, like my father before me, as an imperfectly socialized young man in retreat to the natural world. She worried, I think, that the conventional novel, which typically involves a lot of human interaction, would be outside my range. Her particular concern was woman characters. She frankly, even brutally, stated her doubts that I would ever be able to draw a realistic heroine, given my understanding of the female psyche.

Her recommendation of *Fire* and *Storm*, then, was both a suggestion as to a worthy literary path and a strong maternal hint at my shortcomings as social animal.

George Rippey Stewart was born in Nebraska in 1895, a Hemingway contemporary who eschewed Paris for Columbia, where he got his degrees, and then for Berkeley, where he joined the University of California faculty in 1924, became a professor of English, and taught my mother a course or two. Stewart was a passionate and gifted onomasticist (a student of the origin of names) and a prolific writer of literature in almost every form. Had I bothered to look into him, I would have discovered one of the finest semi-forgotten writers of the American West. I did not bother. I had better things to do than read some old professor of my mom's, and for forty years her advice went unheeded. Then last January, as I packed cold-weather gear for a *National Geographic* assignment in Antarctica, *California* suggested a piece on Stewart. It had been a while since I heard that name. "*Fire!*" I remembered. "*Storm!*" Antarctica, where elemental nature still rules, seemed a suitable continent on which to read George Stewart, so I stuffed several of his books in my duffle. I would be a good boy finally and do what Mamma said.

Fire opens with ten pages of preamble. Stewart introduces his first character, a young woman who has fled a broken romance for the solitary tower of a fire lookout. This college girl, Judith Godoy, is a bit mannish—tall, broad shouldered, an unsqueamish killer of rattlesnakes—yet attractive and likable. Stewart's opening with Judith Godoy, one suspects, was a response to a challenge by some woman—Stewart's wife, maybe, or his mother—to prove he could write a believable female. He pulled it off, I think, for whatever my opinion is worth. Judith, the evidence suggests, is a Cal student, an English major, a would-be writer. In the solitude of her lookout tower, her internal monologues are novelistic. She knows it's creepy, even crazy, but in her thoughts she always refers to herself in the third person, "the girl" of her own story. The ten pages of the book's preamble pass agreeably enough in her company, but the tale has not really begun. It is not until the eleventh page that, as they say at Cape Canaveral, we have ignition.

On that page Stewart describes a thundercloud traveling northward across the summits of the Sierra Nevada, above a forest of Jeffrey pines ten miles from Judith's lookout. One of these pines is conspicuous, at second glance, for its vigor and health. "Although the tallest tree in its immediate vicinity, it was much farther from the cloud than the trees on the ridgecrest. Nevertheless, as an individual man and woman will choose each other, and none other, from a whole city of men and women, so the cloud and the tree drew together from the forces within them."

Reading this passage, at sea off the Antarctic Peninsula, I came to attention. Stewart's metaphor was, I thought, a true and brilliant way to convey the relationship between the cloud and the tree, for I could see where this was going, could see the electricity of the relationship shaping up.

The vigor of this particular Jeffrey pine has a secret, Stewart tells us: its roots touch a vein of underground moisture. "This moisture also produced a channel for the electricity, and the charge moved easily through the sappy trunk clear to the top, where a sharp growing-tip offered an excellent point for discharge. Within a few seconds the tree became tense with electrical pressure.

"Then suddenly, in a blue-white flash, for a period of some few millionths of a second, there poured through the tree between cloud and earth, a force equal to that of many powerhouses."

Now off Antarctica I was wide-awake. I had seen the lightning bolt coming—its ionization had figuratively raised the hair on my neck—yet I was shocked all the same. Atop her lookout, Judith Godoy notes the time of the strike and its azimuth reading. As the dark thundercloud diminishes and moves off, she finds her pack of cigarettes. (Professor Stewart, who published *Fire* in 1948, was shamelessly dependent, like other writers of his time—and the actors, too—on the cigarette as prop: smoking gave characters something to do with their hands.) "The girl lit a cigarette. Suddenly she realized that for an hour she had been in a state of excitement. Now with the storm over, she felt herself slump suddenly. '*All passion spent,*' she said aloud."

We realize, if we have missed it until now, that this had been a kind of sex scene—the most explicit and powerful, it turns out, in all Stewart's oeuvre. His more conventional, man-woman love scenes are rare, brief, and leave much more to imagination. The electric affair between sky and earth has resulted in conception. At the base of the lightning-riven Jeffrey pine, a few dry needles heat to kindling point and a tiny column of smoke curls into the air.

In the novel *Fire* many human characters come and go: rangers, dispatchers, lookouts, smokejumpers, pilots, tractor drivers, crew bosses, winos recruited for the fire lines in Sacramento's skid row, all of them adequately drawn, and a few memorable, yet none quite so real as the title character—or the title *phenomenon,* to be accurate.

For its first six days, the fire of *Fire* just smolders, a "sleeper" in the Forest Service language that Stewart teaches us. Stewart digresses for interludes away with various Forest Service types, but returns always to the infant fire. He meticulously describes the little runs it makes, its small acetylene flare-ups as pinecones ignite, its dyings out, its reanimations as the breeze picks up. It is riveting narrative. We know perfectly well that these embers will become a conflagration, yet somehow Stewart, in his careful anatomy of the gestation of the fire, keeps us in suspense. We wait for the fire to catch. We hope that Judith will be the one to spot it. The incipient fire is too closely observed to be the product of pure imagination. Stewart must have worked on a fire-line himself, resting occasionally on his Pulaski or his axe to study as the advancing fingers blackened the duff. Or perhaps he researched the matter, slipping away into the pines to set little controlled burns for his own edification. He is our greatest literary arsonist. Professor Stewart is not just fascinated by the fire he has kindled on the page; he *loves* his fire. The fire has more idiosyncrasy and particularity—more personality—than any human in the book. After six days and 99 pages, the sleeper finally catches, and at dawn Judith Godoy sees a pillar-like smudge of smoke to the east.

It is curious, but now, even as the fire flames up, the book loses heat.

The beginning of *Fire* is better than the ending. This is true of many books, of course, our greatest novel, *Huckleberry Finn*, among them. (Tom Sawyer shoulders his way into Twain's masterpiece, taking over from Huck and Jim, who are truer, more interesting, and more likable characters.) In the case of *Fire,* two things happen, I believe. One is that the fire quickly grows too big and complex for the reader to grasp; it loses personality, and human firefighters fill the void, crowding the foreground, where they confront what is now just a phenomenon. The other thing is that Stewart loses interest. Somewhere mid-book he recognized, I suspect, that his fire was now a runaway and out of his hands. (Paternal devotion wanes a bit when the child leaves the nest.) My guess is that Professor Stewart, prolific author that he was, began thinking already of his next project.

If, in its second half, *Fire* loses some of its narrative drive, then the novel remains excellent as a primer on the fighting of forest fires. Stewart loved discovering how things work—meteorology, ecology, onomatology, firefighting—and his first step always was to acquire the special language of each new field. He blazed the way for non-fiction writers like John McPhee, who also loves discovering how things work, and who also attacks each of his pieces by learning the jargon. Stewart set the stage, too, for fiction writers like Arthur Hailey in novels like *Airport, Hotel,* and *Wheels,* good potboilers in which the characters are cardboard but the airport, the hotel, and the auto industry come alive.

Storm, published in 1941, was a kind of trial run at *Fire.* The organization is the same, with each day of the storm assigned its own chapter, eleven days and eleven chapters in all, just as in *Fire.* Both books are accounts of unfolding catastrophe as witnessed by a group of characters that the catastrophe brings together—the formula for the modern disaster novel, a genre that Stewart pioneered. The most prominent human in *Storm*, a meteorologist, plays second fiddle to the real protagonist, his heroine, the Pacific storm which, or whom, Stewart and his fictional meteorologist whimsically name "Maria." (The National Weather Service liked Stewart's idea so much that they followed suit, designating storms by female names, and later the novel inspired the songwriters Lerner and Lowe to write "They Call the Wind Maria.") For my part, I liked *Storm* less than *Fire,* but this may have been my circumstances: I began the novel in Drakes Passage, as we neared the Antarctic island of South Georgia, in hurricane-force winds of 105 miles per hour. What I would have preferred right then was a book called *Doldrums.*

The Year of the Oath, published by Doubleday in 1950, is a battle tract, George Stewart's defense of academic freedom in the dark days when a red-baiting faction of the University of California Board of Regents tried to impose a loyalty oath on the faculty.

"That was the Year of the Oath," the book begins. "In that year we went to oath meetings, and talked oath, and thought oath. We woke up, and there was the oath with us in the delusive bright cheeriness of the morning. 'Oath' read the headline in the newspaper, and it put a bitter taste into the breakfast coffee. We discussed the oath during lunch at the Faculty Club. And what else was there for subject matter at the dinner table?"

I was in first grade in Berkeley in the year of the oath, the child of two university employees who talked oath in the evenings. I was stunned, in reading *The Year of the Oath*, by how much I absorbed of that turmoil and how much, with Stewart's promptings, I could recall. (The term "regents" is still sour for me. Why, in a democracy, do we persist in using a word like that, derived from the Latin for "king"?) One day in this period, when an FBI agent knocked at the door to ask questions about a neighbor, my mother, the gentlest of women, told him to get the hell off our porch. I witnessed this moment. As my mother turned from the doorway we exchanged wide-eyed glances. I remember how she radiated pride and fury and excitement and apprehension. What had she just done?

"We learned also something about how suspicion arises, and mistrust, and fear," Stewart writes. "Of men whom we had known for twenty years we heard it said, 'You can't be sure of him!' Before then these were only things we had read about in books as having happened years ago or in other countries."

In the roll and pitch of the Southern Ocean, reading Stewart's account of the controversy almost sixty years after the fact, I found myself wondering: has the University of California community—have Americans generally—proved as brave in this era of Cheney, John Woo, Guantanamo, special rendition, and assault on the Constitution as our predecessors proved in the year of the oath?

Earth Abides, Stewart's most famous work, is just the sort of novel my mother thought I could manage: a book in which humanity is not simply reduced to secondary importance, but almost entirely obliterated in a global pandemic. (No social skills required of the writer—no society anymore.) Published in 1951 and set for the most part in Berkeley, *Earth*

Abides is one of the first of the "post-apocalypse" novels, a genre that blossomed after Hiroshima, in the era of bomb shelters and duck-and-cover drills. The book opens with a rattlesnake strike in the Sierra Nevada. The victim, a graduate student named Isherwood Williams, "Ish" for short, passes a few feverish days in his cabin, and then emerges to find himself the last man alive.

As he drives home to Berkeley, down through the Sierra foothills and foothill towns, now mysteriously deserted, Ish begins to guess what must have happened, and his suspicions are confirmed by a *San Francisco Chronicle* headline glimpsed through a store window. "CRISIS ACUTE," the headline reads.

(Many of Stewart's predictions have not come to pass, but in this episode of the *Chronicle* his futurism was weirdly prophetic. After a moment of hesitation at the store window, Ish breaks in and walks to the news rack. "His first shock came when he picked up the newspaper," Stewart writes. "*The Chronicle,* the one he remembered, was thick—twenty or thirty pages at least. The newspaper he picked up was like a little country weekly, a single folded sheet." Well, the *Chronicle* that *I* remember was thick, too. The one I pick up now each morning, sixty years after Stewart wrote, is nearly as slim as a country weekly, and I am daily startled by its lack of heft.)

Ish, reading the brief story under the CRISIS ACUTE headline, has his second shock: some unidentified pathogen is wiping out his species.

In some small particulars, *Earth Abides* feels dated. Ish, on being snakebitten, *takes the razor from a snakebite kit,* cuts Xs across the two fang punctures in his hand, and applies the kit's suction cups. Reading this, I winced, reminded of the dangerous and useless remedy we believed in and resorted to back then. It was our form of genital mutilation, except that we offered up snakebitten extremities instead.

Ish, on his return to a deserted Berkeley, heads for San Francisco. He drives up to the toll plaza of the Bay Bridge and, despite the fact that the tollbooths are empty, reflexively reaches in his pocket *for a quarter.* (Today the toll is sixteen times that amount.) In mid-span, goofing around, he veers left *into the wrong lane* and drives along the left-hand rail. (Bay Area Baby Boomers, reading this, will vaguely remember the time when the Bay Bridge had two-way traffic on the upper span and the trains rattling below. There really was an era when rapid transit to San Francisco was sunlit, not submarine and subterranean, and it involved no popping of ears.)

But for the most part *Earth Abides* reads very new. At its core the book is a treatise on post-human ecology, and this helps explain its freshness. For novelists of the more commonplace sort, those who set out to chronicle their epochs, an eventual staleness of product is almost inevitable. Their raw material—fashion, customs, morals, colloquial speech, the zeitgeist—is in continual change, whereas natural law is not. Good, true description of nature has a long shelf life.

In *Earth Abides,* as in *Fire* and *Storm,* Stewart's observations on animals seem more acute than those on humans. Early in the book, as Ish drives home from the Sierra, alerted now to the human condition, or the lack of it, he is crossing the San Joaquin Valley when he spots something loping ahead in the inner lane. A dog? "No, he saw the sharp ears and the light lean legs, gray shading into yellow. That was no farm dog. It was a coyote, calmly loping along the highway in broad daylight. Strange how soon it had known that the world had changed, and that it could take new freedom!"

Too soon, I thought at first, upon reading this passage. Only four days have passed since the pandemic has run its course, hardly time enough for the coyote to figure this out. Then I ruminated on the canniness of coyotes. I decided that Stewart is right: it would take a coyote no more than three or four days to comprehend the disappearance of its nemesis. Stewart knows his coyotes, not just the shape and color but the inner capabilities.

On reaching Berkeley, Ish wanders the empty rooms of his parents' house, drifts into despair, and then has his epiphany. He realizes that as an ecologist he has trained, in a way, for this moment. "Even though the curtain had been rung down on man, here was the opening of the greatest of all dramas for a student such as he. What would happen to the world and its creatures without man? *That* he was left to see!"

Ish shelves his pitiful little thesis, "The Ecology of the Deer Creek Area," in favor of a vastly grander work, a magnum opus to be written entirely inside his head. ("The Ecology of Earth after Armageddon," we could call it, as Ish himself never bothers with a title.) It really does promise to be a terrific book, the greatest thing since *Origin of Species*, if only there were someone else alive to read it.

An informed imagination guides Stewart's creation of the post-human world. Pigs do well, and soon big feral boars wander the land. Sheep do poorly and disappear—too stupid. Human head lice are doomed—no more habitat. Cattle survive and run with bison. Dogs manage well enough, and cats thrive. Pigeon numbers plunge catastrophically in cities but remnant populations survive. Wildfires rage in California, fed by the fuel build-up of a half-century of fire suppression. (Stewart understood the falseness of the mantra of Smokey the Bear decades before the Forest Service caught on.) Wheat volunteers for a time in unplowed fields, then steadily fades, to vanish entirely except in its Asian and African drylands of origin, where "here and there, the little spiked grass still was growing, as it had grown before an incident called Agriculture." The countryside reverts to nature faster than towns. As fences break down, rectilinear blocks of land lose discreteness and the landscape goes wavy, nothing hard-edged, one thing fading into another.

Residents of Berkeley will find the post-apocalypse particularly grim—or particularly cheering, maybe, for the Luddites among us. Our town is Stewart's exemplar for the decline and fall of cities everywhere. Wisteria and camellias go extinct in Berkeley, replaced by the vines of wild cucumber. Clover and bluegrass give way to dandelions. Existing deodars survive, but are unable to reproduce. Climbing roses go crazy and clamber everywhere. Eucalyptus prospers, of course, unfortunately. There is a plague of ants, mitigated suddenly when some unknown constraint brings them back into balance. Rattlesnakes, wolves, and mountain lions move back into town and hunt the Cal campus. The deer population plunges and then plateaus out. Or so I presume. (Stewart says nothing about deer demographics himself—this is just my own contribution—but a big reduction of the deer herd would follow inevitably upon the reintroduction of big predators.)

Nothing accelerates the erosion of architecture faster in Berkeley, and everywhere else, than leaf-clogged drains and gutters. The enemy of the written word is not fire, as in Alexandria or Nazi Germany or *Fahrenheit 451;* the enemy is rats scrounging paper for their nests.

Doe Memorial Library on the Cal campus becomes sacred to Ish, a reliquary for the wisdom of the ages, and he rodent-proofs that alabaster Greek-columned temple. The Bay Bridge and the Golden Gate Bridge become sacred, too. Clearly George Stewart loves both bridges as much as Ish does, and in the novel both spans are symbolic, monuments to the technical brilliance of the vanished civilization. If Professor Stewart takes a single false step in his deconstruction of Bay Area infrastructure, it is probably here, with the bridges. In what seems today a stubborn act of wishfulness, he allows both structures to remain nearly impervious to change. Stewart died in 1980. Had he lived nine more years, long enough to see the Loma Prieta quake whip along the Bay Bridge and drop an upper section onto a lower, he might have reconsidered.

As with *Fire* and *Storm* and *Huckleberry Finn,* the beginning of *Earth Abides* is better than the ending.

The trouble is that people show up. Ish, it turns out, is not the only human survivor. He hooks up with others, starts a family, and eventually gathers a tribe. He never abandons his study of post-apocalyptic ecology, but he is distracted now by social obligations. Of necessity he becomes a bit of an anthropologist and sociologist, as well. He does a fair job at this, as does his puppeteer, George Stewart, but the heart of neither man is really in it. The novel grows somewhat slack and repetitious. The old Greek unities of time and place are abandoned. The narrative stream, which flowed clear and strong up at the headwaters of the story, gets caught now in eddies, and Stewart does not seem to notice the same landmarks on the bank coming around again and again.

The marginal resurgence of *Homo sapiens* does not *ruin* the novel, exactly, but it surely does muddy it up a bit.

Earth Abides is a seminal work, widely influential. Literary debt to the book is sometimes acknowledged, as by Stephen King, who credits *Earth Abides* as an inspiration for his novel *The Stand*. Other times, we can only wonder. It is too late to ask Michael Crichton, but in his breakthrough novel, *The Andromeda Strain*, survivors of that book's epidemic are immunized by altered blood chemistry, just as the survivors of Stewart's book are immunized. (The secret to Ish's survival, it turns out, was that rattlesnake bite.) *The Road*, the 2006 novel by Cormac McCarthy, is full of parallels: the sketchily explained cataclysm, the road journey, the literate father who is a repository of Western tradition, the simpler son who is too trusting of others, the ad hoc "families" of survivors.

George Stewart had his own influences, of course. Daniel Defoe, surely, in both *Robinson Crusoe* and *A Journal of the Plague Year*. Adam and Eve from Genesis, no doubt, and Jesus in the wilderness from the Gospel of Mark.

The writer Ernest Callenbach (who himself owes a debt to Stewart for his California-of-the-future novel, *Ecotopia*) supposes that Stewart's sensibilities must have been shaped at Faculty Club lunches with brilliant Berkeley scholars like the paleontologist Charles Camp, the geographer Carl Sauer, the wildlife biologist Starker Leopold, and the anthropologist Alfred Kroeber. (The Kroeber connection seems especially likely. I would bet that the name "Ish," if not a nod to Melville's Ishmael, sole survivor of Ahab's crew, is a nod to Dr. Kroeber's friend and subject Ishi, the sole survivor of his tribe and the final "wild" Indian in North America.) I wonder, too, about the crowd that came home to Berkeley from Los Alamos and Bikini—Lawrence, Seaborg, Teller, and the others—physicists who must have helped sharpen Stewart's view of apocalypse. And I suspect an Algerian influence. The pandemic of *Earth Abides* is anticipated by Albert Camus in *The Plague*, and Stewart's Ish, like Camus's protagonist Meursault in *The Stranger*, is in many ways a cipher, a man strangely unmoved by the deaths of his parents and oddly unperturbed—almost happy—to find himself alone on the Earth.

A kind of antisocial rapture, verging almost on misanthropy, animates *Earth Abides*. It is a benign and forgivable misanthropy, I like to think, because I share it, as one of those people happiest in solitude. Stewart simply took this sensibility a little further than normal, annihilating, in a work of imagination, ninety-nine percent of the human race.

A FLOOD STORY

Emily Taylor

A LEGEND is a cause for dispute, but a hole in the ground does not lie. In our part of the world, when you dig deep to find water you'll see the plain facts in the dirt: layers of shifting sand; generations of harvest and vegetation settling down in alternating tan and ruddy layers; a rich black band from the rot of bursting plant growth; and below that rocky debris, volcanic discharge, white chips of ground bone, and the sediment at the bottom.

Water doused out the hearth fires, and we were set afloat. First, the clouds gathered thick, doubled up in humps and layers. Then rain came ramming into the ground, and the creek that was already up high that season overflowed its banks. Muddy waters rose and vomited through the crevasses in the rocks we had rested on in the evenings and beaten our clothes against until they were raw, fibrous rags in the day. Unluckily paired with the rain was a seismic disturbance of the earth's plates, an interrupted dinner on a catastrophic scale. There was a shift, and the waters of an ocean poured into the land like grain being dumped from a scoop. The water cut through the low valleys as it picked up speed, turning marketplaces into ravines, mountaintops to craggy islands, and red dirt to clay.

When the rain first started, we didn't mind it. Rain always saves us from another backbreaking day of work in the fields—no more hauling rocks, splitting logs, and pounding wheat to make it edible. We sat inside and enjoyed the feeling of soft, clean hands for a day. We picked the splinters out of our palms and the gravel from under our fingernails. We smoked our pipes in doorways, watching small rivulets form in the mud that was washing away the paths to the creek. When we work all day we cannot be bothered with much more than pushing food into our children, pulling warm clothing onto their bodies, or scolding them when they are lazy. As the rain fell, we played with them, noticing their new freckles and crooked teeth. Our faces lost the permanent grimace of exhaustion and we smiled in our idleness.

By the fourth or fifth day, the children grew restless, and we began to miss the work. Our muscles were sore from sitting in front of the fire so long, instead of from pushing a cart out of the mud when the donkey had become too tired to pull. We longed for the hard sun on our backs again, burning its way through our thinning, homespun clothing and darkening the backs of our necks.

We watched our eccentric neighbor run to and fro in the rain. We called him by this derogatory title because of his wild obsession with the sea—to which no one in the village had ever been. Since his youth he had been building a large boat in his yard, a hobby that seemed frivolous to the rest of us as his family went without shoes or bread. Our creek was never wide enough for a boat; even in the wet season it was not more than the length of a child. The eccentric also collected stray animals, from small brown rats to long-snout boars, which were caged or chained in his home. A strong stink of damp fur escaped from his house each time the door opened.

As the rain fell harder, the eccentric grew more frenzied to finish the final touches to his boat. He sanded the wood under a canopy, and he and his family began to set themselves apart from the rest of us. The women would snub their neighbors at the market as they bought large bags of provisions. His youngest son kicked another man's goat into a puddle as he walked through town on one of the last days when walking was possible. "Better that the poor thing drowns now," he was heard to mutter.

A week after the rain began, the eccentric drove all of his animals into the sheets of water that were coming out of the sky. Beating them with a stick, he forced them up a steep ramp into the boat. The man looked out at us nervously, pulling at his long beard. He held his walking stick up, pointing it at our homes, a silent warning not to follow, not to climb aboard after him. We laughed when he drove his wife and sons out with the same stick and the sons' wives too. His daughters though, they were inside the house, and you could see them leaning out the windows. Either their father wouldn't let them go, or they refused to sit out a rainstorm with a menagerie. They were laughing at their father, no doubt. He got out and pushed the boat down to the creek—now a river—on a small set of wheels. When they were adrift, he grabbed hold of a rope and shimmied up through the one small window, and they floated off.

The strong swimmers among us set out next. They were a group of young men and women who liked the water since they were children, and even as they grew, they'd steal off in the evenings on the paths to the creek. At the bend, the water collected into a round pool which they had enjoyed swimming in during the hot season. Often we'd hear their voices echoing in a watery din when we sat together in the evenings on the stones in the center of the village. When the creek flooded and the low ground began to disappear, a few of the swimmers with nothing to lose made their way into the rising water and fought the current towards higher ground. They carried small sacks of food, which they balanced on their chests as they floated on their backs. Perhaps it was possible for them to pretend that it was just another night on the water, feeling the reedy bushes touch their backs, instead of raindrops and the floating detritus of the marketplaces, the floating jugs and wares and drowned animals and people.

The nobility left quickly as well. The ruler had his servants build a makeshift fleet of boats similar to that of the eccentric. They mined our fields and roadways for precious trees, banging together boats in a matter of a few days. The richest landowners were allowed on with their gold and possessions and families. When those royal boats came through the low country, some of the helpless people, the ones who rented an attic loft of a house, a shed, or a small squat of land, asked for salvation. If not places for themselves, they cried, for their children.

Mothers tossed their babies over the bulwarks, threw them over the rails. The guards deflected the bundles, leaving broken children to wail in the water.

Then there was the first man who made a raft from the beams of his roof. Once the water rose past the second floor of his home, he took all the provisions he could balance and his dog, and he set off on the raft. The dog wagged its tail as they floated away. No doubt it thought that this was the greatest adventure of its life. It probably was. The rest of us soon followed suit, because the creek that had become a river was now turning into a sea. It was encroaching from both sides, creeping under the doors and lapping at our feet. We helped each other disassemble the houses that we'd worked to fortify our whole lives. Men and women worked side by side to pry the beams off the rafters and to pull the frames out of the windows and the floorboards from the ground. The children scavenged for rope, for vines, old clothes, anything with which a raft could be tied together. They were happy to have a task, to be allowed to run in the rain, glad of the destruction, and joyful in the mud.

Scraps of wood or anything that would float were in high demand. People hacked the legs off their kitchen tables to barter or sell. The ones who got gold usually ended up regretting it and used the same gold a few days later to buy back only two of the four legs. The market price of wood rose daily. Of course, there were some who took the gold without a thought. They didn't believe that the water could rise that high, and they shut their doors to the community. They barricaded their homes, stuffing the cracks between the boards with cloth or food scraps, sitting tight to wait the water out.

Besides the stubborn ones, there were plenty who had no means to build. These were the poor, the old, the lame, the ill, and those who had not homes to break apart and float on. We all tried to think of them, while frantically hammering and tying together our rafts and piling on our possessions. We went out to find our aunts who lived in huts alone and knocked on the door of the old couple with the daughter whose mind never advanced beyond that of a child. We helped them to find a place if we could. We gave them our scraps of wood. When the waters rose to the point where there was no land to speak of, and what was left of the houses started to come apart at the seams, we pounded the pegs and nails through the logs so fast they often split, and we wound the ropes so tight our hands bled. Everyone who had built something to float on was floating, and we banded together to form a floating village, rafts tethered to one another with ropes. We set up barrels to collect rainwater and kept scraps of wood for repairs and kindling. People built floating pathways between rafts from tree bark, cloth, and cornhusks, and that way we could visit each other and smoke our pipes together under tarps because believe it or not, it was still raining.

And as the more fortunate of our village rose on rafts, the rest died. They were swept, swirled away, and their scraps of wood disintegrated. Their faces disappeared behind the rain, and they were covered by water. The sky was so dark that they had no light to guide them to the surface and as often as not they'd fight their way to earth instead. An occasional shout sounded through the gales, muffled by the creaks of wood breaking in the current and the steady beating of water against water, the slapping of wave against wake. To be honest, we could have saved a few that terrible night in the wet darkness, but our rafts were thin, and we sat there quietly calculating their integrity against the cries of the drowning. We sang to our children so they would not hear and remember.

On the first morning, the bodies floated swollen in the water which rippled in the battering currents. We came across bodies decomposing under bridges or caught against downed trees where they had tied themselves in exhaustion to rest. But they had drowned anyway when the water rose past their necks.

Gradually, anything recognizable about where we had come from disappeared. We could see the mountains far away at times when the clouds thinned, but we couldn't try to head for them, because with all of the rafts tied together, there wasn't a way to propel ourselves. The current was too strong for oars in the water to do any good.

One morning we woke up to find our rafts colliding with those of a neighboring town. We were on unfriendly terms due to an incident involving a charlatan peddler. They had not seen fit to warn us that his tools were made of weak metal or that his medicine would make a cough worse. When these people drifted towards us, there were shouts of anger on both sides: "Get out of our town." Each side tried to push away the rafts of the other, but the way things were spread out, and the way the current of the water was taking us, there was no way to split up. The ropes connecting our rafts became hopelessly entangled. And it still rained. We glared at each other across the churning water. Eventually, we cut the ropes free and separated. "So long, I hope you all drown," a woman yelled. It wasn't clear to which village she belonged.

The sound of rain falling on water all day and night nearly drove us to madness at first, but soon it was barely noticeable, a staccato tension in the back of our minds. We tried to keep the children close, but they were intent on exploration, so we let them. They started scaling ropes, daring each other to walk across logs. They created small swim areas if there was a large enough gap between rafts. We let them swim because the murky water was clearing and though the currents were unpredictable, the children had to use their energy somehow—lest they'd sink us all. The rain had slowed to fat, lazy drops. The children became skilled at navigating under the floating village and could pop up in front of their home raft just before bedtime.

In all of the frenzy of the harried building of the rafts, no one had noticed that some of the young men in town had grown impatient with the idea of floating with their families. They had gone off and started building their own raft along with the eccentric's abandoned daughters. The older women cursed the eccentric for leaving the girls, and the older men looked across at the raft where the young men and women could be seen, arms around each other. One of the girls was singing accompanied by an improvised instrument of five strings stretched across a small barrel, her curly hair swinging with each strum. They looked like they were having a better time than those who were saddled with families and crying babies whose noses ran constantly from the dampness in the air.

At night we felt the soft currents and the nudge of our neighbors' rafts. We listened to each other's coughs, moans, and nightmares. We lay on our backs with our arms under our heads and looked through the rips in our tarps and the rips in the fleets of clouds for the stars. One night we lay awake listening to a woman give birth to a child. When it was finally born and quieted, we wondered whether it would know a world besides this one submerged in water.

We floated along like this and lost track of time. You shouldn't believe anyone who says they have an accurate account of the days and nights at sea. The light stretching across the water in the morning can be confused with the light leaving on the opposite side at night. The days were each the same; there were no crops to plant, and the moon was covered most of the time. We slept and ate when we liked. The days passed. That is all there is to say. We collected rainwater to boil for drink on our communal fires. We cooked, and we rested. We talked and argued and the children played. It could have been weeks or a year.

Our food consisted at first of moldy potatoes and porridge. Occasionally we'd come across something floating that didn't look like it was too long dead, a cow, or a chicken, and we could roast that and eat for a day. But those things were starving enough before they died, so they didn't do us much good. They added flavor to the soup with a tough, rubbery chunk here and there at which to gnaw and from which to suck the fibers.

When the water cleared of rubbish and silt, the fish returned. They followed our drifting village, eating our scraps. We made lines and hooks to drop in the water, nets and traps to sink and drag. The fish were fresh but rubbery, as if toughened by the churning water and the disruption of their river. They followed us perhaps because they had lost their way too. Their spawning pools upstream were gone, along with the reeds among which they had hidden to avoid being scooped up by birds.

The sun burned through eventually, and when it did, the rising vapors were so thick that you couldn't see your friend sitting across the raft from you. The mountains, which had been our landmark, were gone, and our neighbors were gone. We were each alone again, with our lungs filling with moisture, hurting from saturation, and mildew growing around us at alarming rates. One old man sat with a patch of moss growing off his back. He had grown too lazy to wash, and the seeds had germinated in a dirty clump of hair. He didn't mind—he said the moss kept him warm.

One day, we saw the enormous floating carcass of an animal in the distance. At first it appeared to be moving and struggling. When it came nearer it became a flock of birds fighting for space on which to land and rest their mottled wings. We had seen many weary birds drop into the water and die. This flock, though, took turns flying and resting. They looked at us as they drifted by and we at them.

The mountain grew noticeably larger. There was a slow draining, like when you pull the plug from the bottom of a barrel. We waited for the earth itself to resurface. The currents shifted in the waters until we were rocking back and forth in the wind that had risen up. Our stomachs were disturbed violently, and the babies were constantly vomiting. It was a fight to get milk to stay down in their stomachs for even an hour. After a few days, the fierce wind settled into gusts, and after the gusts, there was a stillness. When the water stopped forming small white caps, we could look down into the shadowy depths and see the sunken earth for the first time.

The ground was soon only waist- deep in water, and we began treading through it, eager to use our earth-legs again. The sun burned, and the sky deepened its blue. Dampness rose from the wood of our rafts, and as they dried they sizzled and cracked with warmth. They were washed white by the brightness of the sun from above and reflecting off the water. The new world was all whites and blues, and our blanched faces lifted and were tickled in a warm breeze.

When the water drained to the point of puddles in sand, we homesteaded where it left us. Our new village was an erratic circle of ramshackle establishments, built of mud and scraps. We raised our rafts as roofs once again, and we slept underneath them, but missed the openness of the sky we had enjoyed while floating. Neighbors stayed close because we were used to this closeness, having been alone together on the water.

The ground had been flattened as if stamped down by the feet of giants. In other parts, steep slopes of dirt formed and stark ribbed plateaus, and then the wind began to hollow out curves, starting anew. The wind also dropped off the seeds from far away mountaintops, and the saturated ground made for easy growth, wild and uninhibited sprouting. After the sprouting, low-lying plants grew, and then shrubs, and then forests.

Our young children barely remembered the delicate green color. They pointed and laughed, and when they saw berries and tasted them on their tongues, it was the world reborn in their mouths. Our makeshift homes built from waterlogged wood and tarped over by dirty sheets were also the hosts for seeds. The plants sprang up, vines binding together the logs, covering roofs, and mildew drying out in the wind and becoming food for hungry bugs.

The insects swarmed in from their places of safety, and having their fill of carcass, now found live meals a great pleasure. They made straight for the eyes, for the nostrils, the inner ear, warm tender spots of skin. Birds circled down in pursuit of them and found a great feast. Our plant-covered houses became covered in caked bird droppings, which formed a thick crust on the roofs as the birds made their nests in the branches of our makeshift homes.

The burrowing creatures must have had a strategy, because they came back in great numbers. The bigger mammals made their way down from the mountaintops, where they had settled together. The few stray humans who had been able to swim there rode horses down from the peaks. They reported a few other human settlements along the patterns of the sinking water, and we found a neighboring village not too far away. The old nobility was diminished in size, but a new one would rise soon enough. The creek had also returned, and the water rushing through the underground pockets gushed out fresh and cold from our new wells. We planted our crops and rounded up livestock. We strained our backs again every day under the sun.

We didn't find out about the eccentric and his "new civilization" until years later, because they had floated very far away. A young man who set out on an expedition up river came back with the story. He told it one night around a bonfire, black eyes smiling with the punchline—they claimed that everything on the earth had sprung from them. "But old man," the boy said, "I've never seen you before in my life." We sat around on a circle of driftwood, laughing so hard we almost rolled into the fire.

CALIFORNIA

Jennifer Elise Foerster

I HAVE BEEN to the crater.
There were miles of chrysanthemums.
Palm trees swayed to the hum of the gas pumps.
Poppies lit up the hills and were eating the oak.

I gathered the acorns, dreamed in the ashes.
The white flock lifted from the chaparral
like a tattered wedding dress.

Planets were wheeling in the fault lines.
Pearls gathered at the coastline.
I was traveling the shore in a wooden boat
re-stringing the continent's necklace.

Dragging a rack of whale ribs,
I carried the relics in my mouth,
met a woman named California,
could not pull her voice out.

I went to the arcade of angels,
offered my bucket of shells—
in exchange I was given a map of hell.

I hopped its dark barges,
dreamed beneath the fireworks.
There was a carousal on the beach and I
galloped the black stallion, offered my map

to the roller-skating cashier. In exchange
she gave me a pterodactyl's tear.
I strung it on a thread,
wore it around my neck,

then rode the Daly City train
where I sat beside a geologist.
He gave me directions to the sleeping
volcano. The clouds were

oysters, opening and closing.
I trapped the blue pearl,
offered it to a fisherman.
In exchange he gave me a dragon-scale kite.

I dozed beneath its shadow,
drank horchata at the cantina,
tangoed with a sailor beneath the bone dry moon
then rented a motel room

between two highways. From there
I could see the hills burn, the sky
shatter. I pushed a rickshaw of fossils
through deepening mud.

My dreams were the treasures
of a sinking boat as I awoke
to the black horse gnawing
hot gravel, the maps
burnt to ashes in my mouth.

JUNDEE AMERIKI

Brian Turner

Many the healers of the body.
Where the healers of the soul?

—AHMAD SHAUQI

AT THE VA hospital in Long Beach, California,
Dr. Sushruta scores open a thin layer of skin
to reveal an object traveling up through muscle.
It is a kind of weeping the body does, expelling
foreign material, sometimes years after injury.
Dr. Sushruta lifts slivers of shrapnel, bits
of coarse gravel, road debris, diamond
points of glass—the minutiae of the story
reconstructing a cold afternoon in Baghdad,
November of 2005. The body offers aged cloth
from an abaya dyed in blood, shards of bone.
And if he were to listen intently, he might hear
the roughened larynx of this woman calling up
through the long corridors of flesh, saying
Allah al Akbar before releasing
her body's weapon, her dark and lasting gift
for this *jundee Ameriki*, who carries fragments
of the war inscribed in scar tissue,
a deep, intractable pain, the dull grief of it
the body must learn to absorb.

THE TAO OF THE COW

Bruce Patterson

I ONCE LIVED ON a farm in the San Joaquin Valley. Less than three years out of the army, alone, broke and chased by war demons, I wound up on the farm by accident. Or since, strictly speaking, there are no such things as accidents—or luck, or fate—I should say that I wound up on the farm the way one thing leads to another, and that to the next, and so on until you arrive at something else entirely with another thing coming.

Working in an onion field on land as flat and level as a lake, herbicided, pesticided, fertilized and fumigated, the birdless sky a dusty dome, the Sierra, Tehachapis and Diablos hidden behind a wall of industrial haze, with tractors on the chalk-line horizon crawling like bugs on a windowsill and lowing like lonesome cows, at least I was about as far away as I could get from root-bound, vine-choked and muddy/slippery mountainsides. "Anti-jungle," the San Joaquin was, and I very much appreciated that. Now I just needed to figure out where—it wasn't here—I belonged.

That's how the farm's milking cow helped me out. I milked that cow a bunch of times, my cheek and ear to her side listening to her stomachs gurgling, my hands pulling and squeezing her teats, her steaming jets of milk rhythmically squirting into my frosty milk pail, and one morning I realized why she was allowing me to get away with it. The reasons were obvious and simple, of course, but the implications for me struck me as profound. While I had no clear idea about what I wanted to be when I grew up, then and there I resolved that, no matter what, I wasn't going to become a two-legged milking cow.

According to cow cosmology, the entire universe is divided into just two elements: *Food* and *Unfood*. A cow's moral code begins and ends with: *When in Unfood, go to Food. When in Food, stay*. My dad was a reformed hustler and when I was a little boy he warned me never to become conceited because conceited people are always the easiest marks. For one thing, since they are convinced that they as uniquely talented individuals are entitled to all they can get their hands on, like fish they always rise to the bait. Even better, because they assume they already know everything they need to know, they never learn anything. Whether it is to a pool hall, a card table, the stock market or a milking stall, they always come back for more.

Am I accusing milking cows of being conceited? Yabetcha. She lets you milk her in exchange for a feedbag full of cow candy, be it alfalfa and molasses, rolled oats or whatever. So long as her mouth is full of candy, she won't lift her nose out of her feedbag or worry over what you're doing to her ass end. But woe to you if she runs out of candy before she runs out of milk. She'll lift her head up, see what you're doing and, feeling cheated, her pride wounded, she'll kick over your milk pail just to spite you. She might even kick you if you give her the chance. If her head wasn't tied and she wasn't stalled, she might buttonhook around and snort a pint of snot into your eyebrows. Worse, she might drop her head and run right over the top of you. If she does, then you'd best hope the ground is good and squishy.

To avoid such humiliations, when it comes to handling any kind of large animals, the First Commandment is: *Thou shall not get thyself runned over.* Unless you're a rodeo cowboy. If that's the case then it's amended to read: *When thou art throwed by thy equine or, lo, verily, thy bovine, thou shall not get thyself runned over.*

Of course, not many rodeo cowboys are temperamentally fit to be following most any kind of commandment all the time. They're bound to sin at least a little bit and the most sinful of them have broken so many ribs during their careers that they tinkle while they hobble, one hip rolling counter-clockwise. In recent times there's been folks willing to call rodeo organized "cruelty to animals." They'll say the same with regard to horse racing, too. I suppose you could even find some folks who'd denounce milking a cow as inhumane and uncivilized. I mean a farmer could just as well shoot a milking cow in the brainpan and haul her off to the cannery to get chopped up into gourmet dog food. The same as rodeo and racing stock could have never been born.

Once on TV I watched a network newscaster grill an old cowboy about the nature, types and extent of animal cruelty on the rodeo circuit. The old cowboy was sporting a horseshoe tattoo across his forehead, his nose was lying over like a broke bale of hay and one of his shoulders was hanging lower than the other. "All'n all," the cowboy cautiously ventured, "I reckon the livestock gets treated pretty good."

By the way, did you hear the one about the rodeo cowboy who showed up at the Pearly Gates? When St. Peter asked him what was the noblest thing he'd ever done in his life, the cowboy told him about how one time he was enjoying a quiet beer in his hometown watering hole when six loud, crude and nasty outlaw bikers barged in. Immediately they started in at harassing one of the local girls and the cowboy couldn't have that. So he stepped into the middle of them fellahs and he told them that they could either behave themselves or he'd knock them down and drag them out one-by-one.

"Hmmm," St. Peter said, impressed. "How long ago was that?"

The cowboy glanced at his wristwatch. "That'd be about ten seconds ago."

THE ARCHITECTURE OF PELICANS

Carolyn Cooke

IT BEGINS, of course, with cows. You walk the rungs of the iron cow-grate, slip between the fence and the gate into the zone of Black Angus and Holsteins, the tags in their ears twitching as the herd turns toward you, stolid and inscrutable. Sometimes, they run. It is a decision not made lightly—cows prefer rumination to sudden action—but like any overly domesticated mammal, they're prone to small anxieties and panics.

The earth rumbles, and the herd hightails it across the field, usually in the most direct path away from you, but sometimes not. Sometimes the herd runs beside you, eyes wide, unable to correct, and lands, sullen and embarrassed, in a grove of scrub pine just where you're headed.

After a while, when the cows have arranged themselves at some mutually satisfactory distance, you let the dogs off the leash. So much open space brings on a kind of madness and the dogs run in wide, whizzing arcs that blur at the edges. You walk along the barbed-wire fence past the old AT&T housing that looks over the trans-Pacific cable to Hawaii, already talking intensely about the deep subjects—sex at midlife, how best to work, long, involved stories about the past (childhood, men, mistakes, choices, witchy coincidences) or stories about people you know that unravel like 19th-century novels, or as if you were Freud or Jung, and your subjects were splayed on a *récamier* like Manet's Odalisque, prepared for intense inspection or analysis. The walk, with talk, takes an hour and a half. If you were different people, content with one pleasure at a time, you might walk in a companionable silence, humbly (or arrogantly) letting in the visions and the salt air, allowing yourselves to be passive, penetrated. But you are greedy girls—you walk and talk. Your goal is to cover ground—skim a certain surface of the world, and at the same time go deep. The story is, for this purpose, a sinkhole. It drops suddenly, like a body from a plane, defiantly vertical, creating depth abruptly, where before all attention had been, as it usually is, on horizontal movement—velocity, trajectory.

A squadron of pelicans flies architecturally just beyond the headlands, honing themselves into a sharpened line. You wonder whether taking flight is the pelican metaphor for going deep—an avid, upward plunge into the sublime.

At some point the rear pelican moves to the front and the front pelican moves to the rear. The bird at the front uses the most energy, so the stronger pelicans agree to trade off. They know how to use their bodies to create a spontaneous aerodynamic structure in the air; they know how to flow. In flight, the birds are at home, maybe even most at home, in their most familiar structure. Such surges of consciousness in a group require planning, communication, subtle agreements like the cows make when they decide when and where to run.

The pelicans fly above the caves and the rock arch and the sea stack, a mesa of shale perhaps an acre around. The sea stack seems marooned, impossible to reach, too tall and vertical to climb, the sheer walls 30 or 40 feet high and slick with waves. But there is, as there almost always is, some man-made artifact of iron or wood impaling the air.

This is the real Pacific rim, the jagged, crumbling edge of the continent. The waves toss ionized particles up the walls of the sandstone cliffs in which twenty or so cormorants are nesting, their long black swanlike necks rubbing and curling against each other. You walk dangerously close to the edge, spying, testing, reminding yourselves that the ground you walk on is temporary, these arrangements—conservancy lands, towns, cities, states and nations—are temporary. You walk along the bluffs then peer respectfully into the actual sinkhole, an inverted cone in the ground perhaps 35 feet across. The sinkhole is too steep to climb into, so it's impossible to determine what kind of opening or pothole leads to the bottom, and where the "bottom" might be—an underground world of hollow galleries, stalactites, stalagmites, siphons and slender, sandy supporting columns harassed by subterranean streams constantly straining against the membrane that holds back the Pacific. You might be able to wriggle down or fall, Alice-like, into this other world, but you might not come back again; the whole Army Corps of Engineers could not save you.

What we think of as "underground" is well within the area of the Earth's crust. Beneath are less hospitable regions: sedimentary rock, metamorphic rock, the granite layer, the basaltic layer, and deeper, hotter places approaching the earth's core—the sun at the center. Walking now across the clifftops you feel at the top of the world, though sea level is just one precipice away. Seventy-five hundred miles distant Everest soars above us, dwarfed in turn and immediately by the dimensions of the troposphere, the stratosphere, the mesosphere, the thermosphere, the mile posts before the outer edge of the atmosphere and, 500 miles out, the beginning of space.

The dogs return, stand shoulder to shoulder and contemplate the sinkhole before running off again.

You walk on, discussing a recent experience with a psychic in Willits. How did the psychic know about your cancer scare? About the dead boy in the pink house? About the Ducati motorcycle? What do you do with information like that? How do you tune in to or tune out other bandwidths out there?

You come to a line of scrub pines, buried up to their necks in duff and covered with a delicate hanging moss. The grass, which last week contained dog-violets and iris, now holds mud-loving flowers: fringed downingia (bluebells).

The surface changes, day by day, season by season, layer by layer. What you think of as "the land" or "the cattle ranch" is really a roll of sod laid out over the sandstone and shale. You imagine living horizontally across the earth, traveling south to San Francisco or east to Boston—but this is a kind of fiction. In fact, you live vertically as much as horizontally. To travel from the coast to the ridge is to move across more antisocial layers of sandstone, shale, schist, limestone. The pygmy forest at the crest of the ridge a few hundred feet above sea level is made of lime, of oyster shells.

You come to the midway point of the walk, at Lighthouse Road, the lighthouse winking a quarter mile away. (The great Fresnel lens was removed from the cupola last year by a crane, and installed in the museum downstairs.) Your first job in Point Arena was as a lighthouse "keeper," sitting for four hours at a time on a vat of mercury which served as a bearing for the lens, and telling the story of the lighthouse, the French lens, the families who lived here before the 1906 earthquake damaged the original lighthouse and the tower had to be rebuilt. People used to go crazy living here, fogged in on this blowy edge of the ocean. It's like residing in a glass of milk. The mercury was crazy-making, toxic. Hat makers used mercury to secure hatbands; hence the term "mad as hatters."

You turn and walk back, past the vernal pool at the edge of a cliff. Water cascades down into an inlet in the foaming ocean, where hundreds of giant sea cucumbers lie tangled together, hairy heads and long bodies surging and ebbing with the tide like drowned dolls. The dogs step into the quiet pool to drink; gulls spray out into the sky.

Toward the AT&T houses, the grass grows denser and taller, in clumps, between which lie muddy troughs wide enough to pass through. The going is slow, though—a knee-high thicket. Suddenly, a cry, a scream comes from somewhere in the grass around you. You fall back and disappear into the grass, nowhere familiar. You are down, gone. You assume that you have been taken, and might be eaten.

Instead, you have stepped over a baby doe so new she's still wet, her mouth still open from her cry of surprise. You back away—unsteady, hulking. Then, when the fawn is safe from the dogs and from you, you hightail it toward the gate, embarrassed, past the cows.

THE MERE MORTAL

Louis B. Jones

CARLA HAPPENED to be kneeling outside the poultry enclosure when she heard her daughter Amanda in the milking barn telling the new boyfriend, "My father is a beatnik. He hates life up here. He calls us '*montagnards*.' He really loves North Beach. And he's in the right place, too, in North Beach. Because he's into porn—something I approve of. Well, he isn't 'into porn,' but he made his money writing an erotic book using the author name Francesca Weld. It's the only book he's sold so far. All his serious work frightens people. People are just too stupid for it." Judging by the sounds inside, the boyfriend was toying with the latch on one of the milking stalls.

Carla went ahead and decided she was actively eavesdropping—which is a mother's right sometimes, or possibly even duty—while she continued crawling around in the grass gathering vagrant eggs into her Carhartt-jacket pockets. Domesticated fowl are so improvident, they leave behind their big white ova in seeming happy forgetfulness. Amanda inside the barn carried on: "My sense is, the Internet is going to save womankind. The Internet will give out so much free, downloadable erotic stuff, males won't come out in society anymore. They'll just stay home. They won't want to get married. Or date. Because dating is expensive and scary. They'll stay inside all day pointing and clicking and stop being a problem out in society. Totally different world."

She was leading this polite, tall glee-club tenor—named Eric—on a tour of the farm's goat operation. It was the second time Eric had been brought to make an appearance here, and Carla liked him. He was a product of the county public-school system locally, but he had applied to eight colleges and been accepted at most of them. All that labor, of filling out applications and writing personal essays and scrounging up recommendation letters, it made Carla tired just to think of it. Amanda hadn't had to bother with applications because she was accepted early, a legacy on her father's side. Lately she was saying she wouldn't go at all, not to Brown, not anywhere, because colleges are all complicit in the war machine and the global-warming cartels, and because back east you can't eat local-organic year-round. The whole East Coast is totally backward.

To everything she said, this Eric, in his purity, had a way of listening with utterly persuaded passiveness, enraptured, while his eyes kept falling to her mouth, her throat, waiting for the moment when he could fasten his own mouth there. At least that's what Carla liked to imagine, or hope. The comedy of love—this young love in particular—was something she observed with certain secret biases, because despite her age and position, this boy Eric was the first male in years who'd inspired her dormant old girlhood crush. His full, beige lips with one pimple at the corner, his strong neck and general uprightness, were altogether the kind of traits that unlocked her own mischief. Or would have if she were thirty years younger. A mother after a certain age in her irrelevancy doesn't try to repress such stirrings—she rather observed them in herself with a little proprietary gladness. Realistically she only hoped her daughter wouldn't mistreat the boy. He was innocent despite all that intelligence. Or innocent because of the intelligence: all the braininess depended on the naiveté. Amanda by contrast was positively jaded. She even seemed to speak with a yawn today.

The sound inside the barn was of Eric opening the stainless-steel cupboard on the far wall. There he would discover an array of scalds, teat dips, all the not-very-effective mastitis remedies she had to employ instead of prostaglandins so Calafia Farms could keep its organic certification. There'd been a little silence, then Eric said, "I wonder if it's uncomfortable." By the muffledness of his voice, he was probably reading labels on bottles. "I mean for the goat. Being milked in this industrialized way?" Apparently he had no response to Amanda's opinions about the pacification by porn of a nation of males.

"Oh, and the most picturesque thing is Antonio. You've got to see him," said Amanda. "He takes the goats out. But he's hardly worth his wage anymore, 'cause at this point that's all he does: the goats. They go out grazing in groups of thirty at a time. Old, fat Antonio. He actually has a shepherd's crook, and he takes them down in the live oaks. Your Spanish will get a workout. He speaks no English at all. Like, he's been in this country for years, but he still only speaks Spanish. So it's just him and his goats in life."

Meanwhile Carla, like a child at Easter, was crawling deeper into the grass behind the barn. Maybe domesticated fowl somehow know. Know which eggs are fertile and which are the duds, and so are liberated to neglect the lifeless ones outside the henhouse. Then, egg laying for a hen is like menstruation. Had she ever found a fertile one outside? She couldn't think of an instance. There was one time years ago when her husband cracked an egg over a bowl for his omelet and released a blue and brown packet, fetal toothpick-bones, a beak, a huge staring lidless eye. That was surely one of the first occasions of Steve's admitting to himself farm life wasn't for him and San Francisco had begun calling him back, because he walked straight out of the kitchen and wouldn't return until she'd disposed of the embryo. Oh and then she horrified him, she poured it in the dogs' bowls, yolk and embryo together, over their Ralston Purina. Poor Steve amidst the barbarity hung his head and gently closed his eyes. They had been married for maybe six or eight years at that point. Strange how you can know somebody so long, and so deeply, and still truly love him, then and now, and it never dies. Steve was *her* particular shot at love in her lifetime. As much as anybody ever does, she'd hit the target, marrying Steve. He had, upon the lawns of Berkeley, arrived in her sight as a handsome package of great genes, carrying a tennis racket. He was like a remnant of an elfin aristocracy that was now extinct, or had almost entirely vanished to enchanted western isles. So she'd acquired him, right there at Sather Gate on the campus, she reached out and took him. Him and his delicate ear and throat, his patrician drawl, his finickiness about language, his tennis, his recordings of weird modern orchestral music that sounded to Carla like horror-movie scores. The great assumption they shared and treasured, always, was his superiority. In the performance that was their marriage, *he'd* been the ballerina lifted in flight, upon *her* shadowier support. That was how she'd wanted it too. If she could have, she would have done the whole thing again the same way, right up to the discovery of that bloody omen in his omelet batter. Whether that particular egg had come from the brooding shelves or from out here in the grass, she had no possible way of reckoning now.

Amanda's voice went on, speaking of Antonio, "Him and his goats *and* his Blessed Virgin. And the memory of his sainted mother. And his wine. He has a name for each individual goat. There's Innocencia, Mercedes, Serena, Modesta, Guadalupe, Isabella, Soledad. On and on. He actually knows which is which. I mean, there's ninety-some goats in this parlor alone, but you can ask him, 'Hey, Antonio, *como se llama este chivo?*' and he'll say, 'Maria,' 'Juanita,' 'Placentia.' He is *totally* rustic."

Carla got up from her knees. Eight brown eggs—and a slate-blue ninth one from the Connecticut hen—lay nestled in her jacket's flat outer pockets, in danger of being crushed in the grip of Carhartt canvas. Holding the pocket rims lightly open, she went around to the front barn door.

Amanda was leaning on the rail of a milking stall. "He has a corncob pipe. He does," she said, watching her mother come in. "It's too warm these days, but a month from now he'll be wearing a poncho. An actual wool poncho. If we went and found him right now, he'd be hanging out with his goats, with his pipe and his shepherd's crook, like, sitting on a hummock, or a tummock, or whatever it's called."

She was draped against the railing, shoulders thrust back, her navel exposed above her jeans in its perfect baby fat, still unmutilated by ring or by steel stud, her breasts flattened into oddly high shapes by the new kind of bra Carla didn't entirely disapprove of, but of course could never consider wearing herself.

Eric, who had been looking out a window over the valley toward the buttes in distant Sierra County, turned and said, "Hi, Ms. Levinson."

"Hello, Eric. You're invited for dinner. This Antonio you're hearing so much about knows where to get mushrooms, and I have a risotto.

So. Now, Amanda, I could hear you outside, and you are a most *informative* fascinating guide! I think we won't have any secrets left after you're finished telling Eric everything about us. Just don't bore him."

"Eric *is* boring, Mom. This is the most exciting day he's had all year."

"I'm definitely not bored, Ms. Levinson." He was smiling, and his cheeks were ruddy.

"And, Amanda? Your father is not a pornographer."

"Well, it's the only book that ever sold."

Carla had to laugh—and laugh with pleasure, because something about Amanda-logic was irresistible. Amanda herself was irresistible. Suddenly of late she was thrilling, indomitable, her fairy hair, her delicate complexion and big blue eyes, her bright fever matching Eric's, their cheeks *competing* in blushes. Nonsense rules, when there's love in the room: all bets are off, all rules are suspended, and an egg-scavenging, lint-haired mother ought to make herself scarce. She didn't belong here where the air was misted with infatuation, or call it lust, indeed like the amazing blood-mist in a poultry abattoir, so radiant was the whole situation, so that Carla actually had to turn her face from the blaze, toward the door. Carrying her pocketfuls of lifeless eggs, she went out, saying, "I'll be up in the kitchen adding little dribs of wine to the rice." Her describing her own plans as trivial, in comparison with the thing that was happening behind her in the barn, was perhaps supposed to act, somehow, as license for them to get physically nearer each other. "Anyone who would *like* to come up and help with dinner is welcome."

While she was walking off, she didn't hear them speak. Probably a good sign. She hadn't forgotten what it was like, the power to, by the slightest gesture, and from a distance, make a boy stand or leap or twitch or expand or shrink: Amanda had *fulfilled* her childhood Harry Potter fantasy—the years rush by so fast, it seemed like only the previous summer—when she'd had an all-consuming ambition to be a sorceress in a world of stupid Muggles and mere mortals; she used to fling the scythes of her little-girl fingers at people as if churning storms. In that milking parlor it was humbling, being in the same room with all that actual sorcery. Humbling even to the girl's mother. Let her use it while it lasts; because people tend to forget, *it is* the ultimate reason for everything else, the reason for barns and goats and harvests and colleges; the reason for new brassiere designs and beatnik fathers and Eric's perfect SAT score and the real estate underfoot and the paperwork Carla does all morning in her office. A young girl is the flower upon all that root and stem.

Up the lane ahead, the last gold sunlight of afternoon lay hard upon the side of the house. Sixty miles beyond and higher, on the crest, the remote peaks of Desolation Wilderness were bathed in that same afternoon light, above the shadows that climbed the lesser mountains. First dusting of snow on top. Winter arrived early up there. It was a place she had never visited. Lived within sight of all these years but never traveled to. A domain of serious backpackers, it was a place she had reached a point now of someday wanting to visit. Alone and not with a hiking party. It was a more arduous kind of hiking up there, involving serious equipment. And there would be a lot of silence, silence as you climbed higher, the way a canyon gets quieter in autumn after the foliage has fallen and the animals have departed. Here at this lower elevation, in the end-of-day warmth by the sheds, swarm clouds of fruit flies made shifting mounds, buzzing, undulating over the heaped pears, which had been harvested but in their abundance ignored, so that now they were turning to slick goo, a feast for the flies, in bushel baskets and cardboard boxes against the potting shed. All for Antonio to shovel into the compost heaps. The old bushel baskets could be hosed off for another year.

It had felt good being on her knees and crawling like a child at her age. It had felt rejuvenating. By contact of soft turf, kneecaps are physically healed; and her own knees had been wrecked during the years of high heels. Crawling, just crawling, is obviously therapeutic for the spine too. Grown-ups ought to spend more time on their hands and knees. In only four years, the whole goat operation had prospered so quickly, the entire muddle of business success had overtaken her so fast, alone in her years of triumph (except for Amanda!), Carla spent all her time now in the office, indoors, very little time anymore in the barns or the gardens. Every morning, the whole morning long in her ergonomic chair, she, in Amanda's phrase, pointed and clicked. But in her case it certainly wasn't Internet porn, it was banking and marketing, flashing past in quick windows, it was promotional searches, e-mailing, purchasing, hiring and contracting, memos for sales and operations and clients' correspondence, paying bills. Absolutely everything now can be done on computer, it's all so convenient, it's deadly, it is death. Just now, crawling on all fours had uncoupled her vertebrae, so her hips seemed to swing better going up the dirt lane. A few minutes near the therapeutic smell of horseshit gives one a feeling of being years younger, like that kind of therapy-by-smell people do. Most days the routine odors, for her soul, were—what was it?—printer toner, the Vaseline Intensive Care on her hands, coffee after coffee, the smell of coffee in the telephone receiver's perforated plastic disk like halitosis. At this point in her life, with Steve long gone and only dull men in these foothills, Carla might easily—might wisely—begin thinking of herself as one of that race of "older single women" who everywhere are a useful element in society, and admit she'd long ago given up all art and artifice, to become one of the chapped, sun-hatted, mannish happy gals, the kind of women she used to look down on, when she first moved up here, seeing them in the IGA wearing men's work clothes, confirming her private generalization that the countryside was the reverse of the city: the females here are overweight and unblessed, the men good-looking. In San Francisco, it was the men who didn't bother. At least in her circles. It was the women who had the goods. Made an effort. Worked the magic. Took up that responsibility.

Anyway, she was suddenly aware that Amanda and Eric were following her, coming up the lane from the barns. They were going to join her in the kitchen. Rather than, say, move deeper into the outbuildings. Or travel on into the woods and maybe catch a glimpse of the legendary gnome Antonio. Or even go down to the pond to feed the swans. What did this portend? It would seem they wanted *her* as audience for a while, rather than frankly facing each other. They wanted a chaperone! So, when Carla arrived in the kitchen, she poured herself some wine. She would be sociable. On the stove she started the flame under the risotto again, ladled in a dose of broth, tilted in wine, gave it a stir, adjusted the flame lower.

She unloaded her nine eggs, intact, upon the polished marble countertop, its black mausoleum luster as fathomless as an ocean: she'd always regretted putting in those marble slabs, preferring the irregular Mexican tiles, which Steve had insisted were trite and impractical. *She* was trite and impractical. It was years now, and she couldn't get over disliking the marble slabs, increasingly. The black mass reflected the nine eggs in its surface, as nine duplicate effigies of eggs in the underworld, supporting them on their nine tangent points, rather than swallowing them up. In the mudroom she hung up the Carhartt she loved so much it might see her out of this life. In the mirror there, her tress of loose hair looked good. Funny, to be adjusting her looks for a clueless boy who could be her child. She stood up more crisply the collar of her shirt.

The two kids were coming up the porch steps. "Amanda, when is your movie?" Carla spoke through the screen door. "Risotto likes to take as long as possible."

"I'm not having any. I'll eat cheese and apples and nuts."

She had been proclaiming lately she would eat only raw food for the rest of her life. Maybe tonight, however, she would relent and have some risotto, because it would smell good. Amanda's radical diets came and went fast, entering her life with fanfare, accompanied by speeches and homilies, as well as politics and metaphysics and plenty of recommended reading, then later slipping away quietly without notice. Carla liked to think it came from her own Jewish side, this wrestling with dietary regimens having moral implications. By contrast, Amanda's father, whether down in Mexico or at the ballpark or wherever, would happily put in his mouth anything that was set before him *without even lowering his eyes to look at it*, literally!

With the exception of the chicken embryo. That was something that got Steve's attention.

Amanda was lifting the lid of the kitchen laptop. "I'll see," she said. Meaning, when movie showings were scheduled. As the screen came to life, Carla imagined, weirdly, that an invading blaze of true "Internet porn" could come storming in, from somewhere, from nowhere, from the heights of cyberspace: those shiny, inflated-looking people who tumbled in camera angles. Sometimes in her work she came across those blasts of dreary obscenity and clicked on past, pausing for a minute to contemplate the farce and horror of it, the odd, stunted lives of the actresses and actors. No doubt Amanda, by her age, had been irradiated by such images. You can't avoid it. In every recess it flourishes yeastlike with a force that's explosive.

But of course no such thing happened. The screen was just the mother-of-pearl gray background, with all her little icons labeled.

"Now, Eric. Are you under any special dietary restrictions? I'm not using chicken broth in the risotto, I'm using vegetable broth."

"No, ma'am. I'm not a vegetarian. It smells wonderful."

"Well then, since Amanda's not eating—and at the risk of offending her morals—maybe I'll sauté the mushrooms in a strip of bacon. Would that be all right, Mandy? That won't drive you from an unclean, defiled place?"

Amanda kept her eyes on the screen. "There's a showing at nine o'clock," she said. "We have plenty of time."

"So, Amanda, why only *raw* food?" Eric asked with an avidity only a seventeen-year-old could have, eager to learn something new, something that might make him change his ways, change his diet, and his life, forever.

"I'll tell you why," Amanda said, lowering the lid on the computer. "See that gas flame? Under that pan? Because of that flame—and a lot of things like it—shorelines are being polluted, women and children are being killed in far-off places where American foreign policy is. Salmon are dying in the dammed-up rivers, coal miners are dying, like in Kentucky and Mexico and China, and in Nigeria whole tribes are being driven off the face of the earth, not to mention Ecuador."

Eric had a kind of joyful-to-be-defeated grin, fixed and ready, but it was clear to Carla's secret eye, he wasn't impressed so much by Amanda's argument, he was simply lost in admiration of her ardor.

As for Carla, she knew what was coming next: Amanda's elaborate analogy of "sin." She held her tongue and went on cooking, giving the mushrooms a few more chops on the butcher block, then stirring them straight in, leaving the bacon out, because without the animal fat the dish might tempt Amanda. It was hard to watch her subsist on carrots. And cold tofu and jicama.

"You know what Catholics and Protestants do?" Amanda said. "Every Sunday they have to ask forgiveness for the sins they did do and *the things they neglected to do*. Those are sins, too. The things you *didn't* do. Secular people who talk about religion like to claim they don't understand the 'sin' part. They say, 'Frankly I don't feel particularly sinful.' Meanwhile they go out and start their car and burn gasoline that little Iraqi children were killed for. And they know it *while* they do it. They're fully aware. They've been told. They haven't, like, forgotten. While they fill up the tank at the gas station, they know what this costs. Republicans and Democrats and liberals—whatever. They all know. It's murder, and they do it, and they know perfectly well they're doing it. Do it every day."

Eric had started to seem worried. He said, "We were planning to drive. The movie is way over in Grass Valley, and it'll be dark. We can't ride bikes."

"Well, *pfff*, there's always something," said Amanda.

Carla intervened to rescue her daughter, asking which movie they meant to go see.

Amanda moved her distracting body up onto a bar stool. "We're going to see the one where two boys kiss," she said.

"Oh, excellent," said Carla, stirring the pan again. Then in the role of mom at the stove she heard her own voice uttering that opinion. And wondered why it should be commendable.

Well, it's commendable because, when you increase the box-office receipts of a movie about two men who fall in love, you're committing a political deed, raising the prospects of a group that has been excluded from the media and culture establishment. Is that not the reasoning?

Amanda told her mother, "I know, it's not the typical date flick. But I'm training Eric. He's going to be less masculine when I'm done with him."

Eric gave an affable shrug for Ms. Levinson, apologizing for his incorrigible masculinity. Ms. Levinson, the mom at the stove, felt her own heart go pitty-pat, in a remembered way, because of the masculine manner in which, now, he'd folded his arms, sitting there in the kitchen chair, his forearms making cancellation signs to remove his own opinions, and himself bodily, from the conversation. Berkeley—her own school, and the school Eric was destined for—was an excellent place; he would get a top-drawer education. The boy was already famous for his perfect SAT scores. It was the first thing one learned about him, before meeting him. But Berkeley wasn't Brown, it wasn't Ivy League, he would miss out on the social connections. All the phony social stuff is an angle kids underestimate. Then it creeps up on them later in life.

What a hypocrite she had become, at this point. The destiny she would really choose for her—rather talkative—daughter would be to end up with a husband, a husband who loved her, and for her to love him in return. Because Amanda was always a little *too much* in control. One wished for her a husband rather like Eric. But first a great education at Brown. Then graduate school, which is apparently unavoidable these days. Then a career and a dazzling life for a few years in (as she pictured it) New York. Then to be superseded in her profession, by the hordes of *men* out there who simply lower their heads and labor, in their chosen fields, in some single-minded way that one really doesn't wish for a woman. Or, anyway, wish for Amanda. To end up single-minded like her poor father. In his airless room, writing his prickly, political poetry for a small cult. Amanda was, at the moment, informing Eric about the poisonous influence everywhere of testosterone. And right now the main thing Carla hoped for her was simply that she might be a little quieter, a little slower and softer. And for her body, with its winking midriff, to be a little less thrust into the discussion. The new bra compresses girls' breasts with the shape of an unreal virginity, an unyieldingness of the classical Greek huntress-goddess, which surely boys must see as buds to be explored, if they can be brave and impolite enough. As Amanda went on, trying to raise Eric's consciousness above the usual male torpor, he had every appearance of agreeably absorbing the whole argument. Despite his SAT-based reputation, he was a little slow. The SAT isn't life.

The grains of rice in the pan had reached the point of being just about as plump and sticky as they were ever going to be. She added a last ladleful of broth and a drizzle of wine from her stemmed glass, then the Parmesan. And the table was set.

Homosexuality, her daughter went on, is troubling to the middle class and the bourgeoisie because when they settle down in the dark of a theater and are subjected to the big projected image of men kissing—when they're forced to see that—their first thought is *Ooh!* but then they censor that thought and their next practical thought is *Hey, but who's the victim here?* Because when a girl is kissed by a guy, it's clear who the victim is. Who the object is. She's the vessel. She's the treasure. Right? So the economic relationship is clear. But then, love between two men?—or two women?—completely wrecks the economic setup. Marriage is the economic unit of society. Marriage is, in reality, part of the government. Marriage is the smallest corporation. A little taxable corporation. A governable corporation. That's how it's all organized. It's all about property preservation. About mortgages. Everything in capitalism is about property. So with marriage and divorce laws, too, the whole thing is about money, without it being identifiable as prostitution. We in the middle class, we aren't supposed to talk about the love-for-money thing. So the possibility of a love that *isn't* prostitution—like gay people who are in love—makes us look at things we don't want to look at. In a nutshell, to make a long story short, this is why it's going to do Eric some good to sit in the dark and watch two cute guys make out.

This was one of Amanda's well-rehearsed disquisitions. Carla had heard it before and was presently more interested in seeing its effect on Eric. This Eric, though, he was a smooth operator; he just soaked it up radiant with admiration. Carla spooned the risotto into three little painted bowls that would make the sticky mess seem more attractive. She supposed Amanda would, at some point, experiment with girls; but

Eric didn't seem to have it in him, to kiss a boy. She couldn't picture it. She couldn't picture *him* picturing it. Her own middle-aged, middle-class soul was that of a hopeful, bruised liberal, but, still and always, she could be squeamish or craven or fundamentally "trite," in Steve's words. Everything she knew about the embraces between men—of which she knew plenty, more than she really wanted to, having had many gay friends back in San Francisco who tended to confide and gossip, confide indeed all too much, about the riskiest, stretchiest kinds of amyl nitrite-induced grappling in bathroom stalls—everything she knew made her simply worry, just like a mom, about the purely anatomical troubles and hygiene complications, as much as the morning after and coffee with a new friend at Cafe Flore, the entry there into an alienated and ironic tribe, the sadness of that.

Anyway, she lived now in the peaceful bright steamy-windowed kitchen of the bourgeois heterosexuals, compromised by—Amanda wasn't half wrong—the old love-for-money deal, and perhaps gradually turning reactionary, one of society's comfortable folks. She didn't need to confess any of this to her daughter. Amanda would go forth and, with her generation, remake the world. It was all for the good, a mom's not having justifiable opinions anymore, just focusing on keeping the farm solvent, e-mailing the stores, keeping the trucks running. The table was laid, the three bowls smoked at the three places. She seated herself in the candlelight and laid her napkin over her knee, and she lifted a fork, and she seized on a lull in Amanda's lecture, which had pretty much run its course, to turn to Eric and ask, "Eric, tell me, what do you think you'll major in at Berkeley?"

Eric was serving himself from the big wooden salad bowl, tender greens from the gardens above the pond, dressed with bits of the farm's dill cheese. Amanda called Eric's attention to the salad gripped in his tongs. "That cheese in there is famous. Seventeen restaurants—right, Mom?—actually list it by name on their menu: Calafia Farms Cheese."

"Wow," said Eric, looking back and forth between mother and daughter, his big tongs suspended.

"Anyway...," said Carla.

He went back to work with the salad tongs and replied, "I really have no idea what I might major in. But I do notice I gravitate toward the sciences. I find I like the terminology, the vocabulary, the whole lexicon, I have to admit. And I like the little details. I'll bet I end up in life sciences. I don't see myself practicing medicine, really. I see myself in some kind of research." He set the tongs down and passed the big bowl.

It was the most the boy had said all evening, and it seemed to consist mostly of the first-person pronoun, a declaration bristling with *I*s all crowding the sentence as little columnar stand-up versions of himself.

"Typical," complained Amanda: she would see "research" as dominated by corporations. She put down her fork, flopped back in her chair, throwing her arms over the back, and parted her thighs wide in Eric's direction, opening herself up for a thorough, critical consideration of him. Carla, as mother, kept repressing her irrelevant dread of unladylike behavior precisely because she'd certainly had many sprees of unladylike behavior herself, back when the game was afoot. "That's why you are the problem, Eric," Amanda said. "You're so narrow. It's all career. It's an ego game with you, and nobody gets the larger holistic picture. You're all so helpless," she finished—and in that instant her rather fond despair over her boyfriend seemed to melt back into real lasciviousness, Carla saw it, it was unmistakable, that gleam just for a minute there, she was sizing him up. And indeed, they never did go to their movie.

Because after Carla had covered the leftovers and switched off the kitchen lights; after she had watched Antonio pass along the lane amid a small herd of goats *clank-clanking* in the last twilight, carrying his little varmint-protection .22-caliber rifle—in the Mexican manner, slung over his shoulder upside-down so the barrel pointed at the ground—bearing his corncob pipe and his aluminum lawn chair; after she had phoned him down in his trailer to discuss tomorrow's apple harvest and the rental of a chipper and the instructions for the distributor's van in the morning; and after she had put the dogs to bed in the mudroom, she happened to be passing by the stairs that led down to the television area, where things were all too quiet, and where, presently, the sounds of love arose. She didn't move on, though. She stayed there at the head of the stairs. It was sweet to hear. It was beautiful. Little whispers and scoldings and sighs.

If Steve still lived here, he would have found a fatherly way to forbid it. Despite all his bohemianism, he would have been a little enraged. But a young woman had to make her explorations, and somehow by insulting Eric all afternoon she had been buttering him up for this. Love alone—love of mother for daughter, of girl for boy—emerges as the warm stone. Warmed by what? Warmed by the sun of many other summers. And what had Carla done to deserve, or cause, all this happiness, this tranquillity and good luck? Nothing. Her daughter, *she* was the one who knew everything now—so it was time for her to begin the long education in confusion, lying on the old plaid couch down there, personifying the victim she had spoken of earlier. It's terribly hard work being young. A young person must thrust herself into existence, must impersonate herself somehow. Carla wouldn't want to be lying on that couch in Mandy's place, not for a million dollars be young again, she was an old hypocrite at last, growing more ignorant and bewildered by the year. This mantle of ignorance and bewilderment, it's grace all right, accumulating. It's the snow on the distant peaks, calling to her. The secret a mother could never speak of to her daughter (or at least not until they're both older, a pair of ladies having lunch together in a tea shop!) was how fine it is to reach an age when beauty is done with you, when lust has picked you up and used you and then dropped you, and you can revert to being as cruel as nature. Old hag, all evening she'd had those same dried mud-badges on her knees, and she liked it that way.

ASK ME IF I CARE

from *A Visit from the Goon Squad*

Jennifer Egan

LATE AT NIGHT, when there's nowhere left to go, we go to Alice's house. Scotty drives his pickup, two of us squeezed in front with him, blasting bootleg tapes of the Stranglers, the Nuns, Negative Trend, the other two stuck in back where you freeze all year long, getting tossed in the actual air when Scotty tops the hills. Still, if it's Bennie and me I hope for the back, so I can push against his shoulder in the cold, and hold him for a second when we hit a bump.

The first time we went to Sea Cliff, where Alice lives, she pointed up a hill at fog sneaking through the eucalyptus trees and said her old school was up there: an all-girls school where her little sisters go now. K through six you wear a green plaid jumper and brown shoes, after that a blue skirt and white sailor top, and you can pick your own shoes. Scotty goes, Can we see them? and Alice goes, My uniforms? but Scotty goes, No, your alleged sisters.

She leads the way upstairs, Scotty and Bennie right behind her. They're both fascinated by Alice, but it's Bennie who entirely loves her. And Alice loves Scotty, of course.

Bennie's shoes are off, and I watch his brown heels sink into the white cotton-candy carpet, so thick it muffles every trace of us. Jocelyn and I come last. She leans close to me, and inside her whisper I smell cherry gum covering up the five hundred cigarettes we've smoked. I can't smell the gin we drank from my dad's hidden supply at the beginning of the night, pouring it into Coke cans so we can drink it on the street.

Jocelyn goes, Watch, Rhea. They'll be blond, her sisters.

I go, According to?

Rich children are always blond, Jocelyn goes. It has to do with vitamins.

Believe me, I don't mistake that for information. I know everyone Jocelyn knows.

The room is dark except for a pink night-light. I stop in the doorway and Bennie hangs back too, but the other three go crowding into the space between the beds. Alice's little sisters are sleeping on their sides, covers tucked around their shoulders. One looks like Alice, with pale wavy hair, the other is dark, like Jocelyn. I'm afraid they'll wake up and be scared of us in our dog collars and safety pins and shredded T-shirts. I think: We shouldn't be here, Scotty shouldn't have asked to come in, Alice shouldn't have said yes, except she says yes to everything Scotty asks. I think: I want to lie down in one of those beds and go to sleep.

Ahem, I whisper to Jocelyn as we're leaving the room. Dark hair.

She whispers back, Black sheep.

Nineteen eighty is almost here, thank God. The hippies are getting old, they blew their brains on acid and now they're begging on street corners all over San Francisco. Their hair is tangled and their bare feet are thick and gray as shoes. We're sick of them.

At school, we spend every free minute in the Pit. It's not a pit in the strictly speaking sense; it's a strip of pavement above the playing fields. We inherited it from last year's Pitters who graduated, but still we get nervous walking in if other Pitters are already there: Tatum, who wears a different color Danskin every day, or Wayne, who grows sinsemilla in his actual closet, or Boomer, who's always hugging everyone since his family did EST. I'm nervous walking in unless Jocelyn is already there, or (for her) me. We stand in for each other.

On warm days, Scotty plays his guitar. Not the electric he uses for Flaming Dildos gigs, but a lap steel guitar that you hold a different way. Scotty actually built this instrument: bent the wood, glued it, painted on the shellac. Everyone gathers around, there's no way not to when Scotty plays. One time the entire J.V. soccer team climbed up from the athletic field to listen, looking around in their jerseys and long red socks like they didn't know how they got there. Scotty is magnetic. And I say this as someone who does not love him.

The Flaming Dildos have had a lot of names: the Crabs, the Croks, the Crimps, the Crunch, the Scrunch, the Gawks, the Gobs, the Flaming Spiders, the Black Widows. Every time Scotty and Bennie change the name, Scotty sprays black over his guitar case and Bennie's bass case, and then he makes a stencil of the new name and sprays it on. We don't know how they decide if they should keep a name, because Bennie and Scotty don't actually talk. But they agree on everything, maybe through ESP. Jocelyn and I write all the lyrics and work out the tunes with Bennie and Scotty. We sing with them in rehearsal, but we don't like being onstage. Alice doesn't either—the only thing we have in common with her.

Bennie transferred last year from a high school in Daly City. We don't know where he lives, but some days we visit him after school at Revolver Records, on Clement, where he works. If Alice comes with us, Bennie will take his break and share a pork bun in the Chinese bakery next door, while the fog gallops past the windows. Bennie has light brown skin and excellent eyes, and he irons his hair in a Mohawk as shiny black as a virgin record. He's usually looking at Alice, so I can watch him as much as I want.

Down the path from the Pit is where the cholos hang out, with their black leather coats and clicky shoes and dark hair in almost invisible nets. Sometimes they talk to Bennie in Spanish, and he smiles at them but never answers. Why do they keep speaking Spanish to him? I go to Jocelyn, and she looks at me and goes, Rhea, Bennie's a cholo. Isn't that obvious?

That's factually crazy, I go, and my face is getting hot. He has a Mohawk. And he's not even friends with them.

Jocelyn goes, Not all cholos are friends. Then she says, The good news is, rich girls won't go with cholos. So he'll never get Alice, period-the-end.

Jocelyn knows I'm waiting for Bennie. But Bennie is waiting for Alice, who's waiting for Scotty, who's waiting for Jocelyn, who's known Scotty the longest and makes him feel safe, I think, because even though Scotty is magnetic, with bleached hair and a studly chest that he likes to uncover when it's sunny out, his mother died three years ago from sleeping pills. Scotty's been quieter since then, and in cold weather he shivers like someone is shaking him.

Jocelyn loves Scotty back, but she isn't *in love* with him. Jocelyn is waiting for Lou, an adult man who picked her up hitchhiking. Lou lives in LA, but he said he would call the next time he comes to San Francisco. That was weeks ago.

No one is waiting for me. In this story, I'm the girl no one is waiting for. Usually the girl is fat, but my problem is more rare, which is freckles: I look like someone threw handfuls of mud at my face. When I was little, my mom told me they were special. Thank God I'll be able to remove them, when I'm old enough and can pay for it myself. Until that time I have my dog collar and green rinse, because how can anyone call me "the girl with freckles" when my hair is green?

Jocelyn has chopped black hair that looks permanently wet, and twelve ear piercings that I gave her with a pointed earring, not using ice. She has a beautiful half-Chinese face. It makes a difference.

Jocelyn and I have done everything together since fourth grade: hopscotch, jump rope, charm bracelets, buried treasure, Harriet the Spying, blood sisters, crank calls, pot, coke, quaaludes. She's seen my dad puking into the hedge outside our building, and I was with her on Polk Street the night she recognized one of the leather boys hugging outside the White Swallow and it was her dad, who was on a "business trip," before he moved away. So I still can't believe I missed the day she met the man, Lou. She was hitchhiking home from downtown and he pulled up in a red Mercedes and drove her to an apartment he uses on his trips to San Francisco. He unscrewed the bottom of a can of Right Guard, and a Baggie of cocaine dropped out. Lou did some lines off Jocelyn's bare butt and they went all the way twice, not including when she went down on him. I made Jocelyn repeat each detail of this story until I knew everything she knew, so we could be equal again.

Lou is a music producer who knows Bill Graham personally. There were gold and silver record albums on his walls and a thousand electric guitars.

The Flaming Dildos rehearsal is on Saturday, in Scotty's garage. When Jocelyn and I get there, Alice is setting up the new tape recorder her stepfather bought her, with a real microphone. She's one of those girls that like machines another reason for Bennie to love her. Joel, the Dildos' steady drummer, comes next, driven by his dad, who waits outside in his station wagon for the whole practice, reading World War II books. Joel is AP everything and he's applied to Harvard, so I guess his dad isn't taking any chances.

Where we live, in the Sunset, the ocean is always just over your shoulder and the houses have Easter-egg colors. But the second Scotty lets the garage door slam down, we're suddenly enraged, all of us. Bennie's bass snickers to life, and pretty soon we're screaming out the songs, which have titles like "Pet Rock," and "Do the Math," and "Pass Me the Kool-Aid," but when we holler them aloud in Scotty's garage the lyrics might as well be: *fuck fuck fuck fuck fuck fuck*. Every once in a while a kid from Band and Orchestra pounds on the garage door to try out (invited by Bennie), and every time Scotty ropes up the door we glare out at the bright day shaking its head at us.

Today we try a sax, a tuba, and a banjo, but sax and banjo keep hogging the stage, and tuba covers her ears as soon as we start to play. Practice is almost over when there's another banging on the garage door and Scotty pulls it up. An enormous pimpled kid in an AC/DC T-shirt is standing there, holding a violin case. He goes, I'm looking for Bennie Salazar?

Jocelyn and Alice and I stare at one another in shock, which feels for a second like we're all three friends, like Alice is part of us.

"Hey guy," Bennie says. "Good timing. Everybody, this is Marty."

Even smiling, there's no hope for Marty's face. But I'm worried he might think the same of me, so I don't smile back.

Marty plugs in his violin and we launch into our best song, "What the Fuck?":

You said you were a fairy princess
You said you were a shooting star
You said we'd go to Bora Bora
Now look at where the fuck we are...

Bora Bora was Alice's idea—we'd never heard of it. While everyone howls out the chorus (*What the fuck? / What the fuck? / What the fuck?*), I watch Bennie listen, eyes closed, his Mohawk like a million antennas pricking up from his head. When the song ends, he opens his eyes and grins. "I hope you got that, Al," he goes, and Alice rewinds the tape to make sure.

Alice takes all our tapes and turns them into one top tape, and Bennie and Scotty drive from club to club, trying to get people to book the Flaming Dildos for a gig. Our big hope is the Mab, of course: the Mabuhay Gardens, on Broadway, where all the punk bands play. Scotty waits in the truck while Bennie deals with the rude assholes inside the clubs. We have to be careful with Scotty. In fifth grade, the first time his mom went away, he sat all day on the patch of grass outside his house and stared at the sun. He refused to go to school or come in. His dad sat with him trying to cover his eyes, and after school, Jocelyn came and sat there, too. Now there are permanent gray smudges in Scotty's vision. He says he likes them—actually, what he says is: "I consider them a visual enhancement." We think they remind him of his mom.

We go to the Mab every Saturday night, after practice. We've heard Crime, the Avengers, the Germs, and a trillion other bands. The bar is too expensive, so we drink from my dad's supply ahead of time. Jocelyn needs to drink more than me to get buzzed, and when she feels the booze hit she takes a long breath, like finally she's herself again.

In the Mab's graffiti-splattered bathroom we eavesdrop: Ricky Sleeper fell off the stage at a gig, Joe Rees of Target Video is making an entire movie of punk rock, two sisters we always see at the club have started turning tricks to pay for heroin. Knowing all this makes us one step closer to being real, but not completely. When does a fake Mohawk become a real Mohawk? Who decides? How do you know if it's happened?

During the shows we slam-dance in front of the stage. We tussle and push and get knocked down and pulled back up until our sweat is mixed up with real punks' sweat and our skin has touched their skin. Bennie does less of this. I think he actually listens to the music.

One thing I've noticed: no punk rockers have freckles. They don't exist.

One night, Jocelyn answers her phone and it's Lou going, Hello beautiful. He's been calling for days and days, he goes, but the phone just rings. Why not try calling at *night*? I ask when Jocelyn repeats this.

That Saturday, after rehearsal, she goes out with Lou instead of us. We go to the Mab, then back to Alice's house. By now we treat the place like we own it: we eat the yogurts her mom makes in glass cups on a warming machine, we lie on the living room couch with our sock feet on the armrests. One night her mom made us hot chocolate and brought it into the living room on a gold tray. She had big tired eyes and tendons moving in her neck. Jocelyn whispered in my ear, Rich people like to hostess, so they can show off their nice stuff.

Tonight, without Jocelyn here, I ask Alice if she still has those school uniforms she mentioned long ago. She looks surprised. Yeah, she goes. I do.

I follow her up the fluffy stairs to her actual room, which I've never seen. It's smaller than her sisters' room, with blue shag carpeting and crisscross wallpaper in blue and white. Her bed is under a mountain of stuffed animals, which all turn out to be frogs: bright green, light green, Day-Glo green, some with stuffed flies attached to their tongues. Her bedside lamp is shaped like a frog, plus her pillow.

I go, I didn't know you were into frogs, and Alice goes, How would you?

I haven't really been alone with Alice before. She seems not as nice as when Jocelyn is around.

She opens her closet, stands on a chair, and pulls down a box with some uniforms inside: a green plaid one-piece from when she was little, a sailor suit two-piece from later on. I go, Which did you like better?

Neither, she goes. Who wants to wear a uniform?

I go, I would.

Is that a joke?

What kind of joke would it be?

The kind where you and Jocelyn laugh about how you made a joke and I didn't get it.

My throat turns very dry. I go, I won't. Laugh with Jocelyn.

Alice shrugs. Ask me if I care, she goes.

We sit on her rug, the uniforms across our knees. Alice wears ripped jeans and drippy black eye makeup, but her hair is long and gold. She isn't a real punk, either.

After a while I go, Why do your parents let us come here?

They're not my parents. They're my mother and stepfather.

Okay.

They want to keep an eye on you, I guess.

The foghorns are extra loud in Sea Cliff, like we're alone on a ship sailing through the thickest fog. I hug my knees, wishing so much that Jocelyn was with us.

Are they right now? I go, softly. Keeping an eye?

Alice takes a huge breath and lets it back out. No, she goes. They're asleep.

Marty the violinist isn't even in high school—he's a sophomore at SF State, where Jocelyn and I and Scotty (if he passes Algebra II) are headed next year. Jocelyn goes to Bennie, The shit will hit the fan if you put that dork onstage.

I guess we'll find out, Bennie goes, and he looks at his watch like he's thinking. In two weeks and four days and six hours and I'm-not-sure-how-many-minutes.

We stare at him, not comprehending. Then he tells us: Dirk Dirksen from the Mab gave him a call. Jocelyn and I shriek and hug onto Bennie, which for me is like touching something electric, his actual body in my arms. I remember every hug I've given him. I learn one thing each time: how warm his skin is, how he has muscles like Scotty even though he never takes his shirt off. This time I find his heartbeat, which pushes my hand through his back.

Jocelyn goes, Who else knows?

Scotty, of course. Alice, too, but it's only later that this bothers us.

I have cousins in Los Angeles, so Jocelyn calls Lou from our apartment, where the charge won't stand out on the phone bill. I'm two inches away on my parents' flowered bedspread while she dials the phone with a long black fingernail. I hear a man's voice answer, and it shocks me that he's real, Jocelyn didn't make him up, even though I never supposed such a thing. He doesn't go, *Hey beautiful*, though. He goes, I told you to let me call you.

Jocelyn goes, Sorry, in an empty little voice. I grab the phone and go, What kind of hello is that? Lou goes, Who the Christ am I talking to? and I tell him Rhea. Then he goes in a calmer voice, Nice to meet you, Rhea. Now, would you hand the phone back to Jocelyn?

This time she pulls the cord away. Lou seems to be doing most of the talking. After a minute or two, Jocelyn hisses at me, You have to leave. Go!

I walk out of my parents' bedroom into our kitchen. There's a fern hanging from the ceiling by a chain, dropping little brown leaves in the sink. The curtains have a pineapple pattern. My two brothers are on the balcony, grafting bean plants for my little brother's science project. I go outside with them, the sun poking into my eyes. I try to force myself to look straight at it, like Scotty did.

After a while, Jocelyn comes out. Happiness is floating up from her hair and skin. Ask me if I care, I think.

Later she tells me Lou said yes: he'll come to the Dildos gig at the Mab, and maybe he'll give us a record contract. It's not a promise, he warned her, but we'll have a good time anyway, right, beautiful? Don't we always?

The night of the concert, I come with Jocelyn to meet Lou for dinner at Vanessi's, a restaurant on Broadway next door to Enrico's, where tourists and rich people sit outside drinking Irish coffees and gawking at us when we walk by. We could have invited Alice, but Jocelyn goes, Her parents probably take her to Vanessi's all the time. I go, You mean her mother and stepfather.

A man is sitting in a round corner booth, smiling teeth at us, and that man is Lou. He looks as old as my dad, meaning forty-three. He has shaggy blond hair, and his face is handsome, I guess, the way dads can sometimes be.

C'mere, beautiful, Lou actually does say, and he lifts an arm to Jocelyn. He's wearing a light blue denim shirt and some kind of copper bracelet. She slides around the side of the table and fits right under his arm. Rhea, Lou goes, and lifts up his other arm for me, so instead of sliding in next to Jocelyn, like I was just about to do, I end up on Lou's other side. His arm comes down around my shoulder. And like that, we're Lou's girls.

A week ago, I looked at the menu outside Vanessi's and saw linguine with clams. All week long I've been planning to order that dish. Jocelyn picks the same, and after we order, Lou hands her something under the table. We both slide out of the booth and go to the ladies' room. It's a tiny brown bottle full of cocaine. There's a miniature spoon attached to a chain, and Jocelyn heaps up the spoon two times for each nostril. She sniffs and makes a little sound and shuts her eyes. Then she fills the spoon again and holds it for me. By the time I walk back to the table I've got eyes blinking all over my head, seeing everything in the restaurant at once. Maybe the coke we did before wasn't really coke. We sit down and tell Lou about a new band we've heard of called Flipper, and Lou tells us about being on a train in Africa that didn't completely stop at the stations—it just slowed down so people could jump off or on. I go, I want to see Africa! and Lou goes, Maybe we'll go together, the three of us, and it seems like this really might happen. He goes, The soil in the hills is so fertile it's red, and I go, My brothers are grafting bean plants, but the soil is just regular brown soil, and Jocelyn goes, What about the mosquitoes? and Lou goes, I've never seen a blacker sky or a brighter moon, and I realize that I'm beginning my adult life right now, on this night.

When the waiter brings my linguine and clams I can't take one bite. Only Lou eats: an almost-raw steak, a Caesar salad, red wine. He's one of those people who never stops moving. Three times strangers come to our table to say hello to Lou, but he doesn't introduce us. We talk and talk while our food gets cold, and when Lou finishes eating, we leave Vanessi's.

On Broadway he keeps an arm around each of us. We pass the usual things: the scuzzy guy in a fez trying to lure people inside the Casbah, the strippers lounging in doorways of the Condor and Big Al's. Punk rockers rove in laughing, shoving packs. Traffic pushes along Broadway, people honking and waving from their cars like we're all at one gigantic party. With my thousand eyes it looks different, like I'm a different person seeing it. I think, After my freckles are gone my whole life will be like this.

The door guy at the Mab recognizes Lou and whisks us past the snaking line of people waiting for the Cramps and the Mutants, who are playing later on. Inside, Bennie and Scotty and Joel are onstage setting up with Alice. Jocelyn and I put on our dog collars and safety pins in the bathroom. When we come back out, Lou's already introducing himself to the band. Bennie shakes Lou's hand and goes, It's an honor, sir.

After the usual sarcastic introduction from Dirk Dirksen, the Flaming Dildos open with "Snake in the Grass." No one is dancing or even really listening; they're still coming into the club or killing time until the bands they came for start playing. Normally Jocelyn and I would be directly in front of the stage, but tonight we stand in back, leaning against a wall with Lou. He's bought us both gin and tonics. I can't tell if the Dildos sound good or bad, I can barely hear them, my heart is beating too hard and my thousand eyes are peering all over the room. According to the muscles on the side of Lou's face, he's grinding his teeth.

Marty comes on for the next number, but he spazzes out and drops his violin. The barely interested crowd gets just interested enough to yell some insults when he crouches to replug it with his plumber's crack displaying. I can't even look at Bennie, it matters so much.

When they start playing "Do the Math," Lou yells in my ear, Whose idea was the violin?

I go, Bennie's.

Kid on bass?

I nod, and Lou watches Bennie for a minute and I watch him too. Lou goes, Not much of a player.

But he's—, I try to explain. The whole thing is his—

Something gets tossed at the stage that looks like glass, but when it hits Scotty's face thank God it's only ice from a drink. Scotty flinches but keeps on playing, and then a Budweiser can flies up and clips Marty right in the forehead. Jocelyn and I look at each other panicked, but when we try to move, Lou anchors us. The Dildos start playing "What the Fuck?" but now garbage is spewing at the stage, chucked by four guys with safety-pin chains connecting their nostrils to their earlobes. Every few seconds another drink strikes Scotty's face. Finally he just plays with his eyes shut, and I wonder if he's seeing the scar spots. Alice is trying to tackle the garbage throwers now, and suddenly people are slam-dancing hard, the kind of dancing that's basically fighting. Joel clobbers his drums as Scotty tears off his dripping T-shirt and snaps it at one of the garbage throwers, right in the guy's face with a twangy crack, and then at another one—*snrack*—like my brothers snapping bath towels, but sharper. The Scotty magnet is starting to work—people watch his bare muscles shining with sweat and beer. Then one of the garbage throwers tries to storm the stage, but Scotty kicks him in the chest with the flat of his boot—there's a kind of gasp from the crowd as the guy flies back. Scotty's smiling now, grinning like I almost never see him grin, wolf teeth flashing, and I realize that, out of all of us, Scotty is the truly angry one.

I turn to Jocelyn, but she's gone. Maybe my thousand eyes are what tell me to look down. I see Lou's fingers spread out over her black hair. She's kneeling in front of him, giving him head, like the music is a disguise and no one can see them. Maybe no one does. Lou's other arm is around me, which I guess is why I don't run, although I could, that's the thing. But I stand there while Lou mashes Jocelyn's head against himself again and again so I don't know how she can breathe, until it starts to seem like she's not even Jocelyn, but some kind of animal or machine that can't be broken. I force myself to look at the band, Scotty snapping the wet shirt at people's eyes and knocking them with his boot, Lou grasping my shoulder, squeezing it harder, turning his head to my neck and letting out a hot, stuttering groan I can hear even through the music. He's that close. A sob cracks open in me. Tears leak out from my eyes, but only the two in my face. The other thousand eyes are closed.

The walls of Lou's apartment are covered with electric guitars and gold and silver record albums, just like Jocelyn said. But she never mentioned that it was on the thirty-fifth floor, six blocks away from the Mab, or the green marble slabs in the elevator. I think that was a lot to leave out.

In the kitchen, Jocelyn pours Fritos into a dish and takes a glass bowl of green apples out of the refrigerator. She's already passed around quaaludes, offering one to every person except me. I think she's afraid to look at me. Who's the hostess now? I want to ask.

In the living room, Alice is sitting with Scotty, who wears a Pendleton shirt from Lou's closet and looks white and shaky, maybe from having stuff thrown at him, maybe because he understands for real that Jocelyn has a boyfriend and it isn't him, and never will be. Marty is there, too; he's got a cut on his cheek and an almost-black eye and he keeps going, That was intense, to no one in particular. Joel got driven straight home, of course. Everyone agrees the gig went well.

When Lou leads Bennie up a curling staircase to his recording studio, I tag along. He calls Bennie "kiddo" and explains each machine in the room, which is small and warm with black foam points all over the walls. Lou's legs move restlessly and he eats a green apple with loud cracks, like he's gnawing rock. Bennie glances out the door toward the rail overlooking the living room, trying to get a glimpse of Alice. I keep being about to cry. I'm worried that what happened in the club counts as having sex with Lou—that I was part of it.

Finally I go back downstairs. Off the living room I notice a door partly open, a big bed just beyond it. I go in and lie facedown on a velvet bedspread. A peppery incense smell trickles up around me. The room is cool and dim, with pictures in frames on both sides of the bed. My whole body hurts. After a few minutes someone comes in and lies down next to me, and I know it's Jocelyn. We don't say anything, we just lie there side by side in the dark. Finally I go, You should've told me.

Told you what? she goes, but I don't even know. Then she goes, There's too much, and I feel like something is ending, right at that minute.

After a while, Jocelyn turns on a lamp by the bed. Look, she goes. She's holding a framed picture of Lou in a swimming pool surrounded by kids, the two littlest ones almost babies. I count six. Jocelyn goes, They're his children. That blond girl, everyone calls her Charlie, she's twenty. Rolph, that one, he's our age. They went to Africa with him.

I lean close to the picture. Lou looks so happy, surrounded by his kids like any normal dad, that I can't believe this Lou with us is the very same Lou. Then I notice his son Rolph. He has blue eyes and black hair and a bright, sweet smile. I get a crawling feeling in my stomach. I go, Rolph is decent, and Jocelyn laughs and goes, Really. Then she goes, Don't tell Lou I said that.

He comes into the bedroom a minute later, rock-crunching another apple. I realize the apples are completely for Lou, he eats them non-stop. I slide off the bed without looking at him, and he shuts the door behind me.

It takes me a second to get what's going on in the living room. Scotty is sitting cross-legged, picking at a gold guitar in the shape of a flame. Alice is behind him with her arms around his neck, her face next to his, her hair falling into his lap. Her eyes are closed with joy. I forget who I actually am for a second—all I can think is how Bennie will feel when he sees this. I look around for him, but there's just Marty peering at the albums on the wall, trying to be inconspicuous. And then I notice the music flooding out of every part of the apartment at once—the couch, the walls, even the floor—and I know Bennie's alone in Lou's studio, pouring music around us. A minute ago it was "Don't

Let Me Down." Then it was Blondie's "Heart of Glass." Now it's Iggy Pop's "The Passenger":

I am the passenger
And I ride and I ride
I ride through the city's backside
I see the stars come out of the sky

Listening, I think, You will never know how much I understand you.

I notice Marty looking over at me kind of hesitant, and I see how this is supposed to work: I'm the dog, so I get Marty. I slide open a glass door and go onto Lou's balcony. I've never seen San Francisco from so high up: it's a soft blue-black, with colored lights and fog like gray smoke. Long piers reach out into the flat dark bay. There's a mean wind, so I run in for my jacket and then come back out and curl up tightly on a white plastic chair. I stare at that view until I start to get calm. I think, The world is actually huge. That's the part no one can really explain.

After a while the door slides open. I don't look up, thinking it's Marty, but it turns out to be Lou. He's barefoot, wearing shorts. His legs are tan even in the dark. I go, Where's Jocelyn?

Asleep, Lou goes. He's standing at the railing, looking out. It's the first time I've seen him be still.

I go, Do you even remember being our age?

Lou grins at me in my chair, but it's a copy of the grin he had at dinner. I am your age, he goes.

Ahem, I go. You have six kids.

So I do, he goes. He turns his back, waiting for me to disappear. I think, I didn't have sex with this man. I don't even know him. Then he goes, I'll never get old.

You're already old, I tell him.

He swivels around and peers at me huddled in my chair. You're scary, he goes. You know that?

It's the freckles, I go.

It's not the freckles, it's you. He keeps looking at me, and then something shifts in his face and he goes, I like it.

Do not.

I do. You're gonna keep me honest, Rhea.

I'm surprised he remembers my name. I go, It's too late for that, Lou.

Now he laughs, really laughs, and I understand that we're friends, Lou and I. Even if I hate him, which I do. I get out of my chair and come to the railing, where he is.

People will try to change you, Rhea, Lou goes. Don't let 'em.

But I want to change.

No, he goes, serious. You're beautiful. Stay like this.

But the freckles, I go, and my throat gets that ache.

The freckles are the best part, Lou says. Some guy is going to go apeshit for those freckles. He's going to kiss them one by one.

I start to cry, I don't even hide it.

Hey, Lou goes. He leans down so our faces are together, and stares straight into my eyes. He looks tired, like someone walked on his skin and left footprints. He goes, The world is full of shitheads, Rhea. Don't listen to them—listen to me.

And I know that Lou is one of those shitheads. But I listen.

Two weeks after that night, Jocelyn runs away. I find out with everyone else.

Her mother comes straight to our apartment. She and my parents and older brother sit me down: What do I know? Who is this new boyfriend? I tell them Lou. He lives in LA and has six children. He knows Bill Graham personally. I think Bennie might know who Lou actually is, so Jocelyn's mom comes to our school to talk with Bennie Salazar. But he's hard to find. Now that Alice and Scotty are together, Bennie has stopped coming to the Pit. He and Scotty still don't talk, but before they were like one person. Now it's like they've never met.

I can't stop wondering: If I'd pulled away from Lou and fought the garbage throwers, would Bennie have settled for me like Scotty settled for Alice? Could that one thing have made all the difference?

They track down Lou in a matter of days. He tells Jocelyn's mom that she hitchhiked all the way to his house without even warning him.

He says she's safe, he's taking care of her, it's better than having her on the street. Lou promises to bring her back when he comes to the city next week. Why not this week? I wonder.

While I'm waiting for Jocelyn, Alice invites me over. We take the bus from school, a long ride to Sea Cliff. Her house looks smaller in daylight. In the kitchen, we mix honey with her mother's homemade yogurts and eat two each. We go up to her room, where all the frogs are, and sit on her built-in window seat. Alice tells me she's planning to get real frogs and keep them in a terrarium. She's calm and happy now that Scotty loves her. I can't tell if she's actually real, or if she's stopped caring if she's real or not. Or is not caring what makes a person real?

I wonder if Lou's house is near the ocean. Does Jocelyn look at the waves? Do they ever leave Lou's bedroom? Is Rolph there? I keep getting lost in these questions. Then I hear giggling, pounding from somewhere. I go, Who's that?

My sisters, Alice goes. They're playing tetherball.

We head downstairs and outside into Alice's backyard, where I've only been in the dark. It's sunny now, with flowers in patterns and a tree with lemons on it. At the edge of the yard, two little girls are slapping a bright yellow ball around a silver pole. They turn to us, laughing in their green uniforms.

HOW TO CHOOSE A SOUNDTRACK FOR A BANK ROBBERY GETAWAY

Joe Loya

I'VE DONE MANY bad things in my life, most of them criminal. And I have genuine remorse for that rogue behavior, just the way any self-respecting person should. I wrote a whole memoir copping to that lifetime of shame, so I've sort of worked through the embarrassment of thinking I was kind of cool in those days when I was really just a knucklehead. Now all I'm left with, for the most part, is the regret of those detour years.

But I still have a few embarrassing things to cop to from my previous criminal days, one of which I will share with you right now.

The year was 1988. I concluded after my third bank robbery that I needed a getaway song to blast on my CD player while I cruised away with the loot. I reviewed the canon of great music, from Beethoven's "Eroica" to Echo and the Bunnymen's "The Killing Moon," and for some ridiculous reason I landed on "Smooth Criminal" by Michael Jackson.

There I was, driving on highway 5 from San Diego to Los Angeles, a minute from the bank, a clean getaway, thousands of dollars in my fanny pack on the backseat, and I was feeling ferocious. So I pulled out the *BAD* CD case and slid the CD into the player. Then the song began.

Quick violent horns and a loud drum startle you. Followed by the sound of a heartbeat picking up speed. Okay, I could feel how this music would work. I got what just went down. The burst of horns meant a crime had just occurred. Followed by somebody panicking, the rush of adrenaline. Like me at the bank counter threatening the teller that if she didn't give me all the money I'd blow her brains out. She stiffens as her heartbeat quickens.

What next? A pause. Then a strong bass track kicks in. Good. Just like I felt in that driver's seat, sturdy and vital. The song was working.

Then Michael opened his mouth.

What the fuck? This song is about a rape? Or murder? I quickly ejected the CD. Listen, I was no stranger to terror and violence. I'd once made a teller piss herself as she faced the wall in the bank vault. I mean, I had just robbed a bank, for God's sake, so I get that I wasn't in a position to pass moral judgment on other types of criminals, believe me, I get that. But I wasn't about to listen to the Ballad of Annie's Rapist during my pristine getaway.

So I drove the rest of the way home annoyed, feeling cheated for not being able to celebrate my achievement with a triumphant song. I wanted music that made me feel mighty, indomitable, heroic, and historic. Maybe some Wagner. And I don't mean "Wedding March" Wagner. Or "Tristan and Isolde" Wagner. I mean "Ride of the Valkyries" Wagner. Which I happened to have at home.

The only problem with "Ride of the Valkyries" was that I mostly associated it with the beach scene in *Apocalypse Now* where Robert Duvall famously quips that he loves the smell of Napalm in the morning. I didn't mind playing a song that would have conjured up a movie scene, but after the "Smooth Criminal" debacle, I decided that any song choice would have to echo my mental state in that car. And while you can't find more triumphant music than Wagner's "Ride of the Valkyries," the mood of the song would forever be tied to the Vietnam War—for me, anyway, an ill-conceived police action. Basically a defeat, in the end.

Once home, I started plucking the CDs that showed promise off the shelf, and stacked them on my desk. The first was the Allman Brothers' greatest hits collection. Southern rock made an initial strong showing, probably because I dug the hint of violence in the bands' names—like Molly Hatchet, .38 Special, the Outlaws—or because some of their songs were great rock anthems, "Freebird" by Lynyrd Skynyrd being the best example, but also "Slow Ride" by Foghat.

Next was Canadian rock. I picked Neil Young's *LIVE RUST* CD because I love the grinding electric guitar sound in "Like a Hurricane."

The deep dissonant chords toward the end of the song charge me, really make sense on some elemental level. Bachman Turner Overdrive also got the nod. "Let It Ride," one of my all-time favorites, is a hard-charged, drum-driven song, a real shit-kicker, with tight harmonies and a clean acoustic guitar sound throughout.

Not surprisingly, more than a few British bands made the cut. Led Zeppelin, Bad Company, Black Sabbath. No Beatles. But I suppose if you held a gun to my head and forced me to choose a Beatles song I could have chosen "Helter Skelter" and not have had to hold my nose. If not for that song's association with the whole Charlie Manson mess, I may have considered it.

Early on I quietly favored "(Don't Fear) The Reaper" by Blue Öyster Cult, mostly because I loved the line "Caesars don't fear the Reaper." (Stay with me.) I used to tell people that I was Nietzsche's Übermensch, the Superman, alive to stomp all over normal categories of proper behavior. I existed to prove that timid moralities were a thing that were meant to be surpassed. So I had a kinship with every manner of authoritarian—Czars, Führers, Pharaohs, Popes, and Kings—who believed themselves supreme. So the notion that Caesar, like me, did not fear the Reaper, appealed to my gargantuan vanity. The problem was that when I listened carefully to the song, I discovered that it was *seasons*, not *Caesars*, that didn't fear the reaper. And on top of that, the song is actually a love song with way too many "baby take my hand" verses to qualify as dangerous, or darkly textured, getaway music. So I let it go.

Then Led Zeppelin got me excited. I was doing the thing I did when I made the mistake of choosing "Smooth Criminal." I was being too literal as I thought of getaway songs. So "Communication Breakdown" felt like a great fit since metaphorically my bank robberies were ad hoc evidence that sometime earlier in my life my ability to communicate normally had broken down. Led Zeppelin hard rock songs are primal music that is wonderfully able to prime you for any kind of action. You want to confront your cheating husband but are worried about what the cost to your marriage might be? Listen to "Black Dog" first. Wanna march into your boss's office and call him or her a prick? Listen to "Rock and Roll." Been foreclosed on and wanna rob the neighborhood Bank of America? Listen to "Immigrant Song" beforehand.

Slowly it occurred to me that I was picking pump-you-up-for-a-good-day-of-bank-robbery music, not enjoy-your-comfortable-ride-home-and-bask-in-your-glory-after-a-heist music. What I really needed was to match music to my *post*-robbery mood.

So I went to the refrigerator, pulled out a Corona, popped in Pink Floyd's *The Wall* Disc 2, sat down in my big comfy leather chair, closed my eyes, and told myself to think about the way I felt on the drive home from a bank robbery. Which inevitably led me to begin to take stock of the mood I was in as I reclined in that chair. One thing was clear: I felt positively post-coital. Like I'd just shot my wad and I was lying in bed naked, half-drugged by a fierce lusty conquest that had proven to be terribly right. I felt mellow. Otherworldly. Slightly buzzed. Like I had a minor concussion.

Not like the drive *to* a bank robbery, where my body always fought off an anxiety attack. My hands would get sweaty. My stomach would cramp. My head would feel like it was trapped in a tightening vice. Intense fatigue would sweep over me so that if I pulled over to the side of the road I know I could have slept for three hours. My body would be panicked and do everything it could to try to shut down before I got to my dangerous destination. In order to combat my body's mutiny I would summon memories of boyhood humiliations, like the time three boys beat me and broke my glasses in eighth grade. My preacher father's response had been to drive me around our East L.A. neighborhood looking for them, so that he could have me fight them one-on-one, threatening to beat me if I didn't win each fight. My reverie would soon lead me to the time when I was sixteen, when I stabbed him in the neck with a steak knife after he'd given me a vicious beating. Then, in that car, under tremendous physical duress, an incredible rage would jolt me and instantly subdue my body, as if I'd just shot twenty grams of endorphins. I would be overwhelmed by an amazing sense of mission. Outwardly, I was stoic. No more jitters. But my brain would be throbbing with mad purpose. Listening to Ozzy Osbourne would have suited me in that moment. The screams, echoes, and antic-sounds in "Crazy Train," along with the lyrics (I'm going off the rails on a crazy train), all suggested asylum bedlam.

That's what it felt like driving to a bank robbery. Like getting ready to stab my dad. But returning home felt more like the sensation I had two hours *after* I stabbed my dad.

My brother and I ran out of the apartment to my aunt's house, where we raced through the door and I told her that I had killed my dad. (He survived, but I didn't know that at the time.) My aunt drove us to the police station. During the interview a cop told me that he didn't believe that I had to stab my father, that I could have done something else. Ran away, or called the cops. He noticed that I was calmly telling the story. He suggested that they might charge me with premeditated attempted murder. Even I knew enough to know that I was acting rather cool for having supposedly just killed my father. After a few hours, I complained to a female cop that my arm hurt badly and my side hurt when I breathed. She drove me to the local hospital where it was revealed that I had a fractured rib and elbow. The doctors also concluded that I had sustained a major concussion. All talk of charging me with attempted murder ceased, and I was taken to a facility named MacClaren Hall where kids wait to be placed in foster care.

At MacClaren Hall, even though I was beat up and bandaged, I lay on that county cot and wore my wounds as a badge of honor, a "you-should-see-the-other-guy" kinda cockiness. In prison I reread *The Red Badge of Courage*, and I remember that there's this part in there where Henry has suffered head trauma in battle and he talks about how he conceived his "torn body to be peculiarly happy." That's how I felt in my concussive state after bloody combat with my father. Peculiarly happy.

The violence of my childhood was like one fuzzy dream-state. I can now say that my entire crime spree could be understood as my replicating the mood of the home I was raised in. Full of terror, episodic violence, and extreme disassociation from the normal frequencies of human emotion.

In fact, the dominant motif of "Comfortably Numb"—the song I was listening to in my leather chair—resonated with my life's motif of hazard and contingency. It was as if the baroque confusion of my childhood concussions had been given voice in David Gilmour's plaintive guitar licks, in the Moody Blues–like orchestral strings, and finally in the brooding, anguished, psychedelic lyrics.

The song ended and I opened my eyes, and I knew what song I would be hearing after every future bank robbery. Which ended up being approximately 25 more, for the next 12 months.

THE GUTTERING PROMISE OF PUBLIC EDUCATION

Gray Brechin

AND SO YOU students go forth, simultaneously enlightened by your teachers and at the same time burdened by debt from your experience at what the University's PR department still calls the world's greatest PUBLIC university. This debt is something that many of you will share with your parents, so consider it a familial bond like your DNA. As you know, it's going up almost 10% next year, the seventh rise in almost that many years, so as heavy as your burden may seem, console yourselves that you are escaping now, since those who come after you will pay ever more for what was free to me when I came to Berkeley as an undergraduate over forty years ago. Think positive: Concentrate on the added earning power your diploma will give you so that you can pay for your kids to come here, if you can afford kids.

The governor, University president and the regents will tell you that they have no choice and that they feel your pain: state support for the PUBLIC university continues to shrink in good times and bad. The regents heard a report last year predicting that if state support continues to decline, tuition will have to rise to $18,000 in a few years, twice what it is now. They want you to believe that the decline in state support is an ineluctable force, like the law of gravity. Resistance is not only futile, it is virtually unthinkable except for a few rude and immature students and staff who disrupt regents' meetings and occupy their offices.

So it's not surprising that support for humanities and social sciences like geography continues to wither, since these are the disciplines that at their best not only try to teach critical thinking and values, but add to your knowledge of the dimension of time as well as space. Time is dangerous since it stokes memory which is essential for building a civilization. Humanities and social sciences are not big profit centers like business, law, bioengineering, and intercollegiate sports. You're told that there is nothing to be done, since we are living in hard times.

My parents lived in hard times, too. It was called the Great Depression and may soon be called the First Great Depression, like the First World War after we had *another* one. At the bottom of the Depression in 1933, the governor proposed slashing the university's budget. UC's revered president did not simply parrot the governor at that time, however. Robert Gordon Sproul called the governor's position "a facile panacea." He mounted the bully pulpit of San Francisco's prestigious Commonwealth Club to voice his opposition in these words:

> When a nation ceases to encourage and support its universities, it ceases to be a first-rate power. When a state prunes too severely the intellectual life at the top, it produces increasing poverty and despair at the bottom.

Now that was a *public* servant, as well as an educator rather than a shill. There was not a gulf then between the president's million-dollar compensation package and a staff and teaching assistants that qualified for welfare. But that was also very different time, a time about which I've become interested for what it can teach us about how we can escape the increasing poverty and despair at the bottom in our own time. Memory is for learning, which makes it dangerous.

Many of you probably wonder what I do in my messy office hunched over my laptop and surrounded with all that Roosevelt stuff. I'm working with others on an archaeological dig of a lost civilization that our parents and grandparents built in about seven years of far harder times than our own. I do this partly in order to save myself from the pain I experience looking at California's—and the world's—deteriorating environment. I did not want to believe Margaret Thatcher's neoliberal mantra that "There is no alternative" to a constant shrinking of the public domain. In different words but with the same thought, California governors and university presidents have been parroting that line for about thirty years: there is no alternative to constant tuition hikes and service cuts and no new campuses; *there is no alternative* except to borrow and gamble more.

Here I'd like to say that one of my favorite movies is *The Golden Compass* since it posits a multiplicity of universes parallel to our own.

At least one alternative universe is all around us, but we don't see it. It's the enormous legacy of public works created by New Deal agencies in only a few brief years that we in California's Living New Deal project are inventorying and mapping for the first time. Roosevelt's critics say that his New Deal was a waste of money that only prolonged the Depression, but our research and maps are proving them wrong. By putting millions of Americans to work doing everything from laying sewers and running WPA health clinics to painting murals and planting forests, these public works began to lift the economy out of the last Great Depression. Moreover, we all use and rely upon those public works without knowing we are doing so—they have immeasurably improved the lives of generations of Americans who have no idea of the broad shoulders on which we all stand.

Let's go back to public education, for example. Robert Gordon Sproul's long-range vision was very much in the spirit of other New Dealers who proceeded under the odd assumption that it is much cheaper and better for a society to educate rather than punish its own people and others. The Works Progress Administration and Public Works Administration together built over eleven thousand schools and improved tens of thousands more. They favored building schools, colleges, libraries, and museums over prisons.

Most of those schools were so well built and designed that they are still in use today, over 70 years on. Many of you have probably attended them. Many of them are embellished with sculpture, murals, and other artworks—I urge you to go over to see the mosaics representing the arts on the old University Art Gallery just east of Sather Gate, as fresh today as when artists Marion Simpson and Helen Bruton laid them in 1937 for the WPA.

Those buildings speak to us in more ways than just their fine construction and generous amplitude: many have inscriptions such as that on Berkeley High School that tells students "YOU SHALL KNOW THE TRUTH AND THE TRUTH WILL MAKE YOU FREE," or the motto under which you enter Long Beach Polytechnic High School: "ENTER TO LEARN, GO FORTH TO SERVE." Inscriptions on Hollywood High School in English, Latin, and Greek subtly tell you that you can get a classical education in a PUBLIC school as well as at private Exeter or Groton.

My current favorite is on a lovely WPA-built school in Whittier. As you enter the Lou Henry Hoover School, you see this inscription on a wall in front: "WHAT YOU WOULD FIRST HAVE IN THE LIFE OF A NATION YOU MUST PUT INTO ITS SCHOOLS."

That statement says more concisely what Robert Gordon Sproul told the people of California in 1933. The inscription on the Whittier school is signed "von Humboldt," but that is not Alexander von Humboldt, the father of modern geography; it's his brother, Wilhelm, who created the Prussian public education system that made Germany rich and one of the leading powers of Europe. Germany's graduate programs became the model for our own.

You don't *have* to map the invisible matrix of now decaying public schools, parks, hospitals, airports, zoos, museums, roads, sewage plants, dams, stadiums, bridges, forests, lodges, and so on to understand the generosity of the New Deal, to understand the social covenant of shared risk that it began to weave. You can just look at the posters that the WPA produced for the services it provided. They show you a time in which your taxes came back to you in public services that employed millions to do what the market cannot, or will not, do for you.

When I tell students that when I came to Berkeley in 1967 there was virtually no tuition, you can hear their jaws hit the floor. I took it for granted then; no one told me that I was the unwitting beneficiary of New Deal idealism: in 1960—15 years after Roosevelt's death—aging New Dealers like Governor Pat Brown and UC President Clark Kerr put in place California's Master Plan for Higher Education that promised free tuition in the Golden State's then growing system of colleges and universities and access to those campuses regardless of income level. The California public school system was then much copied and the nation's envy; it is now the worst. The regents never told us at what point they abandoned the master plan, but I have an idea.

Thirty years ago, hucksters began to persuade us that we could have a civilization without paying for it, that risk should not be shared but individualized, and more recently that we could fight wars while cutting taxes. We stand today in the ruins of that fantasy, wondering what happened.

Supreme Court Justice Oliver Wendell Holmes said that "Taxes are what we pay for a civilized society." The artifacts of the New Deal suggest that we once had a civilization worthy of the name. We *could* have it again.

You should not wonder whether your child can afford a public education: you should not wonder whether you can afford a child at all. Start rebuilding that civilization. It's an adult world—again, and its problems are up to you. You can solve them if you remember that we did so before, but only by doing so together, and without war.

AFGHANISTAN CAN'T WASH AWAY VIETNAM

Andrew Lam

TRYING TO GOOGLE news of my homeland, Vietnam, over the last few weeks has not been easy. The headlines that showed were anything but Vietnam. Leading up to President Obama's speech on why we need to send 30,000 more troops to Afghanistan, Vietnam has been once again reduced to America's boogeyman.

Here are a few headlines from major news organizations: "Afghanistan haunted by ghost of Vietnam," "Will Obama's War become his Vietnam?" "Afghanistan is Obama's Vietnam," "Vietnam's lesson for Afghanistan," "Vietnam myths haunt Afghanistan."

Oftentimes, indeed, when we mention the word Vietnam in the United States, we don't mean Vietnam as a country. Vietnam is unfortunately not like Thailand or Malaysia or Singapore to America's collective imagination. Its relationship to us is special: It is a vault filled with tragic metaphors for every pundit to use.

After the Vietnam War, Americans were caught in the past, haunted by unanswerable questions, confronted with an unhappy ending. So much so that my uncle who fought in the Vietnam War as a pilot for the South Vietnamese army once observed that "When Americans talk about Vietnam they really are talking about America." "Americans don't take defeat and bad memories very well. They try to escape them," he said in his funny but bitter way. "They make a habit of blaming small countries for things that happen to the United States. AIDS from Haiti, flu from Hong Kong or Mexico, drugs from Colombia, hurricanes from the Caribbean."

I once met a Vietnamese man who made money acting in Hollywood. He had survived the war and the perilous journey on the South China Sea to come to America. Now he plays Vietcong, ARVN (Army of the Republic of Vietnam) soldiers, civilians, peasants. He is a great actor, he bragged. No one recognized his face. Time and again he died, spurting fake blood from his torso and heart. At other times he screamed in pain, reinterpreting his own past. "Hollywood loves me," he said. "I die well."

Hollywood, of course, is free with its various interpretations. From *Apocalypse Now*, which describes an American's mythical adventure in a tropic jungle to *The Deer Hunter*, which shows a game of Russian roulette being played out for money between an American and some Vietnamese, to *Tour of Duty*, in which American GIs rape then blow out the brains of a Vietnamese girl, to Rambo movies in which America single-handedly restores its pride, Vietnam is always the backdrop, the faceless conical-hat-adorned figure.

Watching such movies, Vietnamese old enough to remember the war giggle uncomfortably. These naïve interpretations of the conflict little resemble their own past. Vietnam was a three-sided war, with North and South at each other's throats, but the Americans have insinuated themselves as central to an otherwise complex narrative in the retelling. Some Vietnamese are enraged, but many are resigned.

For what they know and won't admit to the American audience is that for them history is a series of personal impressions. Fact and details and analysis and fancy interpretations can't capture the truth about Vietnam any more than wildly fabricated war flicks can. Instead, Vietnamese living in America tell their children ghost stories and share their memories of the monsoon rains and harvest festivals. I, too, store in my brain a million of those memories and myths, none of which have anything to do with America's involvement in the war. But that is another story.

Vietnam has more than doubled in population, to 86 million, since the war ended. It is a country full of young people, who form a large majority, with no direct memory of the Vietnam War. It is odd to think that 35 years since the war ended, it continues to stoke America's foreign policy fears. The entire country still stands for America's loss of innocence, its legacy of defeat and failure.

A few years ago, I went back to Vietnam to make a documentary, and I did the touristy thing: I went to the Cu Chi Tunnel in Tay Ninh Province, bordering Cambodia, a complex underground labyrinth in which the Vietcong hid during the war.

There were a handful of American vets in their 60's. They were back for the first time. They were very emotional. One wept and said, "I spent a long time looking for this place and lost friends doing the same."

But the young tour guide told me that it was tourism that forced the Vietnamese to dig up the old hideouts. Then, in a whisper, the young tour guide told me discreetly: "It was a lot smaller back then. But now the new Cu Chi tunnel is very wide. You know why? To cater to very, very big Americans."

She did not see the past. She crawled through the same tunnel with foreigners routinely but she emerged with different ideas. Her head is filled with the Golden Gate Bridge and cable cars and two-tiered freeways and Hollywood and Universal Studios. "I have many friends over there now," she said, her eyes dreamy, reflecting the collective desire of Vietnamese youth. "They invite me to come. I'm saving money for this amazing trip."

Here's a young woman who looks at a tunnel that was the headquarters of the Vietcong and the cause of massive bombings years ago and what does she see? The Magic Kingdom. The Cu Chi tunnel leads some to the past surely, but for the young tour guide it may very well lead to the future.

On the eve of the second wave of a U.S. invasion in Afghanistan, I wish to tell the American media, as well as President Obama, that the Vietnam syndrome cannot be kicked through acts of war. That only through a view that's rooted in people, rooted in human kindness, and not historical vehemence, would a country open itself up and stop being a haunting metaphor. That not until human basic needs are addressed and human dignity is upheld can we truly pacify our enemies and bring about human liberty. And that more soldiers and bombs and droids in the sky will never appease the haunting ghosts of the past. Quite the opposite. We are in the process of creating more ghosts to haunt future generations.

Years ago, the poet Robert Bly argued that Americans have yet to perform an ablution over past atrocities. "We're engaged in a vast forgetting mechanism and from the point of view of psychology, we're refusing to eat our grief, refusing to really eat our dark side," Bly told Bill Moyers on public television. "And therefore what Jung says is really terrifying: if you do not absorb the things you have done in your life, then you will have to repeat them."

It may very well be that the tragedy of Vietnam cannot simply be overcome with some supposed military victory but with another tragedy of equal if not greater proportion. It may very well be that a few years from now, when it's all over, the new American tourists can visit the caves of Tora Bora to weep at some hole in the ground, thinking about the futility of it all.

FROM "THE LAST VALLEY"

Mark Arax

EVERY TIME I barrel down the steep descent of the Tehachapi and cross the Mason-Dixon line that divides the sprawl of Southern California from the farm fields of the Central Valley, the same question occurs to me: Am I a fool for believing that this valley's birthright is agriculture, that if God intended a place to be something, He intended this place to be farmland? Nowhere else in the world brings together land, sun, soil, and water in such harmony. Then I think of the fools like me in Pasadena and Valencia and Van Nuys who believed those orange groves would always be orange groves.

It was Saroyan and later Stegner and Didion who taught me that every writer who comes from the land must eventually confront a deep ambivalence about the place that nurtured him. The writer does this one of two ways. He leaves and writes about his place from afar, hoping the distance gives him not only perspective but a rein on his anger and a check on his heart. Or he stays and tries to work it out from within, the past and present knocking heads and confusing his feelings. If he stays, his writing sometimes misses the mark. This is because the immediacy he has gained by being so close to his subject can bring too much heat, too much passion. At the halfway point in my newspaper career, after stints in New York, Baltimore, and Los Angeles, I chose the latter, returning home to the valley, digging my heels into native ground. It has been a messy affair, but I am still here, trying to put my finger on this place.

If I brought a different passion to the stories I did on the valley, most of my editors didn't seem to mind. Whether the issue was growing new towns in the middle of the vineyards or the tens of millions of dollars in crop subsidies that went to the richest families in Fresno, the stakes always seemed higher here than when I was writing about L.A. The reasons were obvious in one respect—it was my home—and yet I sensed a deeper explanation that had to do with how we as a society related to place. I began to consider the different ways—three by my count—that Americans connect to place, each one a way of living.

The first evolves out of the idea that place is moveable, that you can take home with you or create home wherever you are. This becomes an easier proposition because so much of what makes a place unique has been lost in America, swallowed up by the tide of homogenization. If one place looks identical to the other place, then place is no big deal. And losing place is no big tragedy. Place is not only moveable, it is disposable. The second notion of place is the way a historian or social scientist sees it. Place becomes your subject and as a subject it must be kept separate from your soul. You can live in such a place, become a student of such a place, and even find a measure of accord with that place, because it is your home and your laboratory. But the place is never you and the changes that come to it are never taken personally. You live above the fray. This was the sense of place that informed my writing about Los Angeles. The third notion of place is one of deep roots and intimacy, a direct connection between a person and place, right down to its earth. I am bound to this place. You cannot separate me from it. As the land is being remade, where is my place? I am tied to this place, and yet as it abandons itself, does it also abandon me? In this way, place is not simply geography but a spiritual relationship to the geography, and it is this relationship that gets lost as the land becomes transformed. This was the sense of place that I brought to bear in my writing about the valley from the day I touched down in the foggy winter of 1990.

I had arrived at the cusp of an era of stunning growth. A half-million acres of the state's best farmland were being converted to new Targets and Home Depots and terra cotta subdivisions with Orwellian names such as The Orchards. Up and down Highway 99, city council agendas were filled with pages and pages of applications for rezoning.

As far as I could tell, not a single one was ever denied. In the County of Kern, supervisors decided that the planning commission, the last bridle to boom, needed to be eliminated. Developers were building residential tracts without even the sewer lines to service them. In Bakersfield, the most sprawled city in the West, a whole new side of town was taking shape with nothing more than septic tanks. In Fresno, the Planning Department had been renamed the Development Department. The salaries of the development director and all his staff were now funded by the builders themselves; the faster they pushed each project through the pipeline (the fewer questions they asked), the faster the fees from the developers poured in.

The local newspapers, their Saturday and Sunday editions fat with builder ads, weren't in a mood to ask questions either. One question seemed obvious: At a time of boom, why were cities scrambling to balance their budgets? Why had the unemployment rate of 14 percent not budged? Why were drivers getting killed on one-lane country roads that served as the only route in and out of Apricot Estates? Why was the main lobbyist for the building industry driving around town in a fancy car with the license plate REZONE?

I spent months digging through planning documents, sitting through public meetings, and comparing decades of local budgets. What I found did not please the building industry associations or the chambers of commerce or the publishers of the *Bees*. From Bakersfield in the south to Stockton in the north, the boom was scarcely reaping economic prosperity. In a paradoxical twist, growth was actually draining the coffers of every city and town in a 250-mile stretch of middle California. For every dollar that the boom was generating, cities were spending roughly two dollars to provide streets and sewers and cops to serve the new suburbs. To cover the loss, one city after another had taken on record bond debt. The builders had city hall in a classic bind. Cities needed the front-end revenue from property and sales taxes to cover the hefty back-end costs of sprawl. This meant that each new losing subdivision was being approved to pay for the losing subdivision before it. It was a giant Ponzi scheme.

The immediate source of the problem was in plain view. Valley towns, in a lavish gift to a handful of local builders, were failing to charge the development fees that cities to the north and south were charging. In San Jose or Glendale, for instance, a three-bedroom, two-bath house was generating $45,000 in fees—everything from a fee for roads, sewers, and police stations to a fee to beautify downtowns and build parks. Modesto, Visalia, Stockton, Bakersfield, and Fresno, on the other hand, were charging less than four grand for the same house. It didn't take a lot of math to figure out that during a sustained boom—tens of thousands of new houses rising up on farmland—valley cities were forgoing hundreds of millions of dollars to build a better place.

This is why Bakersfield smelled the way it did and looked the way it did. Why the roads were full of peril and a fifteen-minute drive across town—red light to red light—took thirty minutes. (Synchronization is a fee too.) This is why Fresno had one of the lowest parks-to-people ratios in the nation and why downtown had become a roost for pigeons. Why a dozen valley men with names such as Spanos, Bonadelle, McCaffrey, Wathen, and Assemi were multimillionaires making a 40 to 50 percent profit on each house they built, an unheard-of return in the nation's building industry.

With its patchwork services, Fresno had consigned itself to the status of a third-rate city. "It's pretty basic," Walt Kieser, an expert on municipal financing, told me. "Good infrastructure is what the best industries and retailers are looking for when they locate to a city. In Fresno, they've done such a miserable job with the roads, parks, libraries, and schools that they haven't created a nice place to live. Instead, they've allowed developers to just maximize their profits."

In Bakersfield, at least one politician was sorry. "I knew residential development wasn't paying its way," Pauline Larwood, a Kern County supervisor, said. "Yes, I voted for my share of developer projects in other supervisors' districts. I did so because if I wanted something in my district, I was going to need their vote."

In Fresno, there were no such apologies. "Slowing growth is elitist and anti-market and anti-free enterprise," Ken Steitz, a real estate lender who moonlighted as a Fresno city councilman, told me. "If a builder comes before the council and meets all the requirements, I don't believe we have a right to tell that developer no. And let's call developer fees what they are: hidden taxes. We don't need any more taxes."

Had Steitz, a born-again Christian, been more honest, he would have added that he was a drunk and a philanderer in the clutches of a half dozen developers. He and his fellow council members were pushing the view that California environmental laws did not apply to Fresno. Developers needn't fuss with the environmental impact reports that were basic in every other major city. The San Joaquin Valley had overtaken L.A. as the nation's smog capital, but the council refused to consider how the new subdivisions on the far fringe of town were polluting the air. When the city's own economic impact studies began showing that each housing tract was putting Fresno deeper in the red, Mayor Jim Patterson stepped in. The city, he said, could no longer afford to do economic analysis. The studies were shit-canned.

I talked to one longtime builder from Southern California who couldn't believe his good fortune upon landing in Fresno. "The first time I stood at the Development Department's front counter and realized what they were requiring me to do—which was nothing—I thought I had died and gone to heaven," he told me.

To further my indoctrination, I paid a visit to the father of American sprawl himself, Eli Broad. He had built more houses across suburbia than any other man in history, changing the face of cities from New Jersey to California. Now, in a second act that could not have been further removed from those days at Kaufman & Broad, he seemed to be doing penance. He was trying to revive downtown Los Angeles, a core that had been gutted by the subdivisions he had planted across the basin. As we sat in his Sun America building thirty-eight stories above Century City, his office at the very top, he traced his rise from the shy, big-eared son of Jewish socialists to a billionaire philanthropist trying to change the culture of the city he had come to love. To better illustrate his vision of downtown, we got into the backseat of his limo and took a drive.

"You're a very dangerous man," he said.

"Why do you say that?"

"Because you make me feel comfortable."

Then, with a missionary's glare, he made a remarkable confession. The way he and every other home builder paved over the landscape was wrong. The growth they were bringing—cookie cutter houses with strip malls on fertile farmland—was no longer tenable. "The costs of urban sprawl are very expensive," he said. "We've got to build closer in, higher densities and do whatever's necessary to save the farmland." Maybe he really believed it. Or maybe the old developer in him merely understood that the future of growth, or at least the hippest growth, was moving away from the exurbs and back to the neglected city centers.

A few days after my first story appeared in the *Times* exposing the low fees and high costs of growth, I awoke to the heat of a community-wide blowback. The head of the building industry association used his weekly column in the *Bee* to call me a liar. On the news pages, a *Bee* reporter dug up a whole new set of figures that contradicted the numbers I had come up with. The conclusion was clear: I had cooked my analysis to make Fresno and its developers look bad. The popular host of a local radio talk show ranted on the air: "This is the same Mark Arax whose father was murdered in this town in 1972, a crime that was never solved. He's a bitter kid who has let his anger get in the way of objective reporting." A few days later, the *Bee* discovered that its story had been wrong. A city bureaucrat had given the paper false information to discredit my story and make it appear as if developers were paying their fair share. None of it mattered now. In the minds of the powerful, I was the prodigal son who, chip on his shoulder, had come home to dump on the home team.

True, I knew things about the valley, secrets that were whispered but never chronicled in any official way. I knew that Ed Kashian, one of the wealthiest developers in Fresno, had learned how to influence politicians from an old technician, his father. Big Mike Kashian, straight from Detroit, became card-playing friends with my grandparents and was never very careful when he boasted that his buildings downtown, fronts for prostitution, were protected by the mayor, police chief, and district attorney. I knew that Harold Zinkin, Kashian's partner, was having an affair with a councilman's wife, paying her a salary while the councilman was voting to approve his rezones.

And I knew that John Bonadelle, the most formidable builder in Fresno, had been a cattle rustler who was caught three times hauling off steers from neighbor ranches during the worst deprivations of World War II. After a stint at San Quentin, he changed his name from Bontadelli to Bonadelle and went into the construction trade. He was a short, thick man in his mid-seventies who was rumored to have stared down the Mafia in a land deal gone bad. I saw for myself how intimidating he could be during a city council meeting to consider one of his applications for rezoning. He wanted to build hundreds of houses in a part of town that had been deemed off-limits to growth because it lacked water, sewer, and roads. He took a seat front and center where no council member could possibly miss him and waited with a smile that wasn't a smile. The wording of the motion was confusing, and councilwoman Esther Padilla, a Bonadelle lapdog, looked flustered as she cast her vote. She ended up voting, much to her surprise, against the rezone. By a 4 to 3 margin, John Bonadelle had suffered a rare defeat. His face turned red with rage, and he summoned Padilla to the outer hall. I followed right behind and watched as he backed her into a corner. I couldn't hear their words, but Padilla appeared to be begging for forgiveness. After the break, the council reconvened, and Padilla raised her hand to speak.

"Would it be possible," she pleaded, "to return to the last item so I could change my vote?" The council voted again, and Bonadelle got his rezone.

His office sat on old fig ground in the northwest part of town not far from where I lived. When I called to set up an appointment, he did not remember that I was the kid who grew up on Lafayette Avenue just behind his mansion. It took up nearly a full block of Van Ness Extension, the lawn so wide that the USC marching band (his children were Trojans) came there every summer to play at a fund-raiser. In the far backyard, Bonadelle kept a pen of squawking peacocks that occasionally broke out and showed up, in full plumage, on our front lawn. The old cattle rustler had no trouble herding them back home.

I knocked on his office door, but there was no answer. I walked in and stood in front of the secretary's desk, but there was no secretary. From the other room came the sound of snoring, and I followed it to the doorway. There was Bonadelle, cowboy boots on his desk, taking an afternoon nap. I tiptoed back into the lobby and studied the mounted photos of the rare African long-horned cattle he kept at a small spread west of the highway. At some point he awakened and invited me into the conference room, where I proceeded to ask him about every rumor I ever heard about his payoffs to politicians—cash, booze, and whores. He stopped me only one time to lodge a protest, and that was when I told him I was planning to write a profile about him that would include his time in San Quentin.

"Would you mind turning off that tape recorder?" he asked in a gruff voice.

"Sure."

"Now, I've got a wife and three kids who know nothing about my prison time. And I'm an old man with grandchildren who think I'm pretty special. You wouldn't want to destroy all that, would you?"

He started to horse trade. "I'll give you what you want if you leave that out."

I promised to leave his prison time out of the story, but he gave me nothing that was worth a damn. As it turned out, I didn't need his assistance. With a little more digging, I found out that Bonadelle, in an effort to get his housing tracts green-lighted in the little boomtown of Clovis, had bribed several local politicians. At least one of them, a councilwoman named Pat Wynne, had turned him down flat. At first, Wynne didn't want to tell the story, fearing what Bonadelle might do to her. But the FBI already was in town, snooping around. So she decided to go on the record:

"John Bonadelle invited me to coffee one day and said he thought every pretty girl ought to be driving a Mercedes or Cadillac. I told him

I liked my Toyota. Then he said I could be making $250,000 a year selling real estate, and all I needed was for him to open the door. He said, 'Tonight, when you lay your pretty head on your pillow and think about your future, I want you to think of John Bonadelle.' I kept thinking, 'My God, how blatant. This only happens in cheap paperback novels.'"

The FBI and assistant U.S. attorney in Sacramento couldn't believe how blatant it was: cash handed over in paper bags at the country club; politicians selling votes for a new set of car brakes, an oil job, a contract to build a fence. Before it was over, sixteen politicians and developers pleaded guilty or were found guilty. Farid Assemi, the builder who liked to finger a string of worry beads and play bridge on the international circuit, came to a teary-eyed deal with the feds. His main lobbyist, Jeff Roberts, the man with the REZONE license plates, took the fall and was hauled off to prison. Right behind him was old man Bonadelle.

I went to federal court to hear the guilty plea of Big Bob Lung, the blustery city councilman who had whined that my reporting was nothing more than the get-even of a murdered man's son. The evidence showed that Lung had sold his votes to Bonadelle for, among other things, a new blue suit. As he stood up to come clean, I couldn't believe my eyes. He was pleading guilty wearing the same blue suit.

LABOR WAR IN THE MOJAVE

Mike Davis

THE BIGGEST HOLE in California, with the exception of the current state budget, is Rio Tinto's huge open-pit mine at the town of Boron, near Edwards Air Force Base, eighty miles northeast of Los Angeles.

Seen from Google Earth, it is easy to imagine that the 700-foot-deep crater was blasted out of the Mojave Desert by an errant asteroid or comet. From the vantage point of Highway 58, however, the landscape is enigmatic: a mile-long rampart of ochre earth and gray mudstone, terminating at what looks like a giant chemical refinery.

At night, when a driver's mind is most prone to legends of the desert, the complex's intense illumination is startling, even slightly extraterrestrial, like the sinister off-world mining colony in *Aliens*.

Terri Judd's labor owns part of this eerie landscape—or rather its void. She's a third-generation borax miner, as deeply rooted in the high desert as one of the native Joshua trees. Every working morning for the past thirteen years, she has bundled her long red hair under a hard hat, climbed up the ladder of a giant Le Tourneau wheel loader and turned on its 1,600-horsepower Detroit Diesel engine. Her air-conditioned cab perches almost treetop height above custom-made, twelve-foot-high tires that cost $30,000 each. She operates this leviathan with delicate manipulations of two joysticks, more high-skill video game than *Mad Max*.

In a regular twelve-and-a-half-hour shift, she ceaselessly repeats the same mechanical calisthenic: lowering her twenty-foot-wide bucket, deftly scooping up twenty-five to thirty tons of borax ore, then delivering the load to one of the mine's plants to be made into boric acid or granulated for eventual use in dozens of industrial applications, from fiberglass surfboards to HD display screens.

Each year one million tons of borax products are fed into hopper cars (800 of which are permanently assigned to the mine) and hauled to the LA harbor for shipment to China and other industrializing countries hungry for the caustic residue of the Mojave's ancient lakes. The Boron pit, which replaced an underground mine, produces almost half the world's supply of refined borates.

Strip mining the Mojave may not be everyone's cup of tea, but Terri—a combat veteran of Operation Desert Storm and a single mom—flat-out loves her job. "What can I say? We get to play with the big toys. I guess I was always a tomboy. I preferred Tonkas to Barbies, socket wrenches to dollhouses."

But she doesn't play alone: Big Brother is looking over her shoulder, evaluating her performance. "In effect, the boss rides with me. The GPS in my loader can be monitored not only from the plant but from Rio Tinto's US headquarters in Denver, or, for that matter, from the global head office in London."

Peeping Toms, however, don't normally perturb Terri. "There are no slackers in the pit. Our productivity is sky-high because borax mining is our family history." Indeed, a Boron workforce shrunk to less than 40 percent of its 1980 size produces record outputs despite a rapidly aging plant; an ornery, dipping ore body; and an increasingly remote and hostile management.

I

Terri acknowledges that her devotion to the mine has been an act of unrequited love. In last year's contract negotiations, Rio Tinto (the British-Australian multinational acquired its Boron facility, U.S. Borax, in 1968 and renamed it Rio Tinto Borax) stunned members of the International Longshore and Warehouse Union, ILWU, Local 30 (Boron), by demanding abolition of the contractually enshrined seniority system and the surrender of any worker voice in the labor process.

According to Dean Gehring, the latest in a succession of recent mine managers, international competition compels a drastic switch to "high-performance teams that have the flexibility to do many different jobs, and we need to reward and promote our top performers. The old contract doesn't allow us to do that."

The company wants a contract that would allow it to capriciously promote or demote; to outsource union jobs; to convert full-time to part-time positions with little or no benefits; to reorganize shift schedules without warning; to eliminate existing work rules; to cut holidays, sick leave and pension payments; to impose involuntary overtime; and to heavily penalize the union if workers file grievances against the company with the National Labor Relations Board.

Rio Tinto, in essence, claims the right to rule by divine whim, to blatantly discriminate against and even fire employees for felonies like "failing to have or maintain satisfactory inter-personal relationships with Company personnel, client personnel, contractor, and visitors."

"The company's proposal," union negotiators emphasize, "would destroy our union, lower our living standards, and give Borax total control over our jobs." On January 30, Local 30 members unanimously rejected the concessions demanded by Rio Tinto.

The company deadline expired the next morning, when Terri Judd set off for work as usual with her lunchbox and thermos. At the locked front gate she and other day-shift workers encountered a phalanx of nervous Kern County sheriff's deputies in full riot gear. Inside the plant, an elite "strike security team" hired by Rio Tinto had taken control of operations.

Delaware-based J. R. Gettier & Associates brags that it is the Home Depot of unionbusting, a one-stop source for security planners, armed guards, legal experts, industrial spies and, most important, highly skilled replacement workers. It even has staff who can operate Terri's giant loader.

The Gettier mercenaries wore sneers and dark glasses as they pushed their convoy past a crowd of angry Local 30 members. "Being locked out," says Terri, "is different from going on strike. Initially there's disbelief that the company is actually serious about booting you out the door. Hey, my granddad worked in this mine. But then you see that caravan of scabs coming to take your jobs, and the betrayal cuts like a knife in your heart."

II

Once upon a time, there were several thousand mining communities in North America; perhaps fewer than a hundred still exist. Boron (unincorporated, population 2,000) is one of the survivors—and all the more anomalous since it is not in the red desert of Wyoming or the hills of West Virginia but in the outer orbit of Los Angeles sprawl. In the boom days of the 1930s it was a textbook company town, where employees of what was then called Pacific Borax—many of them, like Terri Judd's grandfather, Dust Bowl Oklahomans—lived in company houses and used company scrip to shop at the company store.

Unionization (originally by an old AFL affiliate called the Borax Workers Union) ended the feudal era, but the one-employer character of the town remained intact until a bitter, often violent 132-day strike in 1974 forced blacklisted miners to seek new jobs. Some found work at a nearby rocket-test range, while others learned to polish mirrors at an Israeli-built solar power station or applied for guard jobs at the federal prison up the road.

But economic diversity remains limited, and fully one-quarter of Boron's households still punched a Rio Tinto time clock this past New Year's. There are probably an equal number of mine retirees and former employees, so virtually everyone in town has some intimate link to the mine and its turbulent history.

During the 1974 conflict Boron polarized into majority pro-union and minority pro-company factions. There was a famous riot at the front gate in the first hours of the conflict, followed by the dynamiting of several foremen's homes, the blowing up of the mine's power line, episodic exchanges of gunfire, an exodus of managerial employees and de facto martial law during the nearly yearlong occupation of the community by Kern County sheriffs.

The current lockout, in contrast, rallies a far more inclusive local patriotism. Along Twenty Mule Team Road, Support Borax Miners placards festoon the windows of homes and pickups. Skateboarders and grandmothers wear black Union Tough T-shirts. Sympathy with the ILWU is not a condition for loathing Rio Tinto's hireling army of scabs and guards.

III

Day twelve. The lockout is beginning to feel like a reverse siege. It is the town, not the mine, that is under growing pressure. At the Local 30 hall, the "gate watch" crew reports that the sheriff's deputies have become quite relaxed, even friendly, probably because they're engaged in their own contract battle with county supervisors. But the replacements have become more brazen, at one point deliberately bumping into a union member with their van.

One of the organizers gravely notes the incident on his legal pad, then returns to the kitchen, where he huddles with his cellphone. He's calling the Local roster to remind members about next week's big solidarity march. Boron workers are awaiting the arrival of ILWU members from up and down the West Coast, as well as a contingent of mining- and dock-union leaders from around the world.

Across the hall, meanwhile, Terri is arguing with another loader operator, Kevin Martz, over which of them performs the most herculean labor in the pit.

Quantitatively, there should be no contest: Kevin operates a P&H 4100 "ultra class" shovel with a 115-ton payload capacity, one of the biggest machines in the mining world. In a few workdays he could probably dig the Panama Canal by himself. But Terri believes that quality is more important. "Come on, Kevin, you only shovel dirt; I dig ore. I'm high value."

Kevin pretends a smirk, then chuckles. He explains that a mining shift, like an army platoon in combat, relies upon constant ribbing to sustain camaraderie. "Our work depends upon friendship, not competition. In an environment of dangerous machines and high explosives, we have to watch each other's backs."

Neither he nor Terri discerns any rational logic in Rio Tinto's zeal to atomize the traditional work community and promote a dog-eat-dog struggle for bonuses.

"Some genius in Denver or London," Terri says, "believes that you can improve output by adopting the law of the jungle. But without a fair system to determine promotion and pay, teamwork will be undermined and morale will collapse. The mine will become less productive and more dangerous."

Conversation moves to the impact of the lockout on the town's economy. Terri is a major mover-shaker in the Veterans of Foreign Wars, while Kevin is a scout leader and active member of his Latter-day Saints ward.

"Normally the VFW is packed to the rafters on Friday nights for karaoke," Terri explains, "but last Friday there were just three families. Business at Domingo's [a Mexican restaurant made famous by its popularity among Space Shuttle crews from nearby Edwards] is way down, and the town dentist could close because everyone has lost their family dental benefits."

Kevin adds that many Local 30 families, especially those who recently bought homes in now-sunk boom-burbs like Victorville and Palmdale, forty or so miles from Boron, face imminent disaster. "Their mortgages are already below periscope depth, so the lockout is just the final shove out the front door. They'll lose their homes."

Kevin believes that fundamental values are under threat. Like many working-class Mormons—the most misunderstood social group in the American West—he's a good trade unionist but no liberal. Not inaccurately, he sees Local 30 making a conservative last stand on behalf of the decent jobs that allow frugal families to prosper in stable, human-scale communities like Boron.

"My wife's a schoolteacher at Edwards Air Force Base, we've no debts other than our mortgage, our kids flourish in local schools, we love the desert—yet if Rio Tinto continues to play this hand, we'll eventually be forced to leave, perhaps to Wyoming."

Terri, the quintessential Boronite, confesses that she also has been wondering whether pits in Nevada or Wyoming are looking for experienced loader operators. She's optimistic about the union but knows that Rio Tinto wields power almost beyond ordinary people's reckoning. "Will we be a ghost town next year? That's the real issue."

IV

"Where the hell is Bougainville?" someone asks Dave Dorton.

"An island near New Guinea," he replies.

The Local 30 gate-watchers are gathered under a sun canopy, drinking black coffee and talking about the skeletons in the company's closet. Dave, a dashing character who looks like he just jumped off a Viking longship, is "silo chief" at the plant and one of Local 30's many old-school bikers. He says that the lockout has incited new rank-and-file interest in Rio Tinto's notorious history. "It's like waking up and discovering that you're married to a serial murderer."

Last summer the US district court in Los Angeles upheld the standing of Bougainville residents—represented by Steve Berman, the superstar class-action litigator—to sue Rio Tinto in an American court for "crimes against humanity, war crimes, and racial discrimination." Like the case of Jarndyce and Jarndyce in Dickens's *Bleak House*, the suit is moving glacially through the courts against terrific opposition from the corporation and may take years to reach a judgment, but the charges are horrifying.

In the late 1960s Rio Tinto, supported by Australia (and after 1975 by the independent government of Papua New Guinea—PNG), began expropriating land in the fertile center of the northernmost Solomon Island of Bougainville to mine one of the world's richest copper deposits. Millions of tons of pit tailings poisoned ecosystems and devastated local agriculture, and by 1989 the relentless repression of nonviolent protest ignited a full-scale revolutionary uprising. The company appealed to its business partner, the neocolonial Papuan government.

In Bougainville, according to its former commander, General Singirok, "the PNG Defence Force was Rio Tinto's personal security force and was ordered to take action by any means necessary." The lawsuit provides stunning evidence of company/government atrocities in a conflict that led to the death of almost 10 percent of the island's population. (During the Spanish Civil War, Rio Tinto applauded Gen. Francisco Franco for executing the radical miners who had occupied its namesake Spanish property.)

Bougainville is only one item in a long résumé of devastation. The Norwegian government pension fund, the world's second-largest, recently divested $870 million in Rio Tinto stock to protest its "unethical" partnership with Freeport McMoRan in the infamous Grasberg mine in Indonesian-occupied Irian Jaya (western New Guinea). Grasberg is an environmental disaster almost beyond imagination, and as in Bougainville, tribal resistance has been met with assassinations and massacres by the Indonesian army.

If Rio Tinto's operations in the southwest Pacific recall King Leopold's Congo, its industrial relations, from southern Africa to Labrador and Utah, are a state-of-the-art experiment in worker intimidation.

In southern Africa, miners' unions have long questioned whether Rio Tinto, long rumored to have supplied uranium to Pretoria's clandestine atomic weapons program in the 1970s, has ever really broken with apartheid in its treatment of black workers. In February there was a worker uprising at its huge Rössing uranium pit in Namibia over management's unilateral raising of performance quotas and its refusal to address worker grievances. (Interestingly, the government of Iran is Rio Tinto's junior partner, with 15 percent of shares, at Rössing.)

In Australia, where the company exploits some of the world's most important iron, coal and uranium reserves, it has uprooted traditional unions, cut real wages and (as it is now trying to do in Boron) replaced collective bargaining with variable individual contracts.

Aussie miners and train drivers, however, have fought back with wildcat strikes and new organizing campaigns. Their defiance has led the company to an extraordinary solution: a fully automated "mine of the future" that won't require unruly miners or railroad workers. A working prototype is being developed in the remote Pilbara iron range: eleven mines with robotized drilling, automated haul trucks and, soon, driverless ore trains, all controlled from an operations center in Perth, 800 miles away.

Industry analysts debate whether this automated mining revolution will be feasible outside the largest, near-surface iron and coal deposits, so Local 30 probably doesn't need to worry about any imminent augmentation of scabs with robots. But they're urgently trying to decipher the complex and ruthless game that Rio Tinto and other mining superpowers are playing on a world stage.

V

The industrial revolution in Asia is bringing to a climax the struggle for ownership of the earth's strategic metals and minerals that began in the late nineteenth century. For instance, a single merger, between Rio Tinto and the even larger BHP Billiton, would create the world's third-largest corporation (after ExxonMobil and GE), with unprecedented power to set prices for exports of iron, aluminum, copper and titanium.

To put it another way, such a mega-merger could exact enormous rents from the future industrial growth of China and the rest of Asia—something that Beijing, at least, has no intention of allowing to happen (iron ore is China's second most costly import, after oil).

What *Forbes* called "the Battle for Rio Tinto" began two years ago, at the end of the 2000s mining boom, when cash-flush BHP attempted a hostile takeover that was countered by multibillion-dollar blocking offers of new investment from the government-controlled Aluminum Corporation of China.

But as resource prices slumped after the Wall Street crash, Rio Tinto share values were immediately pulled under by the weight of the $38 billion debt the company had incurred to buy Alcan (before BHP did) in 2007. BHP, faced with Rio Tinto's inability to sell its Alcan debt as bonds, as well as the subsequent downgrading of its credit, temporarily called off the attack, while the still ardent Chinese were rudely rebuffed by Rio Tinto's rebellious shareholders, supported by xenophobic Australian politicians.

Rio Tinto managed to survive the first year of recession by cutting thousands of jobs and selling off $10 billion of nonessential assets while retrenching in its core mission of exploiting "large, low-cost ore bodies." Mine managers in its minerals division, which includes borates, were told that future investment in their operations would only reward dramatic cost-cutting and higher earnings, not status quo profits. Labor, it seems, is an especially "compressible" cost.

In the specific case of Boron, the financing of a project called "the Modified Direct Dissolving of Kernite," advertised as the key to the mine's long-term profitability, was made conditional upon achieving "flexibility and accountability in our work practices"—that is to say, scrapping the old collective bargaining agreement with Local 30.

In negotiations, Rio Tinto took the intransigent stand that the crisis in world mining had made such union contracts obsolete. Yet since last fall, Rio Tinto and other ore giants have surfed spectacular recoveries on the wave of China's renewed growth, with iron prices expected to rise by as much as 50 percent this year.

Cash flow from other mineral products, including borates, and surges in mine share prices have been bolstered by a huge influx of investment from pension funds and other institutional investors—probably a speculative bubble in the making.

Then, in a staggering move, Rio Tinto betrayed its Chinese suitors and eloped with BHP. Their love child is a joint-production venture—in essence, a partial merger—that consolidates their huge iron ore operations in Australia, giving them unprecedented price-setting power over the world's most important metal.

Indeed, both Tom Albanese, Rio Tinto's CEO, and Marius Kloppers, his counterpart at BHP, recently warned major customers that annual price benchmarks will become a thing of the past, as the mining combination adjusts pricing to the volatile spot market. China, in particular, could see its steel and manufacturing costs rise by billions.

Beijing's immediate, furious response was to arrest Rio Tinto's top four executives in Shanghai for "espionage" (the charges were later reduced to bribery). Chinese officials talk darkly about the Rio Tinto/BHP "monopoly," although undoubtedly they would prefer to own part of it rather than actually dismantle it.

VI

The future of a small town in the Mojave is thus entangled in geoeconomic competitions far larger and more important than the borate market itself. So what chance do 560 miners and their families have in a fight with Godzilla?

The record of the past twenty years is not encouraging. With some heroic exceptions—the 1989-90 Pittston coal strike in Virginia, the 1990s Frontier Casinos strike in Las Vegas and a few others—international unions have seldom been willing to support a local fight to the last bullet or bitter dime.

But ILWU has a unique street credibility. The pit bull of CIO-generation unions, it bit into the heels of the West Coast stevedoring industry in 1934 and never let go. Industrial unions are supposed to be dying, but the ILWU, despite its modest size, punches hard enough to keep the powerful Pacific Maritime Association sulking in its corner, while ensuring that the docks remain safe and well paid.

As the only union that survived McCarthyism with its left-wing leadership (under Harry Bridges) intact, the ILWU is also legendary for putting muscle behind the slogan of "working-class solidarity." Since the 1960s it has conducted scores of job actions and walkouts in support of striking Australian dockers, California farmworkers and South African freedom fighters. Indeed, in May 2008 the union shut down the West Coast for a day to protest the war in Iraq.

In anticipation of the Boron lockout, ILWU had persuaded members of an international coalition of mining and maritime unions—many of whom have done battle with Rio Tinto—to hold their periodic conference in the nearby desert city of Palmdale. On February 16 the delegates, along with rank and file from other ILWU locals, arrive in Boron for a march to the mine followed by a big Local 30 barbecue.

The overture to the protest is the earthshaking full-throttle roar of shovelhead and twin-cam Harley-Davidson engines. The stevedore-bikers of Local 13 (LA Harbor) emerge out of the desert haze like Marlon Brando's leather clad horde in *The Wild One* (or, better, the Comanches in *Blood Meridian*).

Someone, awe-struck, whispers, "Glad these guys are on our side." Later I count twenty-six Harley black beauties corralled in a reverential semicircle on the street side of the union hall. (The unfortunate owners of rice-burners and pasta rockets have had to remove their imported Japanese and Italian bikes to a discreet distance.)

Carloads of out-of-town ILWU members arrive, then two buses carrying dozens of US and foreign labor leaders. The crowd applauds, people shake hands, someone turns up the volume on "Born in the USA" and the marchers begin to assemble, about 600-strong, behind a banner that spans the entire width of the road: An Injury to One Is an Injury to All.

It's an easy one-mile walk in pleasant weather to the front gate. Local 30 brings a dozen American and Marine Corps flags to the front, and begins to chant, "We Wanna Work, We Wanna Work." The sheriffs are relaxed, but the Gettier security guards up the road nervously shift their feet. As usual, their faces are inscrutable behind dark glasses, but you can almost smell their guilty sweat.

VII

Imagine a picnic jointly organized by the IWW, the American Legion and the Hells Angels. One of the first speakers is Oupa Komane from the

South African miners' union. He has a magnificent voice: "Comrades, I bring you revolutionary greetings from the miners of South Africa!" I look around to see how the "comrades" waving American flags react. Komane gets warm applause.

A battle-hardened copper miner from Utah (where Rio Tinto owns the great Kennecott pit at Bingham Canyon) says, "I can't tell you what I think of this company—not in front of women and children." An Australian warns, "They will kill your town. That's what they did to us." A Canadian talks about more dead mill towns in Quebec, while a New Zealander tells a story about Rio Tinto's sinister role in defeating climate-change legislation in his country.

The fiery head of the Turkish borate workers, whose state-owned industry (Eti Mine Works) was founded by Atatürk, father of the Turkish Republic, brings greetings from the Borons of Anatolia: Kirka, Emet, Kestelek and Bandirma. He scoffs at Rio Tinto's claim that his miners' lower hourly wages (almost $10 in a cheap country, versus an average of $26 in Boron) necessitate the trashing of union rights in California.

Finally, Ken Riley, president of the largely black International Longshoremen's Association Local 1422 in Charleston, South Carolina, and a leader of one of the most courageous fights in modern US labor history, summarizes the case for optimism: "You pick on the ILWU, you pick on the world. When our own international deserted us, they were there. Now we're here."

Later, I take Ken aside and confess my doubts. He shakes his head. "I understand what you're saying, but you're wrong," he says. "This isn't political theater. The first month of a struggle is decisive, and the ILWU is doing a terrific job marketing Boron's importance to the rest of the labor movement. Internationally, our unions understand that we have to organize the logistics chain, from producers to transport to distributor to retailer. This is a new model of power for the labor movement, like industrial unionism in the 1930s, but adapted to the reality of globalization."

"But Boron?" I ask.

"Hey, something new is being born here. It has to be."

Toni McCormick, a pretty, jovial woman in her late 20s, gives me a ride back to my car. The wife of a Local 30 member, she coaches the cheer squad at Boron High. "I'm fourth generation," she tells me. "My great-grandfather's house is still standing, made out of old dynamite boxes held together with chicken wire. Our football team plays in a high desert league with other mining and military towns. Sometimes they have to tackle each other in the dirt because grass won't grow in a saline lake bed."

"Can anything grow in a dry lake?" I wonder.

"Sure," Toni smiles. "Miners can."

DEFINITIONS OF IMPERIAL

William T. Vollmann

IMPERIAL IS GREEN, green fields, haystacks, and wide mountains. Imperial widens itself almost into boundlessness, like the Salton Sea as you go south. Imperial is bright fields, then desert wastes, stacks of hay bales almost Indian yellow. Imperial is a dark field glimmering white with irrigation sprays. *(There appears to be a widespread impression,* runs the 1909 Department of Agriculture Yearbook, *that the fertility of irrigated lands is inexhaustible...the experience of generations of farmers in humid regions is disregarded.*) Imperial is a loud lonely train whistling like darkness. Imperial dreams fragrant vegetable dreams. Imperial dreams resentfully of the wealth that it could have if the stink of death would only depart from the broken-windowed resorts on the Salton Sea. (THIS VALUABLE COMMERCIAL PROPERTY FOR SALE, says a hand-lettered sign in Bombay Beach. In Brawley, somebody who prefers to have it both ways has posted the following announcement on a ruined garage: KEEP OUT! INQUIRE AT OFFICE.) Imperial is the smell of a feedlot on a hot summer night. Imperial is the beautiful, smooth-skinned, reddish-brown fat girl with monumental breasts who replenishes the bowls of salsa and relish in a taco stand in Mexicali. Meat grease glistens upon her gigantic cleavage. Imperial is that nameless bygone California beauty queen in the uncaptioned photograph, and the nameless grave-inmates at Tumco. (Their names exist forever, like the Imperial County line, and if I hunted with sufficient exactitude I could discover them.) Imperial is Barbara Worth, the sentimental heroine of (and here I quote the commemorative edition's dust jacket) A Saga of Love and Rivalries Set in the Pioneer Days of Imperial County. Around the egg-shaped illustration, breathtakingly garish, of dark-haired, cherry-lipped Barbara

Worth in her wide sombrero, staring dreamily past a cactus (*Often as Barbara sat looking over that great basin her heart cried out to know the secret it held*), we're informed: Movie Was Gary Cooper's Screen Debut and (thank God for the quotation marks) "A Clean and Wholesome Book" and "Strong People" • "High Ideals" and finally: Three Years on U.S. Top Ten Best Seller Lists, those years being 1911, 1912 and 1922. *The pioneers in Barbara's Desert were, in fact, leaders in a far greater work that would add immeasurably to the nation's life.* In other words, KEEP OUT! INQUIRE AT OFFICE. Imperial is the slender, wrinkled inhabitants of Slab City, together with their trailers, weeds, and heaps of scrapwood. Imperial is the brown-skinned man who somehow missed every immigration amnesty and who now laments for the good old days of the 1950s when *all we needed back then was just a rancher to give a signature to back us up*. Imperial is solid white farmer-citizens, and the conglomerates who now own so many of them. Imperial is the grocery store clerk who begs every stranger to buy a plot of dust while he can, because the Salton Sea's going to get entirely cleaned up within five years and then values will go through the roof! (You can hardly get away from the Salton Sea in Imperial.) Imperial is the grower who *changed our direction from dates to flowers, especially annual color for country clubs and hotels. They're quite lucrative.* (Annual color in this case meant poppies and petunias. Her corporation raised eighty thousand of each.) Imperial is Cahuilla Indians and East Indian liquor store clerks. But most of all, Imperial is "Mexicans" legal and illegal, and Imperial is also "Mexican-Americans."—They just dig in, a Border Patrolman once told me, as if he were speaking of a strange species of insect. They hide in the weirdest places.—Yes, they dig in, like us. Legally and illegally they establish themselves upon the land, and they try to stay; they want to live. (I can tell you that most of the people who come to the U.S.A. don't go back, said a taxi driver in Indio. Because I tell you, Mexico is beautiful but Mexico is tough.—He'd majored in electrical engineering, but then he fell in love and, as he put it, "went out of college." Now he was divorced, with alimony and child support to pay.) *Imperial is the continuum between Mexico and America.*

TURTLE ISLAND

from *I Hotel*

Karen Tei Yamashita

IT'S NOT EASY to get into a boat with three people you don't know and go rowing off toward your destiny. If someone said, "Hey, get into this boat; it's going to change your life," would you do it? That's the trickery of being young. You figure, what the hell. I've never done this before. You've got time. Youth's supposed to have adventures. Even when there're folks who come rowing back from that trip and tell you what could happen or even warn you to turn around, you think you'll make your own mistakes but not those. But they never tell you everything. The past is always saved in someone's ego, so the really complicated and difficult things can only be known by living them out yourself. When it's all said and done, you too will save the hardest stuff inside your knowing ego. And you won't do it out of meanness, or duplicity, or vanity, but maybe because you just forget and get tired, because you've got to be an elder with a certain distance that they call wisdom, or because they never ask you anyway.

A group self-identified by their Asian features gathered at Pier Thirty-nine under a full November moon, dancing through the usual lace of San Francisco Bay fog. Of course, depending, they could have been mistaken for Indian. It wouldn't be the first time someone recognized the features that claim the same genes that crossed the Bering Strait or canoed across the Pacific. Different tribes is all. The giveaway was probably the hundred-pound sack of Calrose rice. Wayne Takabayashi, a kid, probably high school, in skinny jeans and a pair of black canvas low-tops, was sitting on the sack when Stony Ima sauntered up, lugging a box on his shoulder. "Hey," said Stony to Wayne, "you waiting for the, uh, operation to the island?" He pointed his nose in the direction of Alcatraz. At that hour, it had the surreptitious feel of a dark spy operation, but no one had the code words.

Wayne looked up at a long-haired dude with a headband. "Yeah, who sent you?"

"Olivia. You?"

"Who's Olivia?"

"Does it matter?"

"Guess not. You know JB?"

"Yeah, everyone knows JB. So where is he?"

"Don't know. Where's the boat? Supposed to be transport, you know."

"How long you been here?"

"Half an hour at least. Shit."

"Hey," Stony pointed to an Asian woman walking toward them. "That's not Olivia. Know her?"

Wayne shook his head, waiting for her face to be revealed in the dark. "I don't know. She looks familiar." She had that long, straight hair parted in the middle that tumbled over a navy blue peacoat, but they all pretty much looked like that.

Ria Ishii walked purposefully, her hand gripping the handle of a large canister. Wayne noticed it was a gallon can of Kikkoman shoyu. She put it down next to his sack of rice and said, "So, this must be the place."

Stony shook his head. "Can't be too sure." He pointed at Wayne. "He's been waiting a half hour already and no boat."

"Well," said Ria. "Maybe we're not late."

"That's one way to see it," nodded Stony. "Shit, it's midnight."

Wayne pulled on his beanie and tugged his jacket tighter. The neons from the wharf reflected off the black waters, obscured intermittently by low clouds of fog hunkering over the surface. The wind blew cold against the ocean spray misting his face.

Stony, who had worked up a walking sweat with his load, was wiping the steam off his spectacles. "Good idea, the rice," he approved.

"Yeah, what'd you bring?" asked Wayne, nodding at Stony's box.

"Case of Spam." He smiled. "I figure they're camped out there. This is camping food, right?"

"I guess so." Wayne shrugged. Then he noticed that he and Stony were both staring at the gallon can of soy sauce. They were momentarily mesmerized by the light that bounced off the slapping waves and glinted over the can's gold and red-orange carapace.

"Salt substitute," Ria defended.

No one said anything. They all looked out across the bay at the island, the dark concrete fortress perched on its rocky base, the lighthouse beam sweeping in a constant pulse. Maybe they imagined it, but they thought they could see tiny bonfires and smoke trailing darkly across night skies in the cold wind. When the last prisoner departed from the old penitentiary, he left the island to a single caretaker and his dog. After six years, Alcatraz was again occupied. Now the Rock was Indian land.

Ria broke in, "I met an Indian out there on the street who just pulled in from Oklahoma. He's got a boat hitched to his station wagon."

"No shit. The message is traveling," nodded Stony.

"He needs help with the boat. I told him I'd send him some help. But maybe he could be our way over."

Wayne pointed. "They've got the Coast Guard patrolling. See that boat over there with the lights?"

"That must be why we're stuck here. Something fouled up."

"How about it?" Ria pursued her idea. "One of you stay here to watch our stuff?"

"I'll do it," said Stony. He pointed at Wayne. "You could probably use the exercise."

Wayne was jumping around a bit to warm up. "Yeah," he agreed and accompanied Ria, following a small crowd of late-night revelers emerging from a wharf bar.

"I'm Ria," said Ria.

"Wayne," said Wayne.

"I know I've seen you around somewhere."

"Yeah," said Wayne. "Me too."

They found the Indian dozing at the wheel in his station wagon. The back was packed to the gills with stuff. They knocked on his window.

"Hey." He recognized Ria. "I thought I'd catch some snooze. I been driving for almost three days straight, and anyway, I can't leave the boat. Too risky."

They helped him unhitch the boat, pulled away the protective tarp to reveal a wooden flat-bottomed boat painted a deep green. Wayne scrutinized the boat's name, painted in golden letters. In the dark it took awhile, but he finally read: *The Turtle*.

"I'm Jack. Jack Denny. Some call me Turtle, too," said Jack, shaking hands all around.

They filled the boat with paddles, a small outboard motor, fishing gear, a sleeping roll, and a duffel of clothing. Jack shouldered the front, with Ria and Wayne coming up on either side. They marched down the old pier to the end, Jack's boots making rhythmic footfalls, dancing to avoid puddles of fish blood and the drenched scatter of paper trash and beer bottles. The stink of fish and crab wafted about. At that hour, it was just them and the barking sea lions.

Stony was sitting on the rice and blowing plaintive sounds through a narrow bamboo flute. "Night guard came round," he announced and tucked the flute into an inside pocket in his jacket. "Asked me, was I one of those Indians, and did I know it was illegal to go over there."

"What'd you say?"

"Said I was Japanese, just night fishing like usual. Then for some reason, he started talking about raw fish. Said he knew all about it. Lived in Okinawa. Used the dipping sauce, too."

They all stared at the gallon canister of soy sauce again, and Ria smiled. "Hey," she said, introducing the boat's owner, "this is Jack."

They took the boat down a ramp to a docking slip and gently set the *Turtle* into the ocean. It bobbed there in the dark water, and they could see it would soon become like a piece of straw in the big bay. Even so, Jack looked out and said confidently, "Pretty calm out there."

"Yeah, well, good luck," said Ria.

"So we brought these provisions, see." Stony came forward with his case of Spam. Then everything got arranged in the boat—Jack's stuff, plus the rice and shoyu.

Stony looked up. "Oh man, here comes the guard," he rasped.

"How are you folks tonight?" said the guard.

Stony said, "These are my Japanese friends I was telling you about."

"Fishing crew, eh? Where you heading?"

Stony said, "Oh, Marin side maybe, do some rock fishing."

Wayne picked up one of Jack's rods and handed it to Ria, who examined it like she knew what she was doing. She stepped out in front of the guard to obscure Jack and made casting motions. Under the watch of the guard, one by one they all climbed into the boat. Stony retrieved the rope, and Jack took the paddle and pushed off the dock. Wayne got the other paddle and tried to match Jack's movements. Ria waved good-bye to the guard, who called out, "Bring me back some sa-shimi!" After a short distance, they could hear his mutter travel along the waves: "Crazy Japanese."

"Thanks for covering for me," said Jack, a red man but yellow enough.

"So, now what?" Ria asked.

"So, now we go claim the Rock," said Jack.

"Oh shit," said Stony, looking back at the dock that was receding into the dark distance. "Why not?"

"O.K.," agreed Wayne.

"Just so everyone knows," said Ria, "I've never been in a boat. I'm from the South Side of Chicago."

"Aren't there lakes there?" asked Stony.

"Lake Michigan, but I never sailed it. How about you?"

Stony said, "Just some fishing with my dad in L.A. off Pedro."

"O.K., that's something," said Jack. "How about you?" he asked Wayne.

Wayne shook his head.

"The *Turtle* here," announced Jack, "is making her maiden voyage in the Pacific Ocean. First time she's touched salt water."

"Congratulations," praised Stony.

"And not to make you nervous or anything, but I can't swim either," said Ria.

Jack glanced forward to Ria in the bow. "The *Turtle*'s never let me down, but if there're any other last confessions, we'll hear them now."

Stony said, "Ria, you wanna go back?"

"No, no." Ria practically stood up in the boat, waved, and pointed. "Let's go take that Rock."

"O.K."

Wayne asked, "If we pretend to be fishing, will they leave us alone?" In the distance, they could see what looked like a patrol boat cruising by the east end of Alcatraz.

"Maybe." Ria stuck a rod out and pushed a bit of line into the water, watching its skimming trail follow behind.

Jack and Wayne traded paddling from one side to the other, keeping a distant beeline for the dark Rock. Jack suggested, "Sink the paddle in like this and push back."

Wayne copied Jack's motions and probably thought about the last time he did this, on a canoe ride at Disneyland, but this was hardly the time to admit it.

"Why," Ria asked Jack, "did you decide to come? Oklahoma to Alcatraz is a long way."

"It's time."

"You do Nam?" Stony asked, noticing the medals pinned to Jack's denim jacket.

"That too." Jack paused. "You know the story of the Modoc and Captain Jack?"

Jack jerked the cord back a bunch of times until the motor coughed into life. They all settled into the *Turtle* and stared hard at the destined Rock. The story bloomed around them in a translucent fog.

Who knows—if that night guard hadn't come around to talk about raw fish and make sure they paddled out to fish it, whether three Japanese

Americans would have gotten on a little green boat with a Modoc Indian. And it was the damnedest thing how you could be Indian or Japanese but be just plain invisible. Now, some might say that making it through the Coast Guard blockade that night was a condition of this invisibility, but others will tell you that storytelling in itself is powerful magic, can get you from point A to point B, and you don't know how it happened.

Captain Jack, the man Jack "Turtle" Denny was named after, was the chief of the Modocs when they lived on the lava beds around Lost River and Tule Lake along the far northern border of California with Oregon. That was around 1870, a hundred years ago.

"You know how the U.S. Army can have all the manpower, the guns, the copters, the bombs, and napalm and still be losing the war?"

"Yeah, man."

"So it was the same with Captain Jack and the Modoc braves. It was the costliest battle of the time. Government sent in everything and still they couldn't dislodge the Modoc people from lavaland. Hell, they couldn't even see the Modoc warriors who just disappeared into the landscape, merged into the black rocks and sage."

Outboard motor puttputted its concerted rhythm, and the battle rose from the inky ocean in great detail: bloody guts of the killed and wounded, a frayed army of white soldiers shredded by their own crazed departure through jagged rock. And only a single Indian—his head blown up by his own curiosity—fallen. But like every Indian victory, it's still just a story. If the Modoc could hold the inhospitable lava beds, what pride should remove their claim? The same would be true of the Rock, unsuitable for any occupation other than a penitentiary or an Indian reservation—no transportation, no running water, no sanitation facilities, no oil or mineral rights, no industry, no health care, no agriculture or game, no education. It could be rock, could be lava beds. Story's the same.

Winning a battle could get you a peace treaty, but not necessarily the one you want and not necessarily the one they'll keep. The price of peace, if it has one, is never cheap. "So," said Jack, "when the negotiations went sour, the Modoc council voted to kill the white general."

Now, the operative word here is *voted*, not *kill*; people forget that war is a collective action. The story is that Captain Jack voted to negotiate the peace but was in the minority. And then he was called a "fish-hearted woman" for voting that way. Well, he went back into that peace-tent meeting with five other Modoc representatives and asked to get the Modoc lands back—those same lava beds and the Lost River, and once again, General Canby said no.

"At that moment," continued Jack, "Captain Jack took out the revolver hidden near his so-called fish-heart and shot the general in the face. You could say the general lost face, but not Captain Jack."

Ria interrupted. "I swear it's not the story, but I'm going to be sick."

Jack said, "You'll feel better if you just concentrate on looking out into the distance at the island." But when they all looked, they were staring the Rock in the face, its cliffs rising in gigantic shelves above an impudent turtle.

"What do you think?" asked Stony. "Go that way?" He pointed east.

"Got to be a landing somewhere."

Wayne lifted his right foot from the bottom of the boat and shook out his low-top. "You generally get this much water in the boat?"

Everyone looked down and saw the water seeping through. Stony saw Jack's dismayed expression and jumped down and started scooping the water out with his hands.

Wayne pointed with an oar. "Over there. We can make it."

As the boat approached a rocky outcrop, Ria tossed Jack's duffel, and then his sleeping bag. Jack jumped out and yelled for the rope. "O.K.," he yelled, pulling the tether and directing their escape. "Let's go. Grab his hand!"

When they were all safe on the rocks, Jack looked out at the *Turtle*, slowly filling with water but considerably more buoyant without its passengers. "Maybe we can tie the rope somewhere," Stony suggested, searching around.

"Nope." Jack shook his head. "*Turtle*'s gotta go. Had enough, I guess." He let the rope slip away, and they watched the boat bob around with the provisions—Calrose, Spam, and Kikkoman, the fishing equipment, and the paddles, flung like helpless arms.

"Hey!" a yell came from above.

The four looked up, wet to their waists and almost too frozen to move. A light passed over, blinding them, and then someone said, "Welcome to Indian land."

Someone else added, "Land of the free. Home of the brave."

The fifth day of the takeover would be dawning in a few hours. The feeling of excitement and purpose was palpable everywhere. How many times in your life do you feel that kind of power, the sort that unifies a people in collective pride and knowing? This time, you and your people get to choose. It's not an idle feeling, but one that you pursue in various forms, like singing the same song or cheering the same team or praying to the same spirit. A connective wave carries you to the same infinite space, and you feel more alive than you have ever felt.

Looking up from the bonfire, Ria saw the smoke meet the full moon. Two more astronauts had walked there only days ago, but no one seemed to remember. It was just another Apollo, another moonwalk. On Earth, Indians walked on Alcatraz. "One small step for man, one giant leap for mankind."

Around the fire and after a change of clothing, the storytelling continued. The Indians of All Tribes had a comparative story going about Turtle Island. It seems like several tribes have a variation of this creation story, how the Earth was born from a tiny plug of soil on the back of a turtle. There are usually three animals who go in search of land. Some say the questing animals were an eagle, a loon, and a muskrat. Others interchange beaver and otter. Others put in for the toad. But there's pretty much some agreement that it was a turtle's back and always some minor amphibious animal who came back to the surface of the water with a precious plug of earth. Maybe it's a creation story, but maybe it's also a story about sacrifice and quest.

The morning rose over the island, and they had not slept. They walked to the eastern edge of the Rock and looked out toward the wakening city. Stony drew the flute from inside his jacket. Jack eyed it and asked, "What kind of flute is that?"

"Japanese call it a yokobue." Stony set the thing to his lips and pierced the morning with its birdsong. He blew a high-pitched wild yodel that converged with the barking sea lions, the low horns of passing ferries, and the clang of scattered buoys. Then Stony coaxed Jack: "You never finished your story about Captain Jack."

"Oh, yeah."

Don't think that if you kill a general, the U.S. Army will let you go. History tells us that the white man's pride is located in his laws, such that he will justify his pride and his greed, his great paternity and his superiority, with the great writ of his laws. Everything must follow accordingly. The white man will only give up or lose something if forced to do so by his own laws; in this way, he cannot lose face and continues secure in his pride that his law must be just. And so Captain Jack and four of his fellow Modoc warriors were tried and hung. Two braves, however, escaped the gallows and were imprisoned in Alcatraz. The Modoc brave Barncho died here, but Slolux lived to follow his people to Oklahoma. "Slolux," said Jack, "was my great-grandfather."

A great sunrise blushed behind the hills and towering buildings of the city's peninsula. Wayne pointed to a green speck rowing away from the Rock. Ria scrutinized the floating vessel. Stony said, "*The Turtle*?" then asked for confirmation, "There are two guys rowing, right?"

"Who are they?" asked Ria. "Hey! Come back!" she yelled into the bay uselessly. "That's Jack's *Turtle*!"

But when Stony blew his flute in melodic tribute, they seemed to look back in the direction of its cry.

Jack waved and said, "It's O.K. They're Indians."

"How do you know? From the island?"

"Yeah," he nodded. "Finally, they got away."

"Huh?"

"Shit," said Stony. "What are they going to do with your shoyu?"

RETURN TO DEVIL'S GULCH

Darla Hillard

FORGET-ME-NOTS CARPETED THE banks of Papermill Creek that March weekend my Aunt Ginny and I spent at Marin County's Samuel P. Taylor State Park. It was 1994, and Ginny was in her early 70s. She looked less like my father's sister and more like my own, in her straight-leg Levis and a khaki crush hat that hid her white fringe. The forget-me-nots, feral reminders of bygone days, were appropriate. Ginny was on a quest to find whatever might be left of a secret cabin my Uncle Van and his friends had built in Devil's Gulch around 1930, before the land became part of the park.

"I hope I can remember where it was," Ginny had said over the phone. "It was barely standing when Van and I were last there in the '60s."

I thought it both amazing and wonderful that my uncle and his friends had gotten away with having such a hideaway, trespassers as they were and considering how impossible such a thing would be today.

Back then the Golden Gate Bridge was still on the drawing boards. Nearly every weekend my uncle and his Airedale, Pat, would catch the ferry from San Francisco to Sausalito. Dogs might have been allowed on the ferry, but not on the electric connector train or the North Pacific Coast narrow gauge that ran from San Rafael to Tomales Bay. Once smuggled aboard, Pat would hide under the seat until they reached Lagunitas.

Clyde Polk and Shorty Atkins were Van's partners in crime. Clyde lived in Forest Knolls and Shorty in Lagunitas. They built their cabin from materials scrounged, scavenged, and packed in by the sweat of their backs. Van's sister recalled, "It was a long hike, but the boys carried all the supplies up the hill as if it were a breeze. They harnessed the little waterfall and generated enough electric power for one light bulb to burn a couple of hours. Sometimes we would hike up the slopes of Mount Barnabe and gather mushrooms and feast on them that evening. None of us died, so I guess they were OK." They swam and fished for steelhead in Papermill Creek (since renamed Lagunitas Creek). And, it must be said, they did a little poaching.

Dogs, horses, and camping had been vital ingredients in Ginny and Van's 41-year marriage. She was grieving his long decline and recent death. Now at least she was free to roam again; it seemed the surest way to carry on. That I was to be part of her quest for the cabin was like a bridge to my past, and a chance to rediscover my favorite aunt. The summer I was 12, crazed by hormone overload, she had taken me on their annual pack trip into the mountains.

I'd always been half afraid of my lanky, gruff uncle. That summer I saw that he was in his element camping beside a high meadow, telling stories, trout fishing, and riding Early Dude, a racer he had rescued from the glue factory. He fed my cowgirl fantasies while Ginny fed something deeper, more enduring.

"Matilda and I will be traveling alone a lot now," she explained as we headed out Sir Frances Drake in her small motor home. "I wanted something manageable for an old lady, and I thought it would be safer with an open cab." I had to strain to hear her from my seat in the back; Matilda, an Australian shepherd, had the passenger seat.

In the late 1800s, what became Samuel P. Taylor State Park was a thriving mill town producing paper and blasting powder. The Taylor enterprises also included a fur tannery, firewood collection, and Camp Taylor. Where the campgrounds are today stood a 100-room hotel, dance hall, bowling alley, saloons, riding stable, grocery store, butcher shop, and laundry. Camp Taylor drew families from San Francisco to spend whole summers by the creek. The men commuted to their city jobs by train and ferry—an hour's journey, free of "traffic updates every 10 minutes."

Samuel Taylor died in 1886. Six years later, a nationwide financial panic doomed the town and its industries. Taylor's wife and sons were unable to repay a mortgage for mill improvements. The lender foreclosed and then died, leaving the property to Taylor's widow, Elizabeth. In 1905 Elizabeth, who lived in San Francisco's Fairmont Hotel, posted "no trespassing" signs and ordered the demolition of all the remaining buildings on the old Taylor property.

Though the train ran to Tomales until 1933, ridership declined without the industries and tourists. The streams and woodlands were returned, largely, to the wildlife. Elizabeth stopped paying property taxes, and by 1940 she owed Marin County $11,000. Still, acquisition of the park took five years. The state legislature would have to approve the purchase and the county would have to waive the tax bill. But the hardest part was convincing Elizabeth to sell. Finally, after her son-in-law took over her finances, she agreed to the deal.

Ginny and I arrived at the campground in early afternoon, with time to get settled and take a stroll before dinner. Matilda set the pace, half choking herself in her eagerness for the walk and the promise of a wade in the creek.

Early the next morning we crossed the road and entered the loamy-smelling shade of Devil's Gulch. I picked a forget-me-not for good luck. Our map indicated that the trails were out of bounds for horses, bikes, and dogs. "Well," said Ginny, "if Matilda gets caught we'll just have to throw ourselves on the mercy of the ranger. This quest requires a dog."

We followed the gulch trail until we came to a side gully that looked right, but there was no path up it, and it was thick with poison oak. So we retraced our steps downstream and found the trail to Mount Barnabe, named for Sam Taylor's mule. We crossed over the gulch and climbed up the steep hillside. Ginny was worried. "The cabin was lower down; I don't think I'd recognize the setting from way up here."

The path leveled out and led along the contour. We passed through spreading coast live oak trees, pungent bay laurel, and orange-trunked madrone. "There was an orchard somewhere up the gulch," Ginny said. "Van and the boys would filch a bucket of apples, and while the others peeled and sliced, Van made crusts and did the baking. The pies would be gone as fast as he could get them out of the oven—which was a five-gallon drum."

We had crossed a little side stream and were heading for the next ridge when Ginny stopped. "There's something about this place." She walked back and looked uphill at a tree leaning over the gully. She looked down. Fifty feet below the trail lay an old piece of corrugated tin with red paint still showing through the rust. "It's part of the roof! It had a red advertisement painted on it. I remember that madrone, too. Oh goody! We've found it!"

We made our way carefully down the steep bank. Broken boards were nearly obscured by trees and bushes along the gully where Matilda lapped at a thread of water. Ginny poked in the loose earth and found an S-shaped section of pipe. "It's part of the hot water system. These coils were under the stone fireplace."

"Pancakes for breakfast," I said, picking up a rusted syrup tin. "They must have had good times here."

"Oh, yes," replied Ginny. "You know they came even in winter, rain or shine. They always had a good supply of wood. Shorty composed a poem that they left tacked to the door. It welcomed anyone who happened by and asked that the cabin be left as it was found. I never met Shorty, but Van's spirit is sure all around here."

Chickadees chattered in the trees. Sun warmed the hillside, and our thoughts turned to lunch and the beers, cool in their newspaper wrappers at the bottom of our daypacks. Ginny caught Matilda's leash and got a free haul back up to the trail.

"It looks like the cabin just eventually fell down," I pointed out between bites of my sandwich. "I'm surprised the park staff didn't clear it out, but I guess most of the visitors wouldn't have ventured out this far in the early days. They just let nature take its course."

Ginny looked down into the gully. "Van and his friends were sorry to give up the cabin, but they had no regrets that we got a park and not 'Taylor Estates.'"

Ginny died last year, at 86. We scattered her ashes with those of Matilda, under a sugar pine in the mountains where years ago she had done the same for Van. Beloved remains enriching the soil of one of their favorite retreats. Surely by now the few traces that remained of my uncle's cabin are gone, buried or consumed by the soil of Devil's Gulch. But the cabin's story will endure, the kind of gift that our family can carry in our being from generation to generation, an ode to our love for wild places.

FROM *LIFT*

Rebecca K. O'Connor

PEREGRINE BEGINNINGS

FALCONRY IS A religion, a way of thinking, a means of experiencing life. True falconers are compassionate, clear-eyed straight-shooters. We've touched nature's senseless violence, clung to her stray miracles, and this alters our beliefs. It is a religion for which we are often persecuted. And at the center of falconry is a holy war for the peregrine.

Fifty years ago peregrines were considered vermin to be shot on sight. Many states had bounties that made sighting the gun on narrow wings profitable. Hawks and falcons were thieves that robbed humans of fine game, fattened chickens and lofted pigeons. There were few groups of people who valued the raptor. Yet the falconers valued them more than anyone. To the falconers there was nothing more perfect than a peregrine. Then the sea change came.

In the years before I was born falconry was nearly eradicated for the sake of the peregrine. The cosmopolitan falcon had remained a steadfast beloved to the falconer for more than three thousand years, but during the years of my childhood these birds nearly disappeared from North America. The falconers were just as mystified as the conservationists and then horrified when the blame was placed on their sport, on the few that loved them the most. Falconers were named nest-robbing soulless pirates.

The North American Falconers Association formed a committee "for the preservation of falconry" and waged a war for their rights. The falconers saved their art, keeping it legal, but lost the right to trap a peregrine. In order to preserve the privilege to hunt with raptors, we forfeited the wild take of *Falco peregrinus*.

Birds were no longer trapped on the beach to fly a single season and released on the migration. Eyasses were no longer tenderly tucked in a jacket pocket to be rappelled down the sheer face of cliff eyeries. Yet the falconers were determined. If they couldn't borrow them from the wild then they would breed them. And the falconers succeeded where the scientists did not. I didn't know it when I was eight years old, but the falcon on my roof was a miracle of desire.

Then the peregrine began to resurge as a wild population and burgeon as a captive-bred resource. When I was in high school the long-wingers, falconers who preferred the flights of the long-winged falcons, had their choice of flighted companions from many different breeding projects even if they weren't allowed to borrow them from the wild. As the captive-bred peregrine became more accessible, surprisingly the war resurged as well.

Scientists didn't believe that falconers could be successful breeding the falcons when others had failed. Surely, the falconers were laundering wild birds through fake breeding projects that couldn't possibly be producing young.

Across the United States Fish and Wildlife agents knocked on the doors of sixty falconers. Search warrants in hand they tore through homes, mishandled birds, interrogated falconers, and confiscated their falcons. Described as "clumsy, clueless, ham-fisted, jack-booted storm troopers" they turned the falconry community upside down and heralded the beginning of Operation Falcon.

Some of the falcons confiscated were returned after lengthy, arduous, and expensive court battles. Others perished in the hands of the agency. Our government was convinced that falconers must be passing off wild birds as captive-bred young in their breeding projects despite the lack of proof. Tried in the media, we were all dubbed international falcon smugglers.

There was little truth to the accusations. In fact, the trial revealed that the main perpetrator was an undercover agent supplied with illegal birds by the government. He had been paid to set about entrapping whomever he could snare. Again the falconers fought for their rights, for the sake of their love of the peregrine. Again they won, but the damage was done. Federal agents, state authorities, and worse, the public had tried the falconers in the media and proclaimed them wildlife criminals.

The peregrine is off the endangered list. Young wild birds are now abundant and pester our trained falcons in the field. We long for the short-term company of a truly wild peregrine but wonder if we'll ever be allowed to trap them again. It's doubtful.

Driving home in silence, Adam somewhere in his own head, I think about how the falcon on my fist is the fruit of several bitter wars, his breeding the result of passion pushing science. Had the falconers given up, had either of those battles swung the other way there would be no license for my religion and I wouldn't have a peregrine.

When I was an apprentice, you could not put a captive-bred peregrine on your license, possess it legally, unless you were a master, a falconer with five years of experience. I've been a master falconer for some time now, but have never had a peregrine. I have a lot of excuses why. Peel those excuses away and I'm just afraid, afraid to fail, but this year I'm flying a peregrine anyway.

In February I turned thirty-two. There's nothing monumental about the number except that not long after my birthday I woke one morning with a memory that made it something more.

I'm seventeen and someone reads my palm. I can't see her face, just long dark hair, frizzing about her cheekbones, but I can hear the even tone of her proclamation. She says, "You will live to be thirty-two." Her voice is scratchy, unnaturally throaty.

She traces a line at the center of my hand that leads between my thumb and forefinger as if she is reading. She doesn't laugh or even smile, just traces a few more lines and drops my hand.

I can't even imagine living another fifteen years, so I shrug it off and turn away without looking back. I mean to forget it. I don't believe in the foretelling of death. No reputable fortuneteller would say such a thing, even a novice. It's against the rules.

Somehow, though, this girl had planted the thought and it reverberated like a ringing alarm when it was time to recall it, when somehow I found myself thirty-two. I keep bringing the memory back, trying to make the girl lift her face so that I can see it, bring out the details so that I can remember where we were, but I can't draw out more.

I know the lines of my hands now. I've studied them carefully, these etchings I was born with versus the white lines I once foolishly carved on my wrist. I don't know which is more of a portent, features or scars. Still, the lifeline that surrounds my thumb looks endless and strong. It is crosshatched over and over at its beginning stretch, a sign of hardship and stress. It smoothes out in what's sure to mark my thirties and that has always left me hopeful for the future.

Madame Christine read my palm five years ago from a room in her doublewide at the edge of the Florida swamp. I had stopped on a whim, twenty dollars in my pocket, half my grocery money for the week. The bird show at Disney's Animal Kingdom didn't pay well, but I was hoping for a bright future. Madame Christine told me I was born under lucky numbers, but that I just hadn't gotten the luck yet. She promised it was coming and said I was going to live to be eighty-three. I asked her how she knew and she pointed to the left on my palm and said, "Right here," but I didn't see it.

I don't believe I'm going to die, but all the same, this year has become a big "What if?" What if this is it? I wanted to see more than thirty-two. More than that, I didn't want to waste this year. What if I never have another chance to fly a falcon?

I think about how the lines on my palms meet to form an "M" scrawled much like a child crayoning birds in the sky above stick figures, wonder if a life with birds was always in my future. Birthright or self-infliction, the falcon is the future I want.

"Why haven't you ever flown a peregrine?" I ask Adam. He shrugs.

"You've got plenty of places to hunt ducks," I say, wondering why someone who has flown birds for seventeen years would choose never to fly a falcon. He has access to much better terrain for flying long-wings than I do.

"I would rather fly a goshawk," he says without looking at the peregrine on my glove. "Besides, I've seen plenty of guys fly falcons. I've had my fill."

I run my finger over the falcon's longest toe, then press my fingertip to the point of the talon until the sharpness of it stings. It's fragile and powerful, a perfect contradiction. The bones so narrow, I could snap them between two fingers, but the strength of his piercing grip could draw blood from my bare skin in an instant. I can't imagine how you could ever get your fill.

"I hope you'll come watch this guy fly anyway."

"Get him in the air and we'll see," Adam says.

TO TAME A PEREGRINE

It isn't hard to wake at dawn when you can hear the stirrings of a falcon outside of your room. I lie in bed a moment, eyes closed and smiling. I had zip-tied a bell on the screen perch so that I can hear the falcon adjust, know if he bates, note if he gets back up. As the sun starts to light the room, the bell rings faintly, responding to the gentle vibrations of the falcon scratching his head. I listen just a little longer, knowing that my sudden appearance will cause him to tighten his feathers and think about flight. I hear him rouse, a hum of feathers that have all been lifted from the body and shaken down into place. My flannel sheets are too warm and I envy his feathers, warmth that can be adjusted precisely, individual muscles raising each shaft, allowing air to cool between skin and down. Then my African grey parrot calls, "Coffee?" in a believable intonation of my voice and the bell silences, the spell broken.

It's June and this is the low desert, one hundred degrees at midnight, no matter how dark the night or how many scorched acres are converted to lush lawn. The only time it's comfortable outside is at dawn. I pad over to the falcon in my pajamas, a tank top and boxers. I slip on my falconry glove, double-layer elk skin, cut from a tracing of my hand and sewn to fit and protect the skin just past my wrist, but I still feel naked and exposed when the falcon glares at me. I have too much skin showing, too many fragile parts, but I step him up on my glove.

I tell myself he's just a falcon, a tiny thing despite his giant temperament. I've hefted eagles on this same fist and haven't lost any appendages. Even the first red-tail hawk I flew as an apprentice falconer was twice this peregrine's size, thick-toed and broad-beaked; she was far more dangerous near my soft eyes and brittle finger bones. This head full of reasoning does nothing to override the chill in my gut when the falcon meets my eyes. He knows he's stronger than me and I'm not going to change his mind. So I keep his jesses tight, his feet close the leather glove as I walk outside to tie him to a perch on the patio.

The falcon needs to get in the habit of eating at dawn, have an appetite when we would normally be flying. He needs to learn that meals come off the lure and then we'll begin training in earnest. Without a lure the only way to get a falcon back is through a sacrifice of live game. Raising pigeons for slaughter is hard on the soul and bad training besides. Sure, you could throw a pigeon or some other farm-raised game into the wind, draw the falcon down from the sky with a fluttering meal, but that's not training; it's only a reminder of what a wild heart is unable to resist.

Back in the kitchen, I take the quail I thawed during the night and cut it in half down the center, a leg on each side. I bought five freezer bags full, each stuffed with twelve farm-raised quail, three rows of four, carefully lined up so the bags stack nicely next to the vegetables and the ice. No different than chicken or Cornish game hen really, except that they haven't been cleaned or dressed. I tell everyone that they serve Coturnix quail in fine restaurants, but my friends still jump when they reach for ice to put in their sangria. I've learned to be strategic about when I thaw quail. Nothing ruins a dinner party faster than the words, "Um, there's a dead bird in your sink."

I put half the quail in a sandwich bag and then in the bottom crisper drawer for later. I pour myself a cup of coffee and then grab the lure so that I can tie the other half of the quail on it.

I made the lure the night before with much flailing of stitches and no shortage of needle-prick fingertip blood. It's ugly, this thing that I've made to signal the falcon to come back to me. It's an oval pouch, stuffed with plastic grocery bags to fill it out, flaps of leather at each side that vaguely look like wings, two grommets punched in the center so that I can run a string through them and attach some tempting food and another string sewn in the top so that I can swing it. As I tie on the food I think it looks like a bulbous lump, a tiny flat football, but it will have to do. At least the quail looks palatable.

Although I've never tried cooking any of this quail I've bought for years to feed my meat-eating birds, I think that it looks delicious. Not delicious in the way a spoonful of ice cream melts into sugar and cream on the tongue, but in the way a can of tuna at the end of a day-long hike seems to reach to your marrow. The opened quail looks like sustenance, like life. When I toss the lure in front of the falcon and step back, he jumps on it, eyes huge and wings out. I don't move, but think to myself, *Gotcha.*

I'm five years old stretched as long as my body will allow, my belly to the grass. I've got a salt shaker balanced in my right hand in the tips of my fingers as far out as I can stretch my reach. The salt shaker is in danger of tumbling from my tiny grasp, but I will it to remain. I try not to move. If I drop the salt shaker, I'll have to start again.

The sparrows picking through the seed I have strewn in the lawn are letting me get a little closer every time and I think this is it. I've been working on this all afternoon.

I don't want to keep one, not really. I just want to be closer. It isn't enough to watch. I want to hold one, to examine its toes and tiny talons, to examine where its beak hinges shut, to feel its feathers in my palms. I'll let it go right away, I promise silently. Then, at last, they are close enough.

I tighten my grip on the shaker enough to hang on as I jolt the crystal canister and toss salt in their direction. At least three of the birds have their backs to me, which is perfect because I have to hit a tail.

Everything moves at once, flying salt, flapping sparrows, but I am certain I saw bits of salt bouncing from one bird's tail. I saw it. Yet, the bird still flies away. I sit up for a moment trying to understand what has happened, but I know what has happened. It didn't work. It isn't going to work. I begin to wail and run for the house, the salt shaker pressed to my chest.

"Why are you crying?" my grandmother turns and asks as I fumble with the screen door to get inside. She seems worried and I'm sure she'll understand.

"Granddad said if I sprinkled salt on their tails," I suck in a sob and continue, "I could catch one."

"Howard," my grandmother yelps and I think I can hear my grandfather chuckling in the living room. I cry harder.

I settle four feet from the falcon on the ground, legs crossed, sipping my coffee. The falcon pauses to stare at me in between quick bites. I watch him without looking straight at him, raise the cup to my lips, scratch an ankle. I make this a game, moving only until his body indicates I'm about to make him nervous. To win I need the falcon to eat with his wings tight against his body, tearing at his meal with relaxed dips of his beak, no interest in my motions. If I keep playing this game, eventually I'll be able to stroke his long thin toes while he eats from between my fingers without a flinch. I need him to believe that I will never rip anything from his feet, never take anything he hasn't given up willingly.

I rub my nose and freeze when his wings drop to cover his food protectively. Hand to nose I wait for him to relax again and think that this is going to be a long haul, but I hate birds with bad manners, birds that mantle and scream. A bird like that is the sure sign of bad falconry. More importantly, a bird like that is miserable.

I have friends that mantle when they eat, usually men from a large family of brothers. They eat with their arms protectively stretched around their dinner plates, their heads bowed, gulping down their food. I worry about them, if they ever think they get enough to eat and if they ever believe that anything truly belongs to them. It makes me want to slowly ease my fingers beneath their elbows until at last they relax with the certainty that I would never snatch a morsel from their plate. Their posture is the same as a raptor concealing its food in the wild, where bigger predators abound and meals are easily taken or killed over. My falcon could be robbed or ripped into a meal by a hungrier raptor, but I want him to learn that meals are safely eaten in my company no matter the dangers that loom above. Wish I could do the same for my friends.

Half of a quail is a small meal and the falcon finishes quickly, jumping off the lure on the ground and to his slightly higher perch. He rubs his beak side to side on the edge of the perch. It looks as though he's sharpening it, but he's only cleaning his beak, feaking. It's the motion of a raptor that feels well fed and comfortable on his perch. It makes me smile. Someday he might even feak on my glove. For now though, I'm satisfied with this morning's worth of progress. I scoop up the lure, leave the falcon to get a drink of water from his bath pan and go inside.

There will be a few more days of this and then I'll have to find a field where I can fly him. I'll quit garnishing the leather pouch, despite Tom Austin's admonitions, but will step him up on the glove for a meal once he's grabbed at the lure. He'll come to understand the lure is a cue—that grasping it, then catching it, results in a meal.

At some point I'll make a mistake reading him and he'll get distracted and fly off. One thing at a time, though. Tomorrow he'll jump for the lure the length of his leash. The next day I'll tie him to a line and urge him to fly to it from ten feet and then twenty. I'll double the distance every time he comes without hesitation, go slower if he isn't sure he wants to fly. He's got to be certain before I can be certain.

Watching him from the sliding glass window I wonder how the season will go. I've trained or helped train at least one hundred birds over the last eight years. I've flown birds for shows in Florida, Ohio, Texas, and Australia, as well as here at home. Free flight shows demand precision training and as much faith in yourself as in the birds you encourage to fly back to your hand. Still, falconry is different. Hunting with a bird is harder, more dangerous, the natural risk of being a raptor just part of the deal. When seventy-five percent of fledged raptors don't survive their first year, you have to know you're up against the odds. Nature doesn't make exceptions for falconry birds.

I turn away from the window, reminding myself that he doesn't belong to me, that nature can take him back any time she wants. In fact, the government can do the same. As far as U.S. Fish and Wildlife is concerned, that bird on my patio belongs to them. They can knock on my door and take him for any reason they see fit. No amount of begging, reasoning or billable hours to an attorney will make a difference. When the feds come you have to be careful.

My mentors have taught me to treat game wardens and nature the same. Never volunteer information, never underestimate, but always be respectful. They are neither friends nor enemies, but dangerous just the same. Falconers should foresee every possible danger; keep their facilities, equipment and papers in order with every detail recorded either to document the whims of nature or to prove there are no whims to their falconry. The birds don't belong to us, but any one of us will tell you that in the end it doesn't make a difference. Nothing can take away the hours that we've already stolen in the field. This morning I woke to the sounds of a falcon stirring and shared his breakfast, gaining a tiny bit of his trust. That's mine to keep.

Christopher Robin has great friends. I know this because mom has been reading me Winnie-the-Pooh. *I close my eyes as she reads, "Once upon a time, a very long time ago now, about last Friday, Winnie-the-Pooh lived in a forest all by himself under the name of Sanders."*

I try to keep my eyes closed, but I open them and giggle when Pooh climbs the tree after the bees and breaks the branch. I don't want to go to sleep. I want my mom to stay perched at the edge of my bed, the dark crown of her head peeking over the spine of the stiff book, her voice sweet and sounding like a smile.

My room is small but stuffed with things for little girls. The miniature reading chair my grandparents gave me with its red and orange blocky armrests is my favorite, but there are plastic baubles, plush toys and books everywhere. There are many books, mostly golden books, some with crayon-scribbled pseudo-letters from my hopeful hand. The books are my favorite toys even though I'm not old enough to read.

I don't have to read now though because I can hear my mom's voice as I drift off into the sleep I am struggling against. I will hear it every time I open a book about Pooh. Her sing-song storytelling lull will be mine to keep along with the black and white photo on the bedside table. I will dust off the photo even after it is hidden in the drawer and recall her words years after she's gone.

A week later in the field, the falcon is tied to parachute cord, a long piece attached to the swivel that hangs from the leather straps, the jesses at his ankles. I secure a transmitter on his tail in case my creance of parachute cord fails, and so he can get used to the weight. I place him on a perch in the center of the yellowing soccer field and walk away, my back to him.

Forty feet away, I slip a squirming starling from my pocket and before I have a chance to think on it further, toss it in front of me. I need to know he understands, that he has no reason to balk at a live meal. There isn't a moment to wonder if the peregrine comprehends, he's already on his way and I'm occupied with managing the lines, stepping back, moving behind, avoiding a hitch or a tangle. Then it's over.

The falcon and I look at each other, both startled. Then he bows his head slightly over the bird in his feet, snaps the neck and looks back up. He allows me to meet his gaze, seeing deep into his falcon's eyes and I understand that I could keep this predator on a line forever, but he will never be my pet. Over that shared look our relationship changes just a bit, because suddenly, we both grasp an obvious truth. I am looking into the eyes of a wild peregrine. It's so soon, only ten days, but it's time to let him fly free.

BLUEBELLY LIZARD, OR WESTERN FENCE LIZARD (*SCELOPORUS OCCIDENTALIS*)

Rebecca Solnit

THE BESTIARIES, OR books of beasts, of almost a thousand years ago contained much we no longer believe. There is no stone in the heads of toads that neutralizes poison and there are no unicorns at all, so the ability of their horns to likewise undo poison is not particularly helpful either. Those old books were compendiums of known and imagined animals, of eagles and dragons and elephants, with lore about their powers, lives, and meanings, often moral and religious meanings. They were also compendiums of sheer wonder, but the sense of wonder that emerges from scientific knowledge is at least as great, whether it's about the Belding's ground squirrel of the Sierra Nevada that hibernates about eight months a year or the elephant seal that not only can hold its breath underwater for an hour but often does so for twenty minutes or more at a time while sleeping on the shore. Or the blue whale, whose heart is bigger than an American bison and beats about six times a minute, a tenth the speed of ours, or the hummingbird in flight, whose tiny heart beats a thousand times a minute.

Toads can't counteract poison, but bluebelly lizards, it is now known, have a mysterious property in their blood that eliminates Lyme disease from the infected ticks, in their nymph stages, that bite them. They may be why the West Coast is so much less infested with this pernicious disease than the East. The bluebelly's blood now is as marvelous as the toadstone then. But it's important to celebrate the bluebelly for its own sake, for its twenty long toes as delicate as eyelashes, for its ball-bearing eyes, for its grainy camouflaging stripes in tones of dust and shadow, for the secret blue bands of its white underside—two long vertical lines and more blue on its chin, ranging from a soft sky blue in the young and female lizards to a fierce azure that saturates the males in rut.

The official English name of this creature is the western fence lizard, but they were all over the West millennia before fences were, and the California kids I knew called them bluebellies. Bluebellies were everywhere in the California hills when I was growing up, darting away from us, sometimes—like many other lizard species—shedding their tails when one of my brothers tried to catch them, so that the tail stayed behind flapping frantically, a tactic thought to have evolved to distract predators. I have seen thousands of bluebellies, held dozens, perhaps hundreds, but only twice have I seen the intensely blue males in rut fight each other, scrabbling and separating and gripping, doing pushups on the rocks betweentimes. (The pushups display their blue undersides and are thought to impress females.) Once they were under live oaks on Mount Tamalpais near the Golden Gate, once they were on the warm granite of the trail up Little Yosemite Canyon; both times I watched until all sense of scale fell away and I might as well have been watching sapphire dragons. But it is not the exceptional moments or exceptional beasts that are grounds for wonder. The everyday bluebelly found everywhere in California but the deep deserts and highest mountains is, with its purifying blood, its underside of sky, its speed and its talent for survival, already a small astonishment.

VIRGINIA LOWRY AGUILAR

(September 17, 1927 – May 23, 2008)

Judith Lowry

My grandparents, Robert and Edna Lowry, had a large family. Of their twelve children, only five lived to full adulthood. This was not uncommon in the early part of the twentieth century. Three babies died at birth. The flu epidemic of 1918 took baby Tommy. That same year, little Leo, barely two years of age, was killed on the front porch of the family home when a hunting rifle accidentally discharged in the hands of a young cousin. Two decades later, Robert, the eldest son, suffered a fall from a horse and was knocked unconscious for several days. After that he began exhibiting unusual behavior. He was eventually sent to Napa and the state mental hospital, where his condition only worsened over time. Then his health failed and he was sent home to die at the age of twenty-eight. My grandparents contacted an Indian doctor, who worked hard to save him, but it was too late.

The six remaining Lowry siblings were Viola (Vi), Jesse, Stanley, Leonard (my father), Juanita, and the youngest, Virginia. Except for Aunt Vi, who married a Klamath man and went to live in Sprague River, Oregon, they all lived out their lives in Susanville. I love and respect the memory of all my aunts and uncles, but it was with Virginia that I shared the closest bond, although it wasn't supposed to be that way.

My mother and father met during World War II. Mom was an Australian "war bride" from Sydney. My dad, with Virginia and her husband, Bob, drove down to San Francisco to meet Mom's ship when she arrived in the United States. The tone between the ladies was immediately established when Virginia asked my mother what she thought of the city by the bay and Mom haughtily pronounced, "I think the city needs a bath." From then on, and through the years, Mom and Aunt Virginia had a contentious relationship. Mom resented Dad's loyalty to his family. She felt misunderstood and outnumbered by the Lowrys' tight-knit clan. They found her strange; not only white, but foreign to boot, and with an attitude. So with every family gathering the alienation grew and when my folks divorced during my senior year of high school, we lost nearly all contact with Susanville and all the relatives.

My adult years were different. I went back to Susanville when I was twenty, to reconnect with my dad and my family. Mom wasn't happy about this at first, but later, when she was dying, she and Virginia got together and made up. That remarkable act was a great gift. In the years to follow I came to know my aunt and learn from her, and this is what I can share.

SINGING HER HOME

Virginia did a little beading, but apart from that did not practice any traditional skills like weaving or gambling games or indigenous songs or language arts. But in her soul, and through her loving and energetic life, she lived her time on Earth as true to the spirit of our ancestors as anyone I ever knew. She worked hard at everything she did. Like her ancestors, she earned every calorie she consumed, starting as a little girl with a job picking fruit with her parents in the Central Valley, and later working at the fruit-box factory in Susanville when she was a teenager. Although legally too young for employment, she and her friend Ramona pestered the boss for jobs for weeks until they wore him down. It was an auspicious day for that factory when they hired this vibrant, beautiful young woman whose work ethic was best expressed in a phrase she often uttered: "If you've got time to lean, you've got time to clean." Whether on the job or volunteering (something she did a lot of), if there were a busy kitchen and people to feed, be it the veterans' reunion dinners, fundraising at the Indian taco stand, or her favorite, funeral suppers, one would generally find Virginia among the throng of workers lending solace and serving comfort food to the mourners.

Even in her elder years, when we would press her to take a seat to rest and let us do the work, she would decline by saying, "If I sit down I'll just get all stove up [broken up]. Better to keep working."

Her vernacular was peculiar to a certain era and a certain cultural rearing. It made her storytelling charming. She never said "Indian," she said "Indin." Nowadays we say "NDN," but back in the old days that's how they naturally said it. She took pride in her high-desert upbringing and her rural ways. She loved her parents and had good memories of them. She said she wished that her mother had lived to see television and her father had lived to see a power saw. Her generation had a much more direct experience with life than we do today. She talked about the way "scratch chickens," which dined on grubs and insects, tasted, and how crisp and clean and cold the drinking water used to be. "We had the good life," she would say.

She disliked New Age spiritualism and was critical of younger folks reinventing the Indian. It was years before I could get her to go to our tribe's medicine lake, high in the mountains. "Just an old fishing lake," she would say. But the day we finally went there with her son, Dugan, and she saw the lake for the first time, she was truly impressed by its tremendous physical and spiritual beauty. We saw a bear that day, too, which she took as a sign, and when we were trekking back to the car she spied some coins on the dusty trail. "Somebody must have dropped some money." She picked them up and counted a couple of pennies, a nickel, and a quarter. "This quarter has my name on it!" she exclaimed. Indeed it did. She took it home and kept it as a charm.

In her tidy home she never left a bed unmade or a dirty dish in the kitchen sink. She did not own a clothes dryer until she was eighty years old. She hung her wash on the line in her back yard in the summer and in the garage during rain or snow. Her towels and sheets were always soft and smelled good and fresh. She devoted herself to her family and raised her children to be responsible and caring people. Indeed, Virginia's greatest source of pride was her son and her daughter.

Dugan Aguilar is one of the preeminent photographers of traditional California cultures. His reverent and poetic images are published and exhibited throughout the state and across the country. He is well thought of by his subjects and elders for his humility and respect. His mother recalled the day young Dugan hit four home runs in a Babe Ruth game in Elko, Nevada. He was subdued and thoughtful on the ride home. When they got back to the house, Virginia observed that he was quiet about it, as others gave him praise for his day's performance. She told me she held her own feelings in herself, as if to show her joy would burst some spell in the room. "He didn't let the pride show," she said softly, "but all evening his eyes were shining like diamonds." Years later, when Dugan was away at the war in Vietnam and she would begin to miss him and worry, she would take herself out to her back porch to sit and gaze at the familiar summit of Diamond Mountain (Yotim Yamane) and say inwardly, "He's just over that hill," and feel comforted. Susanville was her universe. "God's country," she called it. All the pageantry and drama of the world and life played out before her in that little town. She never longed to stray far from her mountain home. She relied on the strength that her bond with the land provided.

Aunt Virginia delighted in calling to report every advancement her daughter Jo received in her job with the Department of Forestry. Jo has always been a steadying influence on tribal and family matters. Like her mother, she has the unity and protection of her family utmost in her mind. Steady as a rock, her mother's best friend, she now steps into eldership, which can be a lonely place at first. But soon the spirits of our own elders drift back to us in our memories and in the very things we might think, or say, or do on a particular day. How often have we heard our mother's words coming out of our mouths? They come back to us in the faces of our children and grandchildren. They come back to us as we observe ourselves aging and resembling them in the passage of time. In the end, much of the pain of loss is replaced by abiding gratitude and spiritual assurance.

Auntie regularly kept me updated on the goings-on at home in Susanville. We loved gossip and made no bones about it. Not too many years ago, Virginia had been feeling poorly, so I drove up to see her. I took something very special that I had discovered among my late father's things. It was what you might think of as a little medicine bundle. After a searching look from her eyes and my nod of approval, she curled up in her chair, unfolded the fragile old letters one by one from their envelopes and read, with great relish. As the tale of her brother's youthful misadventure with two beautiful young women revealed itself to her from those perfumed pages, her eyes grew bright and a smile of wicked satisfaction warmed her face. She was practically purring, and afterward she perked up so much that she decided we should go out to eat dinner. Such, apparently, is the therapeutic value of a really juicy story.

Virginia was the last of a generation that endured open racial segregation, the poverty of the Great Depression, and the World War, where many Indian men and women went to serve while their families stayed behind to pray. Over time she endured the losses of many friends, relatives, her parents, and all of her siblings. She was the baby girl of the family and saw everyone off one by one. I admired how she stuck around with such spirit, for ten years, without her beloved Bob.

In her later years she spoke of some regrets she had, "the circles" she called them, and the humility she demonstrated in being able to share them was impressive and a lesson not to be forgotten. "Everything comes around," she would say. "The circles always come around." And then she would tell a story or two or three. Some were sad and bitter remembrances. Some were jubilant and some were laced with triumph, like the time she faced down her husband's supervisors over discrimination that had cost Uncle Bob, a Paiute man and a logger, a well-deserved promotion. It was a withering verbal attack, colorful yet ladylike. She would relive it for me sometimes and bring the moment back to life with all its drama, and I could see this young Indian woman standing there in that café. I could see her in her youthful beauty, in her dungarees, her feet planted in crisp white tennis shoes, facing down the bosses and letting them know, in very specific terms, what she thought of them. Magnificent stuff.

On her eightieth birthday, the community center filled to the brim with people who loved her. She partied hearty! Sadly, we were all to meet there again eight months later to attend her memorial. Her graceful passage was well attended by loved ones who came to call, or stayed with her at her house. As her strength waned, her family was there to wash her car, clean up her yard, and replace her tub with a walk-in shower. They labored around her tirelessly and she soaked up every deserving bit of it. But the hardest work fell to Jo, who maintained her own matriarchal duties while devoting herself to this last tender labor of love with her whole heart and soul. Those of you who have been through it can appreciate the many trips to the doctors' offices, and scarier ones to the hospital, tracking dates, procedures, medications, diet, and a host of unexpected challenges.

Virginia's spirit burned very bright until the end. No hospitals, tubes, or drugs for her. She wanted to be home. She spoke with us and even managed some weak laughter that crinkled the corners of her eyes in that signature smile that could light up a heart. In the last days of her life, surrounded by family and friends in the little home she had kept for close to fifty years, she received hugs and kisses and loving words from her daughter and son, grandchildren, great-grandchildren, nephews, nieces, neighbors, and her best buddies and girlfriends. As her body grew weaker and her heartbeats fainter, her mind was as awake and alert as ever it was, and she even chuckled a little at our lame jokes. She scolded God for not coming to get her sooner and then, when we reminded her that although she had a lot of clout in the family and community, she could not rush the Almighty, she said softly, "That's right, I can't boss the Lord." The day after that, in the early morning hours, dozing where she had been seated in her easy chair for the morning news, she slipped away quietly and went Home.

Virginia always had a strong belief that she would be reunited with all her loved ones who had passed away before her. There would be her parents, her husband, and all of her brothers and sisters, as well as many other relatives and friends. Her concept of Paradise was not strictly defined by any religion but rather by her own spiritual perspectives. When my own father lay dying and in that waking dream state some experience at the end, she held his hand like the good sister she was and told him of their family waiting for him. "There's Mom and Pop and Robbie and Vi and Jess..." Before she could go further, he uttered a long sigh and said, "Yes, it's beautiful here!" She helped him to see his Heaven. For what else is Heaven but the warmth and protection of our loved ones?

In her final wishes, she requested no hearse. It was her desire to ride to her resting place on the bed of a pickup truck, Indian style. On the morning of her funeral the men busied themselves around her son's truck tying knots and tugging lines, making sure her last ride would be snug and safe. Many others hovered around making little worried comments about not losing her to a bump in the road.

This brings me to a story that Virginia told me a few months before she died. I tell it here because it so perfectly expresses the way Indian people release the spirits of loved ones. Virginia, always an avid funeral attendee, and more so in her later years, traveled to the funeral of an Indian man she knew who had been a top rodeo champion in his youth, a bronco rider and a big fellow. For some reason this family's way was to have female pallbearers. The procession began with the unloading of the hearse, with the weight of the casket causing the women to falter a bit, and the crowd gasped. Later, exiting the church after the services, the pallbearers, clearly struggling with the weight of their burden, stumbled and nearly fell. Again the crowd leaned in and gasped. At the graveside, the ladies' last tender duty was to lower the coffin gently into the earth. Once again, the heavy load asked a little more of them than they physically had to give and the coffin slipped and fell, banging and clattering its way down the grave's shaft before landing at the bottom with a loud thump. Before the crowd could react and gasp once more in horror, a voice from the back of the group shouted out, "Well Bill, you've had your last great ride!" The crowd erupted in laughter and tears. Everybody was then ready to go and eat. That's Indian humor, and I guess that's why Virginia loved to go to funerals. She lived for moments like that.

Without Auntie to talk to I don't keep up much with the goings-on at home anymore. She was the last of our generation's elders to pass on, and now we baby boomers feel the weight that was on their shoulders pass to ours. I wish I could find more comfort in the younger folks but I can't. Not yet anyway. I still pine for Auntie's company, for her friendship, our talks, the fun times we had. There was a feeling of safety with my elders that I miss. If I were to try to go search for her now, I suppose I would have to go back home to Susanville. Once, when we were sitting at my father's grave, overlooking the town and the valley, I confessed to her that I didn't think I wanted to come back to Susanville anymore because Dad was not there and it would be too painful without him. She looked at me in astonishment and then smiled and said gently, "Oh no, he's not gone. Look around you and you'll see. He's everywhere!"

Beloved Auntie, so are you. You are everywhere, in all the places that we love.

POLAROIDS OF TOM

Burlee Vang

for the granite above you and the earth
below. Flowers for my connection
to the kingdom of loss.
Flowers for memory,
for what passes and stays, stays
but is gone.

—Blas Manuel De Luna,
Flowers for Your Grave

I HAVE A BROTHER who would've been twenty by now, had he lived beyond the seven days in an incubator at Fresno Community Hospital.

"A chubby boy," my father recalls.

"...with bright red lips," my mother adds.

As if a rose petal landed under his nose?

"You and Abel were too young to visit him then," they said.

I was three and Abel was one when my mother went into labor again. We slept with Grandmother, who had pulled our bed sheets and blankets and laid them on the carpet between the couches in the living room. It was a two-bedroom apartment in a complex where all the tenants, like us, were Hmong. I remember my father returning from the hospital one evening, the jangle of his keys, the front door opening with a rush of cold air. He crept lightly by our heads to avoid questions in the dark, like *Where's Mother and the baby? Why have they not come home yet?* Grandmother had often boasted about my fluency in Hmong to relatives whose children could not speak yet—but on this night, I kept silent beneath the blankets, following my habit of pretending to be fast asleep.

This part of my memory is unclear, but I've always imagined my father going into his bedroom and closing the door, the sound of the lock clicking. He would kneel in prayer. After some time, he'd come out into the living room and stand in the dark, perhaps watching us, listening to our breathing. He'd return to my mother at the hospital as quiet as he had come. It was the sound of his car engine that stirred the neighborhood dogs. That, I remember clearly.

"If a dog barks at night and no one is around, it means there is a ghost nearby," Grandmother always said.

The dogs kept barking long into the night. Was there someone—or *something* sitting outside our door? I must've slipped back into sleep by cupping my ears and mulling over my mother's absence. Abel and I had not seen her since the day she left for the hospital, her belly the painful size of a basketball. I'd cry in the late afternoons, staring from our window at the grassy courtyard. Sometimes the children out playing would notice me and break from a game of tag or drop their jump ropes and gather to make weeping faces, which would make me bawl even harder, at least until Grandmother shooed them away like pigeons. And after that, she'd run her old fingers gently through my hair, chiding, "Your mother will not come home, because you're scaring her with all those tears!"

When my mother was released from the hospital, she no longer resembled the woman I knew—not the one with the stern voice who always made sure that Abel and I did not go hungry by finger-feeding us rolled up balls of rice and meat, and then scolding us if we chewed our food too slow. "Eat!" she'd say. "Hmong kids in Laos swallow faster than the two of you!" She had become fragile, her hair tangled in a mess and her skin glowing moonlike. I watched her struggle through the door in my father's arms. Each breath she took was long and heavy, like steam from a boiling kettle. My father laid her on the couch. When they spoke, their voices cracked as if from yelling or crying too much.

Grandmother looked at them with wet eyes. I kept distant until my mother's arms reached for Abel and me. I don't remember if I even asked why the baby was not with her.

My mother had undergone a Cesarean section in order to give birth. But they didn't thread the flaps of her flesh together after the operation. They stapled her shut. When she lifted her shirt to show Grandmother, I saw the metal gleaming like teeth, her belly smiling with pain.

"Don't jump on the couch," my father said. "She is hurt and tired. Let her rest."

I have imagined how the doctors must've pried her open with their mechanical tools—the womb gaping like lips of a flower in bloom—and lifted my brother out, lungs crying for air, eyes pooled with our mother's blood.

There are two Polaroid photos. The only pictures of my parents' third son. There are no dates. No names. I discovered them the year my parents purchased their first house. The photographs had been tucked in a yellow folder among a stack of family albums and folders containing bank statements, tax papers, and birth certificates. I was seven at the time.

In the first photo, my brother is wearing a light blue beanie with his eyes closed and his fists tied in mittens, a frown framed between two rosy cheeks. In the other, the beanie is not worn, his lips parted by a slow yawn. His tongue is visible. Gums pink. Where skullcap and scalp should have grown, his naked brain juts like a red egg from the nest of his head, right above the eyebrows. It was the first time I'd seen him. I took the photos without my parents' knowing and slipped them under my mattress. Some days I'd stay in my room and stare at the pictures, possessed by the mystery of the brother I would never know. Each night I curled a whisper around his name, the letters spelled out in the dark like smoke. There was something haunting about him—though not exactly terrifying, not like the barking of a dog at night. During the quiet hours of REM sleep, I dreamt how infants were handled after death. How they were laid into tiny shoeboxes—little eyes and lips resting in makeshift coffins. "Throw away" is the literal translation of the Hmong word used to describe the burial process. Up until adulthood, I had believed that my brother didn't have a funeral since my parents never mentioned it. I assumed that all infants who died in hospitals were probably discarded like broken thermometers, bloody latex gloves, or a doctor's half-eaten sandwich. Being so small and lifeless, they were probably not worth the time and space of a funeral and burial. Babies swam in my head, all kinds of dead babies—pink skin, black skin, red skin, and yellow skin—all placed inside garbage bags ready to be dropped into hospital disposal bins.

"Throw away." The words would light up in my head.

I kept the photos until my parents sold the house. When my father dismantled our beds, as he was pulling away my mattress from its frame, the two pictures fell at his feet. I don't recall what happened next. Perhaps he placed them back in the yellow folder, or gave them to my mother. Growing up, my family hardly spoke about the third son. Was the weight too much to be carried on our lips, out in an open conversation? I was the oldest child and yet I could not bring myself to question my parents, especially my mother, whose eyes welled up whenever his name was mentioned by accident. What I imagined filled in the dark spaces, became memory.

Grandmother, who arrived in America an old woman, had told my mother to find a husband. "If something terrible happens to me tomorrow, who will look after you?" At fourteen, my mother became a high school dropout and a housewife.

"I needed security and your father was there to provide it," my mother says. "I was not in love."

When I was born, my father was the assistant manager at San Lorenzo's Nursery Company, a flower shop in Santa Ana, where he pushed fifty hours a week for an hourly wage of five dollars and seventy-five cents, which was above the starting minimum.

"From the moment you spilled from your mother, all you did was cry," he says. "You did not stop."

"Even if we held you!" my mother adds. "We had to take turns holding you throughout the night. You were always sick with a fever."

So they called up every Hmong shaman in Orange County, weekend after weekend, to figure out why I was crying, and how to put an end to it. I was possessed, the shamans agreed, and that the spirit haunting me had to be expelled through *ua neeb*—a ritual in which a shaman must enter a trance and ride his magic horse into the underworld, where he would negotiate with the spirit responsible for my sickness. Aside from a few family photographs, the inside of our apartment was covered with endless rows of spirit money, as if gold and silver leaves had sprung out from the walls. During *ua neeb*, incense sticks were burned over bowls of rice and boiled chicken eggs. The sounds of a shaman's gong and finger bells filled the living room, along with the voices of neighbors and relatives who had gathered to witness what each shaman had to suggest after their trance in the spirit world. My crying prevailed in the midst of all this.

"There is no evil or hungry spirit at work here," many of the shamans concluded. "He is only crying with a fever because his own spirit is not pleased with the name you gave him."

"Burlee" had been a terrible choice. My father has told me that "Burlee" is not a Hmong name. To this day, he does not know why or how he came up with it.

So to find a new name, each shaman had to *hu plig*, which, in my case, was the act of throwing a pair of split bullhorns in front of our door and asking my spirit for forgiveness. My name was changed over twenty or perhaps thirty times, although my parents can no longer recall any of the names the shamans gave me then. Both my arms were covered in sleeves of white blessing strings, from wrist to armpit, making me wail even louder from discomfort.

"You must've hated every single name, because you stayed sick," my parents still say.

The shamans had done everything. In the end, my father snipped off all the blessing strings with a pair of scissors, tore down the walls of spirit money as if tearing down the walls themselves, and cursed the ancestors who couldn't help us. He threw everything that had to do with *ua neeb* and *hu plig* into the aluminum tray in which my mother often baked whole chickens.

"If you cannot help my son," he shouted to the ancestors, "then I will not depend on your worthless rituals anymore!"

He struck up a match and lit the contents on fire. The smoke rose into the wind outside our apartment, everything wrinkling in flames, and I got my name back. But I didn't stop bawling. My father placed his hand on my temple, which was still hot with fever. A Christian tenant had seen my father's burning tray and stopped by to suggest an alternative. With little hope and mostly doubt, my father picked up the phone and dialed the local Hmong pastor to come pray for us, to see if his God was worth more than ashes. He arrived shortly with some of his church members. After a few hymns and prayers, I stopped crying. This was our conversion story, which my parents would tell from time to time.

"My son's spirit, or whatever it was, had left him in peace," my father would say with great pride.

"It was as if Jesus had pulled the tack out of his bottom," my mother joked.

Although we became Christians, my grandmother remained a shamanist until the day she died.

"She was not happy that we had abandoned the old traditions," my parents have reminded their children. "She held it against us until the end."

As Protestants, our lives had been renewed through the Christian Missionary Alliance, which hosted a network of Hmong churches across America. We did not dabble in the past anymore, we separated ourselves from all *ua neeb* and *hu plig* practices. Not a single sheet of spirit money ever found its way into our home again, no incense sticks were lighted over bowls of rice and boiled eggs, no shaman was welcomed in to find and coax a wandering spirit. Because my parents had completely swept the old traditions out the door like bones from an old meal, we also stopped calling our dead to eat with us at the dinner table or to fill in the quiet spaces between our living bodies, to join us in laughter and grief. Those who begged in the afterlife would stand outside our home, palms raised like bowls at our windows, our door completely closed to them and to those who would die later on.

I saw my third brother in a dream once. He was not an infant but a small child, walking by. Or perhaps he floated by me, adrift in a sea of bodies, people who appeared to be lost. He whispered his name—that's how I knew it was him. I don't know if we talked. I forgot the look on his face. But I told my mother the next day. What she said, I have forgotten.

There is a history of frequent encounters with "smothering-ghosts" in my family, a type of malevolent spirit known to paralyze its victims in their beds. These attacks occur during the moments before sleep enters the mind or at the point of waking from sleep. Abel is the family member most familiar with these spiritual confrontations. Two weeks after my grandmother died, he woke in the middle of the night to find her slouched at his feet, her fingers wrapped around his ankle. She was weeping. He was unable to move until my mother heard his gasps for air and rushed to his side.

Researchers who have studied this phenomenon call it "sleep paralysis." It occurs in the gradient between waking and REM stage, when the body is disconnected from the brain but still in a fully conscious state. No one can explain its exact causes, and although it is not considered dangerous, scientific reports indicate that a great number of Hmong men have died from these so-called smothering-ghost attacks, their faces often twisted in grimaces of terror. In my early experiences with sleep paralysis, unlike Abel, I didn't have the notion that I was encountering a supernatural force, despite being in a state of immobility. I called it sleep paralysis, not a smothering-ghost attack.

On a night in 2003, I found myself fully awake at four in the morning. I had left the window open, since it was summer. Moonlight was spreading through the blinds and across the room, enough to see in the dark. I was trying to fall back to sleep when my mattress shook from a sudden shift of weight. A child was weeping at my feet. Its small hand reached out and held my calf. A strange numbness shot up from the spot of contact through my entire body and I couldn't move, nor was I able to muster up a cry for help. What should've been screams came out as whimpers. For several minutes, the child held on, enveloping me in its numbness, becoming a part of me, the two of us pausing under the moonlight. We were both weeping into each other's ears.

After my parents moved from Orange County to Fresno and Abel was born, my father became unemployed. He was attending college at the time so they applied for Medi-Cal. During my mother's first and second pregnancies she was able to listen to each child's heartbeat through a Doppler machine. In her third pregnancy, my mother never had the chance to hear her son's heart, that watery ticking inside her. She had gone to a small clinic owned by a Thai couple whose patients were mostly Hmong refugees, speaking little or no English. The physician, who was the husband, had prescribed a bottle of pills for my mother to take for two consecutive months. She kept a regular schedule with him for follow-ups. My father always accompanied her, and at the end of two months, she returned to the clinic with the empty bottle.

This time, it was the physician's wife who met her in one of the examining rooms. When she took the bottle from my mother and read its label, her eyes widened.

"You are not supposed to take this! Who told you to take this?"

"Your husband," my mother said. "He gave it to me two months ago."

"No, no, no. This is not good for you. This is the wrong medication!"

My mother can still recall the shock on the wife's face, how the husband was called immediately into the room. The wife scolded him in Thai for his irresponsibility, but it all ended quickly with the husband apologizing to my parents. The wife tried to maintain a smile—*to assure my mother that she would be fine? That the child in her womb would be born with a normal skull?*

My mother didn't sue them. Nor did she display any outrage toward the couple's error. Her body felt the same way it had felt during her first two experiences with childbearing. It was her assumption that if the baby had been affected by the pills, her body would've felt different. She was having her third son, whom my father had already found a name for, and that was all that occupied her mind.

After she told me about the incident, I wanted to ask her why she didn't get a lawyer then, but I knew she would've answered, "I couldn't speak English well. Your father was busy with school. We were poor and didn't know anyone."

"What was the name of the pills he gave you?" I asked instead.

"I have forgotten," she said. Nor could she remember the reasons why she had to take them.

"There was a funeral," my father mentioned once over dinner. "The church provided money and food. Since we had become Christians, our shamanist relatives refused to help with anything."

"How long did it last?" Abel asked.

"A day and a night," my mother said. "I didn't go. I watched the two of you at home."

"Your mother couldn't bear the thought of losing one of her sons," my father explained. "She also needed rest from the operation. Her cut did not heal yet."

"Where was the funeral held?" I asked.

"Fresno Funeral Chapel," my father said. "On 'A' Street."

"How come we didn't know about this?" Abel asked.

"The two of you were too young then," he explained.

"Where is he buried?" I asked.

"Your father knows," my mother said. "He can take the both of you there—now that the two of you are old enough."

We looked at my father.

His eyes gazed as if trying to trace the footsteps in his mind. "I have lost the way there," he finally muttered. "It's been such a long time. I have forgotten the directions. He was buried outside of Fresno in a small cemetery. That's all I can remember."

Outside the kitchen window the sky was burning, the sun setting like a red yolk behind the roofs and telephone poles. At the dinner table, our conversation began, the silence broken by a funeral. Words fell from our lips as our spoons clinked against the china. My father sounded dry and solemn as he spoke. My mother stood at the sink and ran the water over our voices.

Not long ago, we bowed our heads and said an evening prayer together, our knees on the carpet in my parents' bedroom. My father's voice was a torch leading us to the foot of God, where we thanked Him for our daily bread and asked for the forgiveness of sins.

"Keep us together through the night," was my father's last request. He gathered our names, as if under a swooping wing, into the arms of God.

But my heart was not in prayer then. I wondered if my parents' third son, whose name was not gathered, stood beyond the bedroom curtains, outside the window, wishing himself into my father's words. When I was ten I had watched my father trace the incision scar on my mother's belly, a constellation of staple prints beneath his index finger. They were on the bed whispering to one another.

"After all these years, I still feel the pain if I do heavy work," she said to him.

"It'll probably never go away completely," he said. "The cut was deep."

We live in a four-bedroom house now. I help with half of the monthly payment. The memories of living in a rundown apartment have become distant, but often I imagine how children once played outside our window, chasing one another in the yellow grass. Or how jump ropes arced around the sun from the swing of a girl's hands. I beg these young faces to laugh and cry for me once more. I can be three again.

"We've lost both the Polaroid photographs," my mother says. "The only pictures of him." She can't figure where she placed them after the move. Which move? We've moved so many times. Five apartments, two houses. Boxes were thrown away, left behind in dark closets.

Should I look now in our luggage of heirlooms? In the family's filing cabinet? A shoebox?

If I dig into my mother's belly, will I find them stuck to the wall of her cave?

If I search beneath my father's skullcap, will I be able to trace the footsteps in the curved roads of his brain?

The night my father came home from the hospital, did he close the bedroom door and kneel down to pray for my brother—whisper his name at the bedside before coming out into the living room?

Who were the dogs barking at?

I can no longer tell what I know from what I've imagined. The road that leads to him is without footprints, washed long ago by the rain. It winds through the deep, hot countryside of my mind, past open fields lined with barbed wire fences, beyond Fresno. It curls beneath sycamores, around slabs of rock. Where the road ends, overgrown weeds have taken over, yellowed by sunlight. The gravestone among the weeds can be mistaken for a chipped boulder. Our prayers have not touched this place. Spirit money would burn in this heat. For twenty years, his ghost has called the crawling ants "brothers"—the crow in the bent oak "Father"—and the moon when it is full "Mother." To them he calls with both hands raised like a bowl, his orphan cry so shattering that the night could be glass. I can almost hear it by my bedside. What fragmented memories I have of his birth, I bury them here, next to his grave, on this side of my skull. I whisper his name, "Tom...Tom... Tom...," a drum beating these memories into the dirt that they might bloom like roses, red as his crown, bleeding out of the earth.

MY KITSCH IS THEIR COOL

Sandip Roy

I REMEMBER THE AGE of the underwear smugglers.

When I left India almost two decades ago to come to America, my mother folded every spice I could possibly need into my underwear. Turmeric, cumin, little green pods of cardamom—all packed carefully between layers of underwear, socks and computer science textbooks. I wasn't the only one. I've met Indians who smuggled in mangos, home-made pickles and ready-to-fry puris stuffed with peas. In those days before 9/11, customs officials were not very interested in me—a young, single, brown man from a turbulent part of the world. They (and their sniffing dogs) were much more preoccupied with middle-aged Indian women visiting their sons. They were rifling through their luggage, searching for contraband mangos and gourds.

Fast-forward 20 years.

My friends and I wander out of an Indian movie theater in Fremont on a mellow California evening. The latest Bollywood release opened here the same day it did in Mumbai. At intermission (for Bollywood films must have an intermission), you can get samosas and chaat along with your popcorn and soda. We go shopping at an Indian market off the main drag. It's Sunday evening. All the shops in the strip mall are closed except for this one. Lit by unflattering fluorescent lights, its shelves are piled high with all kinds of things—lentils, ready-to-cook packages of saag paneer, ayurvedic hair ointments, even the chocolate Bourbon biscuits (no real bourbon in them) that I remember from my childhood in India. Then we squabble over which Indian restaurant to go to for dinner. Do we want North Indian? South Indian? We settle for a buffet with both.

What happened?

Well, we did. There are now 2.57 million Indians in the United States, according to the American Community Survey of the U.S. Census Bureau. That makes it one of the fastest-growing ethnic groups. Indians are well-off, generally. Median family income is over $69,000. Indians are educated, for the most part. Seventy-six percent have at least a college degree. The post-1965 immigrant boom, which resulted from a drastic change in U.S. laws about who could come into the country, was followed by the dot-com boom. In her novel *The Tree Bride*, Bharati Mukherjee describes how "an immigrant fog of South Asians crept into America." When the chronicle of Silicon Valley is written by some 21st century F. Scott Fitzgerald, it might well be called, she writes, "The Great Gupta."

India is everywhere. It's in Booker Prize lists, spelling bees and specially-for-you nuclear deals. It's in Sukhi's homecooked chicken tikka masala paste at Whole Foods. It's in Bhangra aerobics classes and Britney remixes. *Newsweek* called South Asians the "new American masala." Five hundred years after Christopher Columbus thought he had discovered Indians, we are truly found.

And I am not sure how I feel about that.

When I first came to the U.S., Americans asked me about that "dot on the forehead." Now, Madonna wears a bindi. Bollywood borrows Hollywood plotlines (well, two or three for one three-hour film). Now, the Kronos Quartet reinterprets Bollywood composer R. D. Burman. Birthday cards are reproducing old kitschy Indian matchbox covers. Body-hugging T-shirts worn by gay guys in the Castro say "San Francisco" in Devanagari script. There are even Bollywood appreciation classes at universities. My kitsch has become their cool.

Of course, not everything has been alchemized into cool. My big, fat Indian wedding might be hot ("I want one," a gay man with a Southern accent told me at my neighborhood lesbian bar while sipping a sweet cocktail), but it doesn't mean the Indian cabdriver, the 7/11 clerk or the Gujarati storeowner are any more acceptable.

Our Krishnas and curries are now public property to be sampled, remixed, chewed up and spat out as millions of cookie-cutter lunch boxes. (Probably Made in China)

It almost makes me nostalgic for the old days when people came up to me and said, "You are from Calcutta? My doctor is Indian. Dr. Harry Patel. I think he's from that other big city—Bombay?" And they would pause expectantly, as if waiting for me to recognize Dr. Patel. Now, they want to know what restaurant I would recommend in the Bay Area for "authentic Indian food, you know, a hole-in-the-wall place where Indians go, not your white-people-Maharaja-Thali stuff."

And I am wondering, do I want to tell you?

But it's too late. In San Francisco's Tenderloin, in streets that still smell of piss, where homeless men shuffle around at the street corner, the clutch of Indian and Pakistani restaurants is brimming with hipsters. There are at least half a dozen Indian restaurants within a couple of blocks. Shalimar was the original hole-in-the-wall, in a rundown neighborhood of junkies and musty SROs. It started out as a place where cabbies could run in for a quick bite. Nothing fancy, no tablecloths, just a bustling kitchen and tandoori chickens turning on the spit. Now, the homeless man standing outside trying to sell a street newspaper greets me with a "Namaste."

Isn't this what we always wanted? Isn't this what we demanded? For other Americans to understand our culture? Acceptance? A place at the table? I guess we didn't fully realize we could also become part of the menu.

Fifty years ago, my parents emigrated to England by ship. My mother pretended to the fishmonger that she had a cat, so she could take fish heads home for a good Bengali fish-head curry. When I moved to the United States three decades later, she told me stories of how afraid they were to cook fish in their apartment, in case the smell upset the Polish landlady.

At my university in the flat plains of Illinois, we also learned that we had a private culture and a public culture. In the grad student apartments, where many of the Indians shared rooms, we could have our tape players on blaring tinny Bollywood songs and watch streaky, pirated copies of Hindi films, while giant pots of communal dal and rice and curry bubbled on the stove. But in public, we learned to leave that culture at home. Boys didn't hold hands on the street like they did in India, we were told. At the department potlucks, we held back on the spices. On Diwali, we didn't have any celebration in the department, even though half the teaching assistants were Indian. Being Indian was for after work. Then we could finally let our guard down and just breathe.

No more. My private culture has become public. At a recent film festival in San Francisco's Castro neighborhood, the theater was packed for Bollywood night. And the audience was very mixed. "Some screenings are 60- to 70-percent white," Ivan Jaigirdar, festival director for 3rd I's South Asian International Film Festival, told me once. "Especially the Bollywood films."

I could see that. My friends and I were cringing even as we were having a grand time. It was a strangely protective feeling. Even as we laughed and rolled our eyes at the excess of it all, we stiffened when we heard the blonde woman behind us sniggering. I was thrilled that this candy-color, emotionally charged melodrama was leaping across cultures and entertaining a diverse audience. But the nagging doubt remains—what really does cross over?

Gaudy and outlandish as they can be, Bollywood films are also an intravenous cultural drip for me. I relate to them somewhere deep inside in a way I, myself, cannot put a finger on. I remember standing in my living room in San Francisco watching an old Hindi movie with my best friend. We oohed and aahed as tragic diva Meena Kumari slowly raised her head, as if the weight of all that gold and brocade was crushing her.

My American friends laughed with us then and at us as we stood in our T-shirts and jeans singing Hindi love songs of indescribable pathos in shrill falsettos, towels draped around our faces like veils. We all laughed together. But my American friends had no idea how we longed in our flat-footed way for Meena Kumari's languid grace, how we tried to line our eyes with hopeless tragedy. And knowing we could never get there, we butchered it all by shrill impersonation, hiding our longing with caricature.

Bollywood is so visually overpowering, so defiant of logic in its Technicolor splendor, that it's just too easy to get caught up in the spoofiness of it all. On-screen, Shah Rukh Khan's face is quivering with emotion. The blonde woman behind me is chuckling at everything—the painful buffoonery of the comic relief, the little kid with the stagy lines, the syrupy romantic scenes where thundershowers and shooting stars appear on cue. The camp crosses over. The heart stays behind, lost in the subtitles. The clock is pushing 1:00 a.m., and the blonde can't believe the movie is still going strong. As one more hurdle shows up before the lovers can reunite, someone groans, "We will be here all night." Those not used to Bollywood don't know it's like running a marathon. After all their knee-slapping hysterics in the first hour, they are now petering out in the final stretch. They are eyeing the exit sign, wondering how long the queue is at the restroom. They are glancing at their watches. They are laughing less.

And I feel a sweet sensation.

As they stagger out of the theater, clutching their heads, looking like they got off a non-stop flight from Mumbai to San Francisco, sick from all the popcorn they devoured, I can't help thinking somehow, in its own way, Bollywood has had the last laugh.

FRONT YARD FRUIT

Ellen Estilai

Most Americans I know are wary of mulberries—that is, if they've ever seen them at all. When I offer the deep purplish-red fruit, some of my friends will say, "Oh, no thanks, I'll pass. They look a little too much like worms." A plate of mulberries brought to a Monday morning staff meeting may remain untouched on Tuesday morning, except by a gathering cloud of fruit flies. Mulberries offend a certain American sense of order. The trees are messy. The fruit is at once unfamiliar yet redolent of the larval delicacies of indigenous Third World peoples. And you can't find any at Safeway.

I try not to take these rebuffs personally, but this attitude offends my sensibilities—not my American ones, but the ones I have acquired after nearly forty years of living with an Iranian husband.

To an Iranian, mulberries are manna. That achingly evanescent period in late spring, when the fruit appears in high-walled courtyards or along village roads, is a time for sharing and remembering. It comes early in the Iranian calendar, a few months after *Nowruz*, the March 20 New Year celebration of renewal and promise. On any day in June, from Mashhad to Kerman, from Isfahan to Tabriz, you will see street vendors, their carts piled high with baskets of white berries or tin buckets of the juicier red ones, wending their way through broad avenues and narrow passageways.

In a swank, shiny, marble-clad apartment in Shemiran, or perhaps under a dusty adobe dome in Dezfoul, a woman turns on the samovar for afternoon tea. She lays out the tea cloth and arranges delicate pastries on a tray and fills a china bowl with white or black mulberries that glisten in the afternoon sun. She calls the family around her and they pass the bowl of mulberries to one another, savoring the warm, dense sweetness and the memories of all the other June afternoons they have done this. As they draw each berry through their teeth, they are left with a tiny filament at the center. Before they realize it, there is only a pile of filaments in front of each person and tea leaves at the bottom of each glass. As the woman gathers up the tea things, the family tries not to think about how short this season is.

Americans lucky enough to have mulberry trees often have an uneasy relationship with them. The Argonne National Laboratory's Ask A Scientist on-line Botany Archive has preserved this question from a forty-year-old father named Timothy:

"I have a mulberry tree in my yard. Can you stop it from producing fruit? It's very messy and kids track it in the house, but I love the twenty-foot tree."

Not only would the average Iranian never ask such a question, he would have difficulty comprehending it. You would have to deconstruct it for him, perhaps with footnotes. You would have to parse its semantic components and break down its sociological underpinnings, and even then he might have trouble getting his mind around it. *What kind of person would resent a mulberry tree?* he might ask. *Who would begrudge a mulberry tree its manifest destiny? What kind of profligate wouldn't just put a sheet under the tree and dry the windfall so he could eat mulberries all winter long?* Of course, an Iranian might also say that people who can't teach their children to take their shoes off before coming in the house should blame themselves, not the mulberries.

Iranians might be perplexed, as well, by the answers to Timothy's question. The two scientists who weighed in online dispatched his query with a clinical dispassion bordering on callousness. The first said, "Guess you have three possibilities: either you would have to pick the fruit and/or flowers from the tree before they fall, or clean them up off the ground, or cut it down." The second scientist said, with grim finality, "While there are fruitless varieties of mulberries, I do not believe there is any way to stop an existing tree from fruiting." In short, if Timothy has an axe to grind with his mulberry tree, he had best employ it to provide next winter's firewood.

While they might be comforted to know that rendering a fruiting mulberry tree impotent ranks low on the priorities of the Argonne National Laboratory, Iranians would no more plant a fruitless mulberry than they would cut down a fully laden one. What would be the point?

That is the very question my Iranian sister-in-law Sekineh asked several years ago on her first visit to the United States. My husband, Ali, was proudly showing his eldest sister our garden with all the roses, herbs and fruit trees he had lovingly planted and tended over the years. We stood in our backyard under the shade of a 35-year-old mulberry tree that came with the house when she asked what had we done with last year's crop. Did we dry the mulberries, make jam? Was there anything left? Ali explained that this was a fruitless variety. There was silence for a moment while Sekineh processed this information.

"What do you mean, fruitless?" she finally asked. "What's the point of that?"

"Well," Ali explained, "it gives a lot of shade in the summer and privacy from the neighbors on the hill above us."

Sekineh was unmoved. For most of her seventy years she had made ends meet elegantly in the center of her widow's tablecloth. She understood doing without, but she had never seen such flagrant disregard for the basic economic principle of gardening, namely that you should get something in return for all your trouble.

"You mean you rake all these leaves in the fall and water every summer and you never get a single mulberry? How could you let this go on for so long? Get me a young sapling and I will graft it onto this tree for you."

My husband, shamed into action, began searching gardening catalogs for fruiting mulberry trees that would thrive in the reclaimed desert of Riverside, California. Before long, he settled on a Pakistani variety that promised long, deep-red fruit, and two Chinese varieties that would yield smaller, round, cream-colored berries. He didn't graft them to the useless backyard tree. Instead, he planted them in a row in the front yard, and waited.

Thus began the education of the neighbors into the transformative power of mulberries.

Now, I must admit that my own American childhood had very little to do with mulberry trees. My knowledge of them was limited to that old nursery rhyme and a very brief experiment with silkworms in my third grade elementary school class. Our teacher had stocked a glass case with a dozen silkworms, and, over a period of a few weeks, we kids plied them with generous amounts of their favorite food—their only food—large, floppy, shiny, green leaves of *Morus alba*, or white mulberry. We loved watching them chomp away at the leaves, getting fatter and fatter, progressing from worm to pupa to moth. One morning, we came to class to find that the moths had emerged from their silk cocoons and paired up, joined at their bottoms, forming six puffy, white V's. We asked what they were doing, but apparently that answer was not part of our teacher's lesson plan. Perhaps because Ozzie and Harriet and Lucy and Ricky were still sleeping in separate beds, and we were several years away from those health class film strips, our questions went unanswered. The next day, the V's and their mulberry leaves were absent at roll call.

It wasn't until I met my husband during my senior year of college that I had any idea mulberries were good for more than encouraging strange silkworm behavior. Ali and his Iranian friends knew the address of every mulberry tree in Davis, California. They thought nothing of helping themselves to the fruit, and during mulberry season, they kept a blanket in the car for harvesting. They were especially fond of *shah toot*, the large, deep red "king's berry," and they wore burgundy-colored shirts on these forays to minimize the appearance of the inevitable stains.

I was often my future husband's accomplice, and the thrill of the hunt made the berries taste all the sweeter. Not that there was much danger of being arrested. We went on our rounds unmolested by property owners; the locals rarely knew the value of what grew in their own backyards. Our friend Abdi, a Ph.D. candidate in agricultural economics, took great pleasure in helping the bankers at Wells Fargo overcome their reticence and take their first bites of the mulberries growing in their parking lot. "You mean, you can actually eat these things?"

So you might ask why, knowing his own shady past, my husband would plant fruit trees in the front yard within easy reach of marauders. I certainly did.

"Aren't you afraid people will just help themselves?" I asked.

"So what if they do?" he shrugged. "There'll be enough for everybody."

This largesse is rooted deep in the Iranian psyche. Iranians are stellar hosts. The culinary excess of a middle-class Iranian dinner party is rivaled only by the potlatches of the Pacific Northwest tribes. British Columbian officials outlawed those lavish displays of hospitality in 1951, but neither the austerity of the Islamic Revolution, the eight-year war with Iraq, nor a chronically shaky economy could put a stop to the Iranian *mehmooni.*

Iranians will find any excuse for a *mehmooni* or dinner party: it could be a new car, a promotion, the return of a child from study abroad...or simply Friday. In fact, it is beholden upon the recipient of good fortune to give *shirini*, or sweets, to friends and relatives.

But that kind of shirini is often more than just a plate of pastries. It can be a ten-course meal that begins with that plate of pastries, followed by fruits, and tea, lots of tea. In the hot months there might be some *sharbat*, a cool drink made with fruit or pussy willow syrup, or romaine lettuce leaves dipped in *sekanjebeen*, vinegar syrup. In the fall, there might be bowls of pomegranate seeds and melons.

A long cloth is laid on a banquet table, or on the floor, and on it are placed bowls of ash, a thick soup, trays of kebabs and roasted meats and chicken infused with saffron, platters with mounds of saffron rice and herbed pilafs, and bowls of various stews—chicken with walnut and pomegranate, lamb with minced herbs, beef and eggplant. These are complemented by an assortment of pickled eggplant and other vegetables and yogurt mixed with shallots, cucumbers or beets.

All of this is followed by more shirini and more tea, along with the host's apologies for the sparse repast, unworthy of his guests, and nothing like the feasts in their own homes.

Iranian generosity is not limited to fancy banquets. It's the glass of tea that begins any business meeting, or the simple, age-old custom of putting a pitcher of water and a glass in an alcove outside on the street for the benefit of parched passersby. In Ali's case, it was the strategic placement of fruit trees for the common good.

Perhaps Ali was atoning for his student days when he planted those trees in the front yard, or he was just being an active participant in an endless cycle. He inherited his love of gardening from his father, who used to say, "People planted so that we might eat. We plant so that others may eat."

So with the first crop of mulberries, Ali set about giving back. He was not only unconcerned that people would help themselves, he was determined to help them help themselves. He started with Mr. Escamilla across the street.

Mr. Escamilla has a first name, but we never use it. Because he was our daughters' seventh grade history teacher, or because of his Old World formality, he will forever be Mr. Escamilla. He and Ali have a front yard relationship, a formal yet genial gardeners' camaraderie. So when the new Pakistani tree yielded its meager first crop, Ali invited Mr. Escamilla to sample some.

"Mr. Estilai, I love these," he said, smiling. "I haven't had any since I was a kid in Spain."

"Let me get you a plate, and you can take some to your wife," Ali replied. But Mr. Escamilla didn't take them to his wife. He stood under the tree, chatting, and obliviously ate the entire plateful.

Ali realized he was on to something.

He took some over to Bart and Vanda, the young couple who live next door to Mr. Escamilla. They told Bart's mother, Christina, who lives down the street, and she came over one day to sample the fruit. Her husband declined ("They look like worms"), but she was enchanted. A few days later, Christina left a little bag of avocados on our doorstep.

One morning, when Ali was working in the front yard, a young couple happened by. The man, in a motorized wheelchair, stopped to admire the mulberries. Ali offered them some and watched as the woman placed one on the back of the man's hand. He carefully drew his hand up to his mouth to eat it, and a slow smile spread across his face. This time Ali put the berries on his hand, one by one. Between bites, Rocky and Laura explained that they were neighbors who lived just a few blocks away. Despite his disability, Rocky loved gardening and managed to orchestrate the planting of many fruit trees and brambles in his backyard. Laura, who grew up in China, was no stranger to mulberries. A few days later, we found a little bag of homegrown strawberries and blackberries on our doorstep, a gift from our new friends.

The arrival of the mulberries only enhanced the seasonal exchange of homegrown fruit that had evolved among the neighbors. Our baskets of figs and peaches were answered by persimmon bread from Bob and Aiko, loquats from Ken and Elizabeth, and plums from Connie and Larry. Our mulberries just kicked things up a notch and widened the circle.

On another afternoon, a man and his young daughter happened by. They admired the tree, and Ali offered them some mulberries. The father asked Ali if he would mind if they helped themselves now and then.

"You're welcome to whatever you can eat right here," Ali replied, "but please don't harvest them to take home. I have obligations."

One such obligation was to save some mulberries for his elder sister Nazee's impending visit to the U.S. Nazee has always been the most self-effacing of women. A widow in her seventies, she has spent most of her life deferring to others—her late husband, her seven children, her six brothers and sisters. When she enters a room, Nazee has a habit of muttering "excuse me" under her breath to no one in particular, apologizing for taking up space. She would never think of taking the last cookie on a plate before offering it to someone else, maybe offering it two or three times. She rarely takes a glass of water without first offering it to the person sitting across from her.

But as she sat cross-legged on our family room floor with the two-quart stainless steel bowl of mulberries Ali had given her in the crook of her arm, a slow transformation took place. While she and Ali reminisced about their childhood in Kerman, she began dipping into the bowl. Slowly, her long, lanky frame relaxed. She cocked her head to one side, laughing playfully, engrossed in the stories. Watching her, I saw the beauty she had been at seventeen.

Soon the bowl held nothing but filaments.

Ali passed by me, bowl in hand, grinning.

"She ate the whole thing," he said with a gleam in his eye, pleased that his sister had been so transported, so transformed.

Last year, when we went to Bart and Vanda's baby shower, we were surprised to find that the man who had asked permission to eat our mulberries was our host, Bart's brother-in-law Ed.

"Oh, you're the man with the mulberry tree," Ed exclaimed upon seeing Ali. "We pass by that tree every day when I walk the kids to school. I tell them, 'When that tree has berries, it's almost time for school to be out.'"

Ed is a true convert. He was so taken with our tree that a few weeks ago he planted his own—in his front yard, within easy reach of the sidewalk.

This was a smart move because mulberry nostalgia can improve property values. One afternoon we returned home from a family outing to find a handwritten note wedged in our door: I was passing by and noticed your mulberries. I hope you don't mind, but I ate some. They reminded me of my childhood in Mexico. I live in Orange County but if you ever want to sell your house, please call me.

We will never sell this house. With every kumquat, every pomegranate and mulberry tree, we become more rooted to this place.

Besides, we have obligations.

OUR GOLDEN STATE

Fred Setterberg

"NOW PAY ATTENTION to me..."

Dad towered above, hands on his hips, sunlight filtering through a cross-hatch of sycamore branches, his smooth, pink scalp illuminated and glistening with sweat. He wore grease-pocked tan chinos savaged at the knees from planting radishes and carrots all morning in the backyard. His canvas hunting jacket was fastened together at the unspooling seams with a foot-long patch of silver duct tape.

"...*You can't just cut their heads off.*"

I shifted my weight, working the flat of one palm into the wet grass, adjusting my gaze so that Dad's shoulder obscured the sun. Several score of yellow dandelions lay scattered across the lawn where I'd neatly severed them mid-stem.

"Why not?"

"'Cause they grow right back, that's why. These weeds ain't no Marie Antoinette and King Louie, you know." He hitched up his trousers by the belt loops and grimaced, estimating my acquaintance with the events of 1789, and then ploughed ahead just the same. "You can't go decapitating these fellas like some crazed Jacobin."

Dad was in a fine mood this Saturday morning, the cool spring air sharpened with the scent of bay salt and arsenic swept in from the landfill at the edge of town. He'd been up since dawn, relishing several hours of complete dominion over the yard. In his hunting jacket's inside pocket, he kept a small notebook and pencil stub, ticking off the chores and projects as they fell one by one.

Crazed Jacobin: Almost certainly, this was a compliment.

"Here. Try this." Dad flung a nine-inch screwdriver into the lawn. It thronged. I would have heard all about it if I'd been the one playing with tools. "Dig 'em out. Every one of 'em. By the roots."

He stalked off and I rolled back on all fours, retracing the zigzag of luminous yellow petals beginning to wither and curl in the glare of mid-morning. Basically, he was saying: Start over. I stabbed the screwdriver into the lawn, imagining it to be the fat belly of Superman's archenemy, Lex Luthor. Only this morning in bed, sheets pulled up to my neck, I had started reading the latest issue of *Jimmy Olsen Comics*—a three-part exploit in which Superman's pal is mysteriously transformed into a human porcupine. I suspected Luthor was behind these shenanigans. *Shenanigans*, meaning mischief, pranks, monkeyshines, or tomfoolery—whatever that meant. I'd come across the word in a recent issue of *Action Comics* in which an inexplicable energy burst from inside a scientist's laboratory strikes Lois Lane and gives her x-ray vision so she can spot Clark Kent changing into Superman in the men's lavatory. Comic books can be very educational. On my third try, the screwdriver found a soft spot amid the gristle of Luthor's belly and sank up to the handle.

My father did not object to comic books, but he argued that greater satisfactions could be obtained by making a necessary contribution to the household. I plunged the screwdriver into the heart of a headless dandelion. It squirmed under pressure, its stem mashed and slivered, but the root wouldn't budge. I leaned into the tool and we sank another inch. Working from the wrist, twisting and flicking, I up-ended the weed at its tip and it flipped out of the ground and into the air like a little man in a flowery hat shot from a cannon. Its crisp tail had broken off. That made me think of a carrot chomped a third of the way up, like Bugs Bunny would do on Saturday morning cartoons. I was hungry. I wanted to go inside, get out of the sun, eat Frosted Flakes, watch TV. Maybe spend some time later with Jimmy Olsen, cub reporter for *The Daily Planet*, a great American newspaper in the city of Metropolis.

A blast of water rattled the pipes along the side of the house. Almost immediately, my nostrils throbbed, registering the tang of iron. My throat burned. Dad out back spraying the roses.

I sank the screwdriver handle-deep into the lawn and hurried into the backyard to watch him work.

Dad was leaning against the compost bin, cradling a brown plastic bottle like the head of a snake slinking out from a dirty coil of sun-baked hose. When he fingered the release valve, the fine, acrid mist of Ortho Home Orchard Spray doused a platoon of aphids tramping across our butter-yellow roses and I gagged. Insecticides, said Dad, had won the war, along with plastics and light-metal alloys and radar and jet engines and a thousand other inventions and improvements. Insecticides and herbicides had saved the bacon on Saipan, flushed Japs out of the bush on Guadalcanal, mowed down mosquitoes and chiggers and tiny blue flies that laid eggs in your eyes and killed men in twenty-four hours and otherwise would have cut a swath through the best army in the world. They probably saved my uncle's life in the Solomon Islands, said Dad—though Uncle Win pointed out that he seldom got to land unless it was by swimming there after being sunk at sea and it was the sharks he had to worry about then.

Yet my father did not apply Ortho to our front lawn, where it might have done some good against the dandelions. Mom disapproved. Dad could do whatever he wanted in his backyard, but the front was public property—at least in the way it got used every day by us kids slithering through the grass, grinding ourselves into the dirt, soaking up through our open pores the lurking vestiges of modern science's most recent realignment of the ordinary molecule, the polychlorinated hydrocarbons and biphenyls that made life out on the patio pleasingly free from gnats, that caused California's Central Valley to blossom into the greatest fruit basket and the best-spread vegetable table the world has ever known, that gave the citizens of suburbia the green gushing pleasure of backyard horticulture, the companionship of flowers, fruits, grasses, shrubs, and trees all year long.

"You done in front already?"

I shrugged, sniffing the air. The scent of Ortho was both repellent and delectable, like the rot of your own athlete's foot.

"I guess so."

"Why do you have to guess?"

"I'm not finished yet," I explained more judiciously. "Not nearly. But I want to help you massacre the snails."

Dad peeled back his lips to expose a faultless set of alabaster false teeth. The army had yanked all the originals, saving him a fortune in dental bills for the rest of his life. "Okay. Go get the Bug-Geta. It's under my work bench."

When I returned with the green and orange cardboard box featuring a menacing gargantuan snail on the front, we sprinkled its contents across a patch of beets, onions, and spinach.

"Dad, can this stuff hurt people?"

We both studied the russet carpet of petrochemicals.

"You an aphid?"

"No."

"A snail?"

"No."

"A slug?"

"No."

"Well, then..."

"But you wouldn't want to eat it," I asked innocently enough, "would you?" Soon as we stopped talking, I'd have to return to the dandelions.

Dad cocked his head. "Look," he said, his voice rising in faint exasperation. "I know what your mother thinks, but there's people in India and China and what-not now that've got enough to eat two and even three times a day thanks to Bug-Geta and what-have-you. There's even a scientist, and this fellow's got himself a Ph.D. from the university—a doctor of plants or animals or insects maybe. And every morning during his coffee break, along with his Nescafé, he treats himself to a nice little meal of a bug poison with a funny name. I believe they call it 2,4-D. And what do you think it's done to him?"

"Nothing."

"Not a damn thing. Said he's even got to enjoy the taste." Dad grinned bumptiously at the audacity of learned men, at progress itself, and then he suddenly tightened his lips and his expression straightened like a clothesline. "Now don't you go snacking on this stuff yourself. It's for snails only. At least," he said, clapping me on one shoulder, "you wait until you get a laboratory of your own."

I laughed along as though I thought I might actually grow up one day to be a scientist, or a farmer, or even the guy at the nursery who sold us the box of Bug-Geta. It seemed the perfect moment. So I asked him.

"Can I have a dog?"

Gil was the youngest brother of Mrs. Bingham, the butcher's wife. After two years in the army and an honorable discharge, Gil decided not to return to Mitchell, Nebraska, so the Binghams let him move into their garage. "Just until something opens up somewhere," Mrs. Bingham explained to my mother. Gil owned a primer gray '55 Buick that he planned to repaint sky blue and cherry out with chrome mags, headers, and a tach once he started working, but for now it sat on the curb outside the Binghams' house and seldom moved before noon. On the driver's side above the gas tank, in four-inch ivory block print, Gil had hand-painted the name of his former girl friend: *Dee Dee Dinah*. They had been engaged back in Nebraska, but the girl found an older man who worked in a bank while Gil was fulfilling his military obligations. Gil was stationed in Germany the same two years as Elvis.

"You ever see him?" asked Benny. The Changs lived three houses down from the Binghams and Benny had talked me and Phil into tagging along. The garage seemed far too dark for the middle of a Saturday afternoon because the Binghams' new boarder had covered the lone side-door window with several layers of the *Oakland Tribune*'s help wanted section. Mrs. Bingham said Gil was still exhausted from active duty.

"More than see."

Gil sprawled the length of his canvas cot, a relic of family hospitality that staggered and whined on its spindle legs every time he shifted his weight. He sparked up a fresh Marlboro and puffed lazy smoke rings into the rafters.

"What do you mean?" demanded Phil, fanning himself with splayed fingers.

"I'm not saying I was his closest friend, you understand. But me and Elvis, sure—we hung out together. Now and then. You see *G.I. Blues*?"

"No."

"You remember the part in the barracks, everybody singing along?"

"We didn't see it," explained Benny. "None of us."

"That's me. Standing next to him. My elbow's leaning on his bunk. He didn't mind. He's a cool head."

Elvis Presley was a cool head. Who could dispute it? At our house, my mother only paid attention to the radio when she heard "The Theme to *Exodus*" by Ferrante and Teicher or anything by Connie Francis (whose real name was Concetta Rosa Maria Franconero, though she changed it so the Protestants would buy her records, too). Dad preferred the news or a Giants' doubleheader with Gaylord Perry and Juan Marichal pitching. It was Benny's older sister Bernice who owned a copy of *50,000,000 Elvis Fans Can't Be Wrong* with Elvis wearing a gold suit that hung on him like damp sheets of cellophane. If anything happened to his sister, Benny said he'd inherit all her albums.

"You ever see Elvis fight?" demanded Benny.

"Nah, he kept to himself. Colonel Tom Parker ordered him to. Didn't want no bad publicity when he got out of the army like me." Gil groped blindly under the cot until his fingers located the dial of his plug-in table radio. Its vacuum tubes warmed to cast an orange glow on the underside of the canvas so that it looked like its occupant was being pan-fried. Twisting the dial through a hail of static, Gil settled finally on "The Battle of New Orleans" by Johnny Horton.

"I heard he knows judo."

Gil yawned, his lips forming an infant's perfect O. He was twenty-two years old, long and sinewy like a knotted rope. He wore thick black frame glasses in the style of Buddy Holly before his plane crashed and they made his eyes look like steelies, the chrome-plated marbles we prized above all others as the most devastating shooters. After the service, Gil had let his hair grow, lubricating the sides with Butch Wax, an indolent chocolate-brown wave teased over his forehead like the horn of a unicorn. He clapped a hand over his mouth when he saw me staring.

"Do you know judo?" persisted Benny. Sometimes Benny was like a little mutt with a rubber bone in his mouth that he wouldn't let go of for anyone.

"Judo's for babies." Gil puffed a smoke ring in Benny's direction. It landed and dissolved on the tip of his nose. "I learned karate."

"My dad's got a black belt in karate."

"No, he doesn't, Benny."

"Benny lies like a rug, Gil."

"I bet your hands aren't registered as deadly weapons with the police."

"I still got to do that," admitted Gil. He cranked himself up on the cot and surveyed the three of us. "You kids want to trade or not?"

"I got some *Archie and Veronica*s," said Benny.

Gil nodded his approval. "Where are they?"

"In my sister's drawer."

"Go get them."

Benny threw open the side door, flooding the garage with the light of day.

"What about you two?"

"My dad doesn't let me read comics," said Phil. "He says they make you stupider."

"I got Jimmy Olsen," I admitted. I didn't feel like I had any choice.

"*Jimmy Olsen, Superman's Pal*, or Jimmy Olsen appearing in *Superman*?"

"Both. I just read the story where Jimmy gets amnesia and thinks he's an orphan and he only wishes he were Superman's pal. But Supergirl's living in the same—"

"Go get it."

"Okay. But what do you got to—"

"Go get it. Then you'll see."

I hesitated. It wasn't that I didn't want to trade, but I knew that my parents were bound to ask where I was going if I rushed out with an armful of *Jimmy Olsens* and I suspected that Gil's garage was not the right answer. Nobody had said anything directly against him. Still, my father had a way of tilting his head whenever Gil got mentioned, while my mother nibbled her lips as though discretely swallowing some uncharitable comment before it escaped to run riot in the world. Gil was too old to trade comic books, even I could see that. And the last time, all he had were two issues of *Casper the Friendly Ghost*, both of them smudged with grape jelly. I was summoning the courage to ask if he had any *Green Lanterns* when the kitchen screen door flew open and crashed against the wall.

"Gil, can I have a ride to the store? We need some things for dinner."

Sandy Bingham lined the door jamb, her torso a seesaw of triangles fastened loosely at the corners—the head of blonde curls bobbing across one shoulder, her hips filling out a pair of green-striped culottes and jutting the opposite direction. Sandy was only three years older than me and Benny, and for as long as I could remember we had all played together on the neighborhood's front yards—Freeze Tag, Simon Says, Mother May I? But ever since starting junior high the previous fall, she had begun calling us "the little kids."

"What're we having, cousin?"

"Pork chops. But we don't have enough."

Gil turned up the volume to "El Paso" by Marty Robbins. He ran his hands down the front of his t-shirt, ironing away its wrinkles. "Then we better get enough, shouldn't we? You know I love my pork chops."

Sandy laughed way too loud and I didn't see the humor. Gil read my mind.

"Elvis loves pork chops. You know that?"

"Un-huh."

"Sure you do."

Gil shoveled his legs off the cot and reached under his bunk to pluck a midnight blue satin jacket from a nest of littered clothing.

He slowly rose, shook the kinks out of his legs, and with a serpentine shrug slipped both arms into the sleeves. A half-moon of hand-sewn gold letters spangled the jacket's backside: DUSSELDORF U.S. ARMY.

"You come back later with that comic book," he told me, "and I'll give you a *Prince Valiant* for it."

"I don't like *Prince Valiant*."

"Come by tomorrow. I might be busy tonight."

"What should we call him?"

"He's so..." Mom ransacked her polite vocabulary for the proper word. "Huge."

"A whopping big name then," suggested Dad.

"He's great!" I squealed and knew I sounded just like a girl.

"Did you have to get the biggest one?"

"The biggest and the best," said Dad. "Am I right?"

"Right!"

"Oh, I don't know..."

"We'll name him after your people," Dad offered. "After some dago."

"We will not call him that."

"One of your emperors. Caligula."

"Who?"

"Or Nero. Nero means black in Italian. Black as sin." Dad drummed both hands on the flat pan of our new family member's rump, and his tail switched like a whip of steel cable lacerating my legs. "I bet your mother didn't know that."

"Why is he drooling? Are they supposed to drool?"

"No, not Nero. Nero had a black heart. Fiddling around when he should have been governing. Let's call him—oh, I don't know...How about Gaius Julius Caesar Augustus."

"Your father was reading the encyclopedia all last night. I don't know why."

"It's kinda...long."

"Augustus."

"Franklin, really. What kind of name is that for a dog?"

"Rome's finest emperor. Of course, they had given up on self-government by that point."

I lay my hand across his forehead as though taking his temperature through the thick coal carpet of fur. The distance from my thumb to little finger wasn't long enough to span his two rheumy brown golf-ball eyes. Part Labrador, part mastiff, part hound of indefinite origins. "A mixed breed," my father had explained at the pound as I pressed my face against the wire mesh cage and allowed his wet pink six-inch tongue to marinate one cheek and then the other. "Just like you." Our new dog was eight months old. Seventy-five pounds. Almost big enough to ride. The animal control officer said he had the rest of the day and if nobody took him home, then that was that.

"Augustus!"

"So be it."

Dad planted a bountiful Valencia orange as the sun shone intermittently between winter's fog and spring's drizzle. Alongside it, he placed a Meyer lemon of the improved dwarf variety. In the shade, he tended columbine and rock rose in the sunlight, geraniums in a red brick planter box and pyracantha for the springtime rattle of scarlet berries. He lavished care upon carpets of lamb's ear surrounding the hop seed bush and phlox selected to attract butterflies and hummingbirds, along with stalks of crimson amaryllis and towers of agapanthus cast in shades of virgin pale and heliotrope. Our backyard remained treeless, but bushy—red azaleas stationed amid eggshell-white and lavender rhododendrons, the redwood fence corners flush with sticky, saucer-shaped ocher flowers branching from the flannel bush, a *Fremontodendron* named for John C. Frémont, who drove out the Spanish, served as the state's first senator, and now had a suburb christened in his own name down the road from ours. Dad told me all about him as we watered, turned the compost, and poisoned our enemies. Everything, he said, grew better in the West.

That was one reason they were pouring into California from every-place now—our neighbors, our future fellow citizens. Seventeen million already and we drew another thousand, another fifteen hundred new people each day. We had become the biggest state in the union, more populous than New York, which hardly seemed worth imagining now, or even Texas—where cowboys still roamed, where Davy Crockett had died defending the Alamo, a place that just *sounded* big, but we were bigger. Bigger and better than anyplace that anybody had ever seen before.

Mom collected magazines that trumpeted the good news and piled them on the end table in case relatives from Massachusetts should come to visit: evidence that she had made the right choice. *Newsweek* put us on the cover, declaring: "No. 1 State: Booming, Beautiful California." *Time* called California "A State of Excitement." *Life* said, "California Here We Come—and This Is Why." We were building houses, highways, hospitals, new universities up and down the state and the best public school system in the country. Just stand at the kitchen sink and you could see the scope of our ambition emerging from the stainless steel faucet, the end result of the California Water Project with its eighteen pumping stations, nine power-generating plants, and hundreds of miles of canals and levees. There was nothing like California back where folks came from, nothing to match us in distant forgotten Kansas, Missouri, Arkansas, Iowa, Alabama. California was a desert, but we were making it bloom.

I concentrated on the dandelions. Every afternoon after school, I plucked at least fifty from the ground. But they kept growing back. Perhaps I'd miss one or two—even Dad admitted that you couldn't get them all—and they'd explode the next day into starry blossoms, thousands of taunting yellow flowers arcing towards the sun only to collapse overnight, turning into prickly globes obliterated by the slightest breeze, their seeds and parachutes unscrewed from their cushion heads and sailing, lofting, floating, and finally descending into the hundreds of hospitable perforations I had created in the moist ground with my screwdriver. The more I picked, the more grew back. A half-dozen sprouted from a hole where a few days before I had evicted a single weed. Each night as I fell asleep, the dandelions etched themselves onto my eyelids, their green-stem plumbing, their flattened yellow helmets, their wicked beige taproots and insinuating tendrils that I could never, ever extirpate for good.

Our neighbors sought long-term solutions for their front yards. The Sandersons paved over their slope of Merion wonder grass and painted it South Seas green, calling to mind a pool of lime Jell-O. The Changs introduced ivy and then sat back to watch it run rampant through the course of a single thirsty summer. Some homeowners did nothing at all, allowing their property to revert to a state of nature, which entirely missed the point of living in Jefferson Manor, where our lawns were meant to be aligned as indistinguishable patches of one-and-one-half-inch tufted emerald carpet reconstituted as a garden of endless duty: as Eden.

In March, Dad and I drove to the nursery to purchase three twenty-pound sacks of Scott's Turf Builder. In April, Dad sowed grass seed in the spots that had parched and spoiled, sousing the soil with a frothy ammoniac blanket of Cope to suppress grubs. In May, we layered more fertilizer and inspected the ground each evening until the seeds sprouted. We watered once in the morning and again at night during the summer—then spread around Weed and Feed to bring the clover to its knees and replace the gobs of nitrogen it otherwise drew from the air and injected into the ground. We attacked the crabgrass with Clout and Kansel and pummeled the remaining insects with another aerial barrage of Cope. When in doubt—it was like washing your hair with Prell—we lathered up and did it all over again.

But mowing and feeding and watering and mowing again had no end. To my father's way of thinking, this was the price you paid, though sometimes he spoke of a devil's bargain.

Leaves had begun to yellow and fold on the Bearss lime—*Citrus × latifolia*, also known as Tahitian or Persian lime according to *Sunset*'s *Western Garden Book*. The culprits appeared to be ants. Dad pinched his thumb and forefinger at the crown of its slender stalk and watched a dozen misdirected workers scramble across the back of his hand. He had worried about lime blotch or scab or greasy spot or even red algae, but the man at the nursery said he'd probably just over-watered, flushing the ants from their nest and weakening the tree until it turned ripe for invasion. We purchased a half-dozen Grant's Ant Stakes. Active ingredient: 1.0% hydramethylnon. The buggers died quickly.

Two weeks later, they were back—and twice as many.

"Is *Dagwood and Blondie* all you got?" asked Benny.

Gil sparked up a Marlboro, inhaled rapturously, and blew the smoke directly into Benny's face.

"Why? You don't think Blondie is bitchin'?"

Benny shrugged. Augustus was sprawled across the cold concrete floor close to the door, where a slim margin of light leaked in through the crack. In the gloom of Gil's garage, my dog looked like a big black boulder, dense and immovable, except when he was licking himself.

"Think about it," advised Gil. "Blondie is bitchin'—that's a fact. And you can have her for two *Betty and Veronica*s."

"How come two?"

Gil swiveled around on his cot and squinted in my direction.

"What about you, kid? What'd you bring me today?"

I made a face that I was glad Gil couldn't see in the dark.

"Speak up. Whaddya got?

I rolled my copy of *Jimmy Olsen, Superman's Pal* into a periscope and casually surveyed the garage. I'd read the issue three times already, but still wasn't sure about trading it. In the featured story, Jimmy drinks a vial of serum that temporarily gives him the ability to stretch every part of his body like a rubber band that will never break. As Elastic Lad, he can peek over tall buildings like the world's biggest giraffe and tie villains all up in knots with his rubber fingers. Once he grabbed a bank robber down the block without leaving his chair (and then he made a crack about the long arm of the law). Serums had previously turned Jimmy into a werewolf, a giant turtle, a Bizzaro World version of himself, and an incredibly fat freak.

"Betty and Veronica," purred Gil, his voice syrupy and spit-filled. "I wouldn't kick either of 'em out of bed. Ronnie's got those big tits, man...I'd come all over them and she'd probably lick it right off."

Benny's head tipped back like he'd been winged by a slingshot. "Man, you're gross, Gil."

"Betty's not so bad, either. Little Catholic girl, probably. Wearing her uniform all innocent like. Hell, they can't keep it out of their mouths. You know what I'm talking about?"

Benny and I glanced at one another, admitting that we probably did not.

"It's just," said Benny, easing away from Gil's cot, "that I already traded you this one before and I'm not really interested in reading it again."

Gil flopped down on his back and sighed. His head rolled my direction and we locked indifferent gazes.

"I bet you two would rather fuck Little Lulu."

"No, we wouldn't!" I objected.

"I bet *you* would," sniggered Benny, the traitor.

"You don't even know what it means, Benny."

"I do too. My sister told me."

"I don't even like Little Lulu," I protested.

Gil kept puffing on his Marlboro, his puckered lips surrounding the glowing red dot. His waterfall was greased thick with Butch Wax.

"You two are a couple of real poker players, aren't you? Holding out on me until I bring out the good stuff."

Benny and I didn't say anything.

"You're pretty smart, aren't you? Be honest."

"I am," admitted Benny.

Gil wiggled his way to the edge of the cot and sat up straight from the belly, like he was still in the army. He muttered to himself about how we had really pulled one over on him this time.

"You," he ordered, pointing to Benny. "Get my duffle bag from underneath."

Benny dove for the concrete, slipped under the cot, and hauled a big duffle out from the shadows.

With two hands, Gil yanked open its string purse and sank one arm down deep, blindly fondling its contents.

"Here it is." He flapped a magazine onto the cot.

I could hardly see anything except Gil's ball-bearing eyes vibrating above the glow of his dwindling cigarette. He reached for the flashlight he kept under his cot. A milky beam splashed across the cover.

"Cool!" said Benny. "Look at his face."

Famous Monsters of Film Land, an issue featuring Lon Chaney as the Phantom of the Opera. He had hardly any hair parted down the middle and the worst set of rotting teeth you ever saw.

"I'll trade," I said.

"No," objected Benny, "I will. Gil asked me."

"Gil asked us both, Benny. I said it first."

"That's a good lesson for you, kid. Take what you want."

I firmly held *Jimmy Olsen* between the pinch of my right hand's thumb and forefinger until my left felt Gil loosen his grip on *Famous Monsters*.

"Wait," Gil told Benny, "I got something for you, too." His hand slithered back into his duffle bag. He grunted with the effort of further exploration. "Yeah, here, it is."

He trained the flashlight on his open hand. Stretched across his palm was a long skin-colored balloon with a puffy tip at the end, like a rocket ship.

"You know what this is, right?"

"Yeah."

"What?"

Benny's voice dropped to a whisper. "A Trojan."

"That's right. Your sister tell you about them?"

"*No*. I just know."

"Gimme *Betty and Veronica*."

Benny handed them over.

"Wash it out before you use it. If you know how to use it."

I wanted to get out of there, but Benny was already at the door. He cracked it open and the light pressed hard against our eyeballs. I grabbed Augustus by the collar and dragged him to his feet.

"And hey, kid," said Gil, settling back down on the cot to read at his leisure Jimmy Olsen's adventures as Elastic Lad. "Your dog stinks."

"He does not," shot back Benny. Benny always stood up for dogs, but he especially respected Augustus. Augustus was huge.

"Smells like a barn in here," said Gil.

Benny straddled Augustus's haunches, hunched over his big head, and sniffed. "He smells good," he reported. "It stinks in here 'cause of you, Gil."

Gil didn't even hear him.

"And hey," he said from behind the comic book, "you tell your sister I want her to come by and visit me sometime, okay?"

I longed for super powers.

Usually, they descended upon an ordinary but virtuous mortal by accident. An unduplicable error in the student chemistry lab. A lightning strike at just the right angle. A bite from a radioactive insect.

In comic books, only the villains plotted to acquire the powers of flight or invisibility or blinding speed, and then they invariably paid a great price. Banishment to the Phantom Zone. Being hurtled to the furthest reaches of the universe by a superhero's shove of superhuman strength. Finding themselves reduced to a quarter of an inch so they fit snugly into the municipal jail of Kandor, the former capital of the planet Krypton that was shrunk many years ago by the green-skinned supervillain, Brainiac, and sealed in a bottle that now safely resides in the North Pole inside Superman's Fortress of Solitude.

In the shower, I watched the water roll off my shoulder to trickle down the naked sleeve of my straightened arm and I wondered what it might take (thunderstorm, earthquake, strange brew radiating from the municipal waterworks?) to transform my molecular makeup so that I was granted the sudden power to shoot streams of water from my fingertips with the concentrated force of a fire hose. Better yet, Yosemite Falls! (Someday we were going there for vacation.) I pictured myself as Shower Lad, blasting villains against brick walls, reducing them to a piteous slosh—a technique I'd seen on the TV news in Birmingham, Alabama. I'd join the Justice League of America, along with Superman, Batman and Robin, Wonder Woman, Flash, and Green Lantern. Together we would battle and bring to justice Brainiac, Bizarro, General Zod, and Mr. Mxyztplk, the imp from the fifth dimension. Almost certainly, I had a vocation.

"When're you gonna clean up after that damn dog?"

I lay on my bed, arms stretched wide and fastened at the wrists, feet strapped to either corner, staring up at the ceiling and into the bald-headed face of evil genius. From a trembling steel cable, Lex Luthor slowly lowered the boulder of kryptonite and I was rendered defenseless into the clutches of the merciless supervillain.

"You hear me? Quit daydreaming and get out there and clean up after that dog or he's going right back where he came from."

Luthor's smooth, pink, evilly hairless skull hovered above, glaring down at me—until I realized that, of course, it was Dad. I bolted upright and slid off the bed and hurried out into the yard.

Next to the compost bin, in the dirt, covered with straw and grass and a conspicuous wide stripe of his own shit smeared across his rump, I found Augustus, sleeping.

One eyelid flapped open, spotted me, slammed shut like a gate.

Augustus was always sleeping.

"Wake up!" I lifted his long black rope of tail by the tip and wagged it for him. "C'mon, boy!" I scratched his head with both hands, drumming my fingertips upon the flat plate of his skull. "Thatta boy, Augustus, good boy!" I slipped my arms around his neck and shoulders, lowered myself onto his back, taking care to avoid the putrid smear at his other end, and I squeezed. His planet head slowly rolled into one shoulder, his features materializing like the man in the moon. A wide ribbon of red tongue washed my mouth. "Good boy, Augustus. Want to go for a walk, boy? Do you?"

Augustus pushed himself up by the front paws, assumed the sitting stance that I tried to teach him, and began to bark.

"Quiet, boy. Quiet."

Augustus kept barking, his pace quickening, the singular yelps now blending into an air raid siren ululation, a hearty yowling with long gummy ropes of saliva dangling from his cavernous maw as he threw back his huge meaty head and gobbled the air for no reason at all.

Dad used a licked-clean root beer Popsicle stick to ladle the fresh pollen of a pink cotton-candy hybrid tea called Bewitched onto the stamen of a lavender Lady Banks climber—forever altering the destiny of his roses. Creating something aromatic, beautiful, or peculiar, something *new*—that was the thing! When cross-pollination failed, Dad resorted to simple grafting, placing five varieties of pears on a single rootstock, showing anybody who cared to observe (I watched, but my mother did not) how to execute a whip graft, cutting both the branch and scion at a shallow angle, binding them together, and sealing the joint with candle wax. Nursing along the graft, watching it take, flourish, blossom, fruit. Sometimes Dad sang to his plants, as Luther Burbank had done, coaxing them along with "They Call the Wind Mariah." Something about vital forces, he explained, an instinct surpassing mere cell division.

And yet reminders of the susceptibility of all living things to accident, pillage, and decay also littered his garden. Rust attacked the roses. Gophers raided his staggered rows of peas and carrots, pulling them underground like Morlocks devouring the Eloi. In the side yard, next to a wreath of wound-up hose and nozzle, Dad planted a regiment of snowy freesias. Natives of South Africa, he bragged, tough as nails and sweet as honey to the nostrils. Augustus thought so, too, and one afternoon he devoured a half-dozen aromatic funneled flowers, leaving only the tooth-sawed shoots. My dog foamed along the pink and black folds of his blubber lips and his breath smelled like Dial soap. We staked him out back with enough rope to slink into the shade once the wrathful sun began to cross our yard.

"You come in now," suggested my mother. "You've been out here working all morning."

Dad snapped shut his Army-issue teeth like an angry tortoise. He glowered at Mom as though she had straight out called him a failure.

For whatever refused to thrive, Dad had nobody to blame but himself, and so he always did. But he also bristled and fumed at the positioning of the sun, the stab of a late spring freeze, the stinginess of seeds bought cut-rate and hoarded over too many winters to produce what they had originally promised. Earlier that morning, I had watched him fling a shovel across the yard and then throttle a wilting sunflower, yanking it out of the soil by the throat.

My mother folded her arms across her chest and stared far over my father's shoulders, the corners of her mouth pinned tight. The end of our block was still fenced off with barbed wire warning against hunters on the prowl, and game birds honked overhead every morning: not a town at all, she sometimes grumbled, but an empty place still making itself up. If a snail devoured his shoots of red chard and spinach, it really wasn't her fault.

I sat on the concrete walkway, both arms wrapped around Augustus, his neck as thick as an elephant's foot. I could sense my parents' uneasiness as each gauged some rivalrous absence in the other. The bay breeze fluttered through my dog's matted black fur and I felt frightened and cold.

One Sunday afternoon, I was surprised to see Dad cheered up within the barony of his bushes, fruit, and flowers by a visit from Uncle Win. They stood alongside the trellis of wisteria, its stalk of violet petals sputtering in the breeze like Roman candle fire. Their heads tipped towards one another in concession to the blood tie and neighborliness. I couldn't even smell an argument.

Dad hefted a lightweight black plastic pot off the ground and fit it into Win's clutches. Then he stood back and beamed. They both admired the plant's tangled sunburst of tiny petals, the center of the flowers swollen into the shape of raspberries.

"Now you need to plant this fella someplace with plenty of sun, and water him good. You understand?"

My uncle nodded. "Sure, Slick. I'll do it today." He seemed touched by his older brother's tenderness towards the flower pot.

"Maybe drop by the nursery on your way home and pick up some fertilizer. Feed and water is the secret. You be sure to feed and water this youngster and you'll get results before you know it. Maybe I'll even rustle you up a few more for your backyard."

Win wrestled the pot into a surer grip, resting its edge against his belly. "What's it called?"

"I'll write it down for you." Dad extracted his notepad and pencil stub from his jacket's inside pocket and bore down hard on the page, studying the results as they materialized. "The scientific name is *Nil kanrf's Deew*. Think you can remember that?"

"What is that, Latin?"

"Old Norse." Dad tipped back the brim to his cap and ran an open palm over the smooth dome of his skull. "The Vikings brought it to Greenland long before the Spanish and the Portagees even set sail. It took a spell to get to California."

"I appreciate that, big brother."

When my uncle left, we all took a lunch break in the kitchen.

"What did you give Win?" asked Mom. She removed a frosted pitcher of blue Kool-Aid from the fridge and found a glass for me in the cupboard. Then she pivoted to face the stove and stirred a pot of Campbell's SpaghettiOs. The kitchen smelled like boiled catsup, but sweeter. It made me hungry.

"What're we having for dinner?" wondered Dad.

"There's Rice-A-Roni, if you want. Or I can take the Chef Boyardee pizza out of the freezer."

"Pizza!" I had already decided.

Dad sampled a mouthful of SpaghettiOs and issued an extravagant sigh of satisfaction.

"Say, when're you going to make that Tunnel of Fudge cake again? I enjoy a good Tunnel of Fudge."

"What did you give Win, honey?"

Dad pulled his pipe out of his shirt pocket and began stuffing the bowl with a sack of Lucky Strike Half-and-Half. He sparked a match, and I remembered him telling me that years ago they used to sell the strike-anywhere variety under the brand name of Lucifers.

"I offered him a nice little specimen of common ragwort." His false teeth parted in a smoky rictus. "*Nilkanrf's Deew*. That's *Franklin's Weed* spelled backwards. It'll be all over his yard by the end of summer."

I laughed. Dad puffed gray clouds over the SpaghettiOs. Mom slammed my glass of Kool-Aid down hard on the Formica table, its blue wave lapping over the rim.

"There is something mean about you," she told him. "Sometimes something mean and small."

I drank my Kool-Aid and they didn't talk. When we finished lunch, Mom joined me in the front yard, down on her hands and knees, rooting out the dandelions with an awkward pull on a foot-long screwdriver that didn't begin to get the job done. I snuck a glance at her face once or twice when she was stooped over on all fours and found that her eyes were as empty and bored and faithless as I feared my own must be.

I came home before dinner to walk Augustus, but he was gone. In the backyard, I found paw prints in the radish patch and a large pile of dog doo that turned out to be cold when I prodded it with my index finger, but no sign of my dog. I thought he might be sleeping behind the fireplace out back, but all I found was his muddy hole and a broom handle ravaged with tooth marks. I wondered if somebody had left the side gate open by accident.

Maybe me.

I jogged into the middle of the street and whistled. Augustus never came when I whistled. I called out his name, though I wasn't absolutely positive that he knew it.

I cut a path down Brook Street, crisscrossing at Yale, Harvard, and Princeton. No Augustus sprawled across the hot tar, no dying dog flopping on his side like the goldfish I'd won at St. Bernard's Easter Festival the year before and spilled one afternoon onto our kitchen linoleum.

Of course! He must have headed to the park. Augustus loved to mark his territory, kill squirrels. He would have remembered the park. Augustus was smart, probably.

"*Augustus*!"

I pictured him at the edge of the swimming pool, lapping up refreshment, urinating into the gutter, diving into the deep end with a deafening splash and sinking to the bottom like a boulder wrapped in bear's hide.

I gripped the cyclone fence with two hands, pressed my face into its mesh, rattled the screen.

"*Augustus*!"

No dog in the swimming pool.

Maybe the eucalyptus grove where he chewed the bark off saplings and bayed at the sea gulls.

"Here, boy! Come home, Augustus!"

In the parking lot, beyond the grove, I spotted a familiar car: *Dee Dee Dinah* inscribed in pale ivory above the gas tank. I dashed to the driver's window, breathless and full of hope. My head bobbed at the open window.

"Gil! Did you see my dog? Augustus? He's black and huge."

Gil gripped the steering wheel with both hands. He cocked his head in my direction and squinted as though he couldn't quite place me. His upper lip curled like Elvis's.

"You talking about a nigger?"

Sandy Bingham was crumpled in the corner of the passenger seat. For some reason, she was crying. She turned her head, concentrating on the eucalyptus grove.

"Did you see him, Sandy? You know my dog. He's gigantic."

"Go away."

I ran home two blocks. The front door was open, which meant my mother or father must be there.

Mom stepped into the living room as soon as I shouted for her.

"Mom, Augustus got out. I looked all over for him. But he's disappeared."

She hesitated, shifted her weight from one foot to the other. "Your father," she stated, as though that explained everything. Her eyes scoured the carpet as if it were rippling with grubs and maggots. "Your father brought him back to the pound. You weren't living up to your responsibilities."

"What?"

"He was too big for here, honey. He was a big dog and he needed a place to run."

"He brought him to the pound?"

"This morning. He felt very bad about it. He did. I could tell.

The existence of Superman raised questions. Why didn't he go back in time using his super-speed to visit Germany before the Nazis and strangle Hitler in his cradle? Why didn't he squeeze coal into diamonds and pass them out to everybody so everybody could be rich? If he was so powerful and so smart and so good, why didn't he irrigate the Sahara desert somehow—he should have figured out how—and turn it into a place where everything grows with plenty of room for everybody and everything.

Superman did not exist. So you didn't need to worry about it. You didn't need to talk. I didn't say a word for days.

I felt sleepy and restless, blurry, vacant—every part of me down to my fingertips too sensitive to the touch, like my skin had been scoured down to the nerve endings. I didn't cry. My father passed me in the front yard while I was rooting out dandelions—I didn't see him. I refused to see him. I felt sick when I heard his voice. I stopped listening. I plunged the screwdriver deep into the green belly of the lawn, but I didn't think anymore about Lex Luthor. I dug up that lawn with a thousand puncture wounds, my screwdriver like a dagger to the heart of every innocent dandelion.

I missed Augustus: I must have. I thought about the times I stuck my nose into his collar of fat, wrapping my neck around his neck while he panted his meaty bad breath and I inhaled the loamy odor of dog, my dog. Then I forgot about him for a day. Forgetting made me furious: I squeezed both hands into bloodless white fists when Mom called me for dinner, retreating into the backyard for as long as five minutes. If they were both sitting at the kitchen table, waiting, I might place the heel of my Keds on the tip of a white freesia and mash it into the soil or yank a radish and lob it over the redwood fence into the yard of some stranger.

Dad said maybe someday we'd try another dog and that made me feel like my insides were bleeding, my guts riddled with BBs. I hated him. I told Mom that I hated him. She said that I didn't and offered to help me outside with the rest of my job. We worked together on our hands and knees, not talking. In an hour, there were hundreds of dandelions scattered across the front lawn like tiny corpses in their silly, stupid, yellow-flowered hats.

Phil asked about Augustus and I explained that he was a big dog and needed room to run. Benny never mentioned him, but he stopped coming by our house for nearly a week. At school, on the playground and in the halls, he wouldn't look me in the face.

Then one night, I heard a small fist pounding frantically on our screen door and I knew Benny was back.

The porch light blazed above him and from behind the grill, he looked like he was shattered into a million pieces. Benny was hopping up and down, actually hopping.

"'C'mon, hurry! Mr. Bingham's got Gil treed."

I slipped out the front door and we tore across the yard, down the block, and onto the sidewalk in front of the butcher's house.

Gil had climbed to the top of the Binghams' sycamore, perhaps seven feet high, and he was now inching along on both feet across the only branch sturdy enough to bear his weight.

"*Daddy, stop!*" Sandy rocked back and forth, her hands wrapped around either shoulder like it was impossible to stay warm.

Mr. Bingham stood next to his daughter, directly below the sycamore, arching up on his toes and swiping at Gil's ankles with a meat cleaver.

"Ernie!" shouted Mrs. Bingham from the end of their walkway. "You're not making it any better."

Mr. Bingham took another swing at Gil and barely missed.

Gil crept further out on his limb, balancing on hands and knees. He was talking fast to Mr. Bingham, not looking down at the ground, not making much sense I thought. Mr. Bingham's white t-shirt was soaked with sweat and his face had turned red and gold.

Gil froze on the far end of his limb.

Mr. Bingham wrapped both hands around the cleaver handle, bending back so far that his spine looked like it might snap, and then threw all his weight forward. The blow severed the branch cleanly, though I could almost swear I saw it freeze in midair for an impossible instant like in the cartoons when the Road Runner screeches over the cliff but doesn't realize it yet—and then it crashed to the ground with a crack and bounced several times across the lawn along with Gil, who rolled over twice and tried to scramble to his feet but fell and was curling himself into a ball when Mr. Bingham got close enough to kick him twice in the stomach, hard.

Lucky for Gil, I suppose, the police were there by now—a pair of squad cars rearing up over the sidewalk with cherry tops flashing, the policemen hustling Gil out of the way of Mr. Bingham's feet, scooping the meat cleaver off the grass, and then placing them in separate backseats. They drove down the street and around the block, and disappeared. Everybody went home after that to get ready for work or school or whatever the next day was going to bring.

"What're these?" asked Dad.

He studied his plate. A large heap of greens occupied the center, pooled in oil. To me, they looked familiar, though oddly placed. Dad sucked on his teeth and kept both eyes pointed down at the table.

"Your dinner," said Mom. She ladled two large spoonfuls onto my plate. "*Soffione*. It's a southern Italian specialty."

I scattered them with a fork, searching for yellow blossoms. The light from the overhead milk-glass fixture bore down on us like the sun. "Dandelions?"

"With garlic."

I could smell the garlic. Some people said it stunk, but I never thought so.

"This all we having?" asked Dad.

Mom served herself before answering.

"Yes."

Dad didn't touch his silverware.

"If you don't like what I give you, you can always fix yourself something else. Nobody's helpless around here, are they?"

Dad prodded his mound and fished up a long green stem on the tines of his fork. He studied his dinner. Then he eased it into his mouth, nibbling delicately with his front teeth like a rabbit.

Mom sampled a forkful. She made a little face and patted her mouth with a napkin.

"You're excused," she informed me.

"I'm hungry."

"Make yourself some cereal. There's a box of Trix open."

"I like Frosted Flakes."

"Mind your mother," said Dad. But his blue eyes roved easily in my direction and he vaguely smiled. I found the Trix in the cupboard. Orangey orange, lemony yellow, raspberry red.

"I'm going back to work," announced Mom. "They need a secretary at the elementary school. Somebody with experience."

Dad kept working the dandelions around his plate, concentrating very hard on swabbing the greens into one of the puddles of oil and garlic that had accumulated at the margins. He didn't look up.

I shook out a bowlful of cereal and poured myself a large glass of Hi-C.

"He's old enough." Mom pressed the weight of both elbows onto the table. "He can come home and do his homework. He can watch television if that's what he wants."

My mouth was full, but I spoke up anyway.

"I'm not picking any more dandelions."

"You don't have to," my father conceded, his voice raised to warn off anybody who might think that I did. "You done a good enough job already."

Mom placed her fingertips against the rim of her plate, pushing it to the table's edge. "If you want, I can still be home in time to make dinner." Her voice was trembling. "If that's still what you want."

Dad eased back from the table, chewing his lower lip. He drew a long breath, his chest swelling indecently before it collapsed. Then he remembered me and winked without actually turning his head in my direction. "Long as we don't get too many more nights of these dago greens, right?"

I watched my mother refuse to smile. Her face looked like marble, pretty and cold.

"Least we're not eating snails like those French people. Right outta the garden, they pop them in their mouths for a little snack. Maybe some parsley and a glass of froggy red to wash 'em down."

I didn't say anything.

Dad forced another forkful into the side of his mouth and ground them with his back molars. "Hey, these are all right." He rose from his seat and scooted over to the stove. "See here—I'm going to help myself to more." He scooped out a generous second serving and set the ladle across his plate. For a moment, he stood at the stove, paralyzed: wondering, I suppose, about that little twitch of unhappiness, his fear and restlessness, where it comes from and how it worms its way into our hearts. What and who, when you came down to it, was really to blame? He was still trying to decide how to return the ladle to its pot while gripping his plate with both hands, knowing that everything now depended on him getting back to the table and finishing dinner without uttering another word.

OM

Chris Abani

1

THE HILLS OF my childhood are purple with dusk and wings—
guinea fowl launched like a prayer to the still forming moon.
I hold Bean's shell to my ear. There is no sea. But only sea.
By my bed, in an empty chair, my shirt unwinds.
I remember my aunt counting the dead in the newspaper.
I never told anyone that every sliver of orange I ate
was preceded by words from high mass.
Per omnia saecula saeculorum.
Spit out pit. Amen.
Juice. Amen. Flesh.

2.

A full moon leaning on a skyscraper. The taste:
qat and sweets on a tropical afternoon.
The dog's black tongue was more terrifying than its teeth.
The gravestone rising out of the puddle was more sinister
than the body we discovered as children swinging
in the summer-hot orchard.

3.

The old woman singing a dirge has a voice of dust.
Sorrow lodged like a splintered bullet next to the heart.
A man once asked me in the street:
Do you own your own bones?

She like the home I come in, I say to Cristina
as we drive toward the Golden Gate.
Bean, I repeat.
She loves the home I come in
and I am alive with fire and scars.
Here is my body, I say, eat it, do this,
remember me—

4.

Even now melancholy is a skin flayed
and worn in dance through the city.
Yes, the city becomes skin too and wears me
as skin and I want to say, *This is my body*, as I stroke
the curve of the fountain in the park.
This is my blood. Drink it. Remember.
The safety of doorways is an illusion.
They lead nowhere.
This is why we build houses.
Sand, when there is no water, can ablute,
washing grain by grain even the hardest stone of sin.
But you, but you, you are a sin that I live for.
Ne Me Quitte Pas. Ne Me Quitte Pas. Ne Me Quitte Pas.
Nina's voice walks in dragging bodies,
dead black men that bled unseen in the dark
of southern nights, shaded by leaves
and the veiled eyes of hate.
And in a poem, Lucille stands in the shadow of a tree
and pours libations for our souls,
for our salt, for our gospel.

5.

Somewhere a man speaks
in the dark, voice lost to rain.

I know this hunger, this need
to make patterns, to build meaning
from detritus; also the light
and the wood floor bare but for the lone slipper
tossed carelessly to one side. I admit the lies I've told.
Look, nothing has to be true
since that picture of hell on the living-room wall lost its terror.
I say I want a strong woman, but unlike Neto
I cannot have the woman and the fish
The war followed.
Children are losing their souls to the heat.
That is to say, poor American soldiers.
The rich have found a way to charge theirs to Amex.
Ask this: what is the relationship of desire to memory?
Here is a boy in the airport café, hair cropped from service.
And he closes his eyes to take a sip of coffee.
And smiles as the dark washes the desert away.

6.

Los Angeles:
A red sky and angels thick like palm trees,
and garbage blown in the wind like cars
and the gluttony of SUVs
in an endless river of traffic.
Through the dark, we say, through the dark:
but do we ever really know?
There is a man in a field and he is searching for God.
Father, he says, Father.
In the distance, birds, traffic, and children.
There is a blue sky. There is a sky blue with night.
The call of the earth is a primitive song,
stomping feet and broken men.
There is a blue sky. And night.

The city is a flock of lights.
The darkness of tunnels like caves is knowledge,
also mortal. Maps are like God.
They are the city yet not the city.
They contain the city but yet do not.
We trace the lines in loss.
Sometimes we find treasure.
Sometimes something fills the mind,
something at which we pause, stopped.
The way a photograph cannot remember the living.

7.

To die is to return.
To fly is to be a bird's heart.
Neither is freedom.
If it were we would have no name for it.
No language. Not even the temptation of wind
blowing a dark woman's hair away from a cliff's edge.
Instead, feathers are brought to my door every day by mystery.
Kindling for a fire, a beacon, an epiphany I cannot light.
This is the body of Christ.
Sanctificum.

FROM *THE ADDERALL DIARIES*

Stephen Elliott

THERE'S A TWENTY-ONE minute video taken in 2005 of a boy's sixth birthday party at a children's gym in Emeryville, a shopping mall–packed landfill wedged between Oakland and Berkeley. It's an ordinary party. A dozen children run races on rubber mats, dive headfirst into foam pools, crawl through tunnels, and flip over horse bars. The soundtrack is filled with screaming and giggling and the instructions of counselors in the background.

Ten minutes in, the camera centers on the mother bouncing on the trampoline with the birthday boy and his younger sister. She's barefoot, wearing a green and white print dress. She doesn't look like a woman with two children, though maybe that's just a stereotype. She's gorgeous and full of energy. She doesn't look like a murder victim and she's nothing like a movie star. Her beauty is warm and lacking in glamour. She's in her thirties, but there's something younger about her. Her focus on the children is so complete it's as if there were no one else in the entire world.

Hours are like weeks at this age, minutes disproportionate to a world children are only starting to notice. These images are all that will last. The dress hugs the woman's hips and floats toward her knees as she falls. The kids jump as high as they can to impress their mother. There are three men who love her. Within a year one of them will kill her. The lens tries to hold her, the viewer rising and dropping imperceptibly, the steady male gaze of the man holding the camera.

At the end of the video all the children sit around a long table. The mother comes from behind her son with a large knife in her hand. She wraps her arm around the boy, holding him against her breast, while she cuts into the cake.

Officer Benson was manning the desk at the Oakland police station when the mother arrived and took a seat in the open vestibule. She came every Wednesday, always early or on time, and Benson looked forward to seeing her.

The husband arrived late with his four-year-old daughter and six-year-old son, playing with the children before surrendering them. Benson thought he was trying to antagonize her, he thought the father stood too close. He'd spent twenty-seven years on the force, enough time to recognize the messages implicit in the way a man holds his shoulders and squeezes his fists, the self-justifying set of a man's mouth. And he could tell when a mother cared about her children and when she didn't. He'd seen it both ways.

The father was not a large man yet he loomed over the wife who ignored him as she zipped the children's jackets and took their hands. It's always like this, the late arrival, the big show, the husband like a kernel of corn shivering on a hot pan as the pretty woman with the soft accent gathers her children together and says goodbye as if nothing is wrong.

But this time something was wrong. Benson abandoned his desk and walked outside. The father crossed the street, opened the door to a small hatchback, and drove away. The lights went on in the minivan as the children climbed inside. The night was clear. The buildings of downtown like dark obelisks framed against the hills in the distance.

The mother waved as she drove off. He nodded then turned back to the station. He was going to give her some advice next time she came in. He was going to tell her in all seriousness, "You better get yourself a gun."

"Remain seated. Court is now in session."

There he is, the husband, the father, Hans Reiser, sitting with his attorneys at a large table in the middle of Alameda County Courtroom Nine. No one would ever notice him walking down the street, but now he's the center of attention. He's small and not quite handsome, with dark curly hair and the beginning of a bald patch blossoming on his crown. His bright lips come to sharp points high on his cheeks, giving him a resemblance to Jack Nicholson's portrayal of the Joker. Two bailiffs sit behind Hans at a small industrial desk, and behind them, after a low wall, are the sixty wooden seats of the gallery.

He's lost a lot of weight in the year since he was accused of killing his wife. Caught on surveillance cameras in the weeks after Nina's disappearance, he was fat with deep rings circling his eyes. He's changed even since I last saw him six months ago during the preliminary hearings wearing yellow prison fatigues, standing in the prisoner pen holding a box full of papers. Now his features are pronounced, as if his face has come into focus. He's probably never looked this good.

The room around him is high and wide with smooth wood panels slicing between slabs of white stone wrapping the walls. Decorated plates separate the top and bottom windows, which offer a view of Lake Merritt. On the left sixteen padded juror chairs sit empty; on the right is a mounted flat monitor for exhibitions of evidence. In front, framed by an American and California flag and a bronze seal of the state, sits Judge Larry J. Goodman, a veteran of capital cases. Compact, with ruddy cheeks, Goodman has a reputation for casualness, late starts, early dismissals, and two-hour lunches. Beneath his robe he wears a T-shirt and jeans. His court hears only three or four cases a year and he knows as well as anyone that if every killer in Alameda demanded a trial, the system would collapse into chaos. "If it's a felony in Sonoma," he's fond of saying, "it's a misdemeanor in Oakland."

Near the witness box stands a portrait of Nina Reiser holding Cori. She smiles at the photographer. The naked child seems huge against her. In the divorce filings Hans accused Nina of having an affair with the photographer. I wait for Hans to look at the picture of his wife and son but he doesn't for a long time, working instead through the great stack of papers in front of him and occasionally arguing with his lawyers. When he does look up, one hour, two hours later, he glances at Nina's picture but nothing happens to his face.

William Du Bois, Hans' lead defense attorney, stands behind Hans massaging his shoulders while they wait. Du Bois' jacket stretches across his broad back. He wears his collar high and tight around his thick neck so he resembles a well-dressed turtle. There have been rumors that Hans will fire Du Bois and defend himself. I watch the attorney's fingers, burrowing into the navy coat, the fabric gathering at his fingertips.

In the hallway the reporters ask about the arguments Du Bois has been having with his client. "It's hard defending someone so smart," Du Bois says. "He can memorize nine thousand pages of discovery so sometimes he catches mistakes in testimony and he gets upset." Then he adds, as if surprised he'd just thought of it, "You'd be upset too if you were falsely accused of murdering your wife."

The court is packed for opening statements. There are a dozen journalists and people who live nearby and have nothing better to do. There are police officers with an interest and a woman who served on a jury that District Attorney Paul Hora argued in front of before. It was his most famous case, the trial of Stuart Alexander, the Sausage King. Stuart was caught on his own security cameras executing three meat inspectors at his San Leandro plant, returning to shoot each in the head. That trial lasted seven and a half months and the killer was sentenced to death.*

"He's a wonderful man," the ex-juror says.

Hora is over six feet tall, trim and rigidly straight. He says he's going to introduce us to someone who's not going to testify at the trial. "She was a mother," he tells the jury, pointing at the picture. "And she would never, *ever*, have abandoned those kids." He shows pictures from the inside of her house. On the refrigerator are photographs of the children above a whiteboard detailing their lunch menu for the next seven days.

"In 2004, after five years," Hora explains, "she left Hans for his best friend, Sean Sturgeon. She shouldn't have done it. Nonetheless it happens." In late 2005 Nina left Sean for Anthony Zografos.

When it's Du Bois' turn, he takes his glasses off and pulls on the bridge of his nose. "Here we have something," he says, squinting his eyes, showing an image from a black and white magazine advertising Eastern European women. Nina smiles above an ad for Nina5972, a

*Stuart Alexander died in prison a year later.

university student looking for a serious relationship. *You see*, he seems to be saying. *What kind of woman has her picture in a magazine like this? A mysterious woman, that's who. The kind that disappears.*

Du Bois refers to the men who had keys to Nina's apartment as "the key club" but he only names Anthony and Sean as members. He shows a picture of Nina and Sean. "An interesting character, Sean Sturgeon. A drug addict. A sadomasochist."

Du Bois portrays Nina as promiscuous, but offers little to back it up. He says she kept pictures of the children around because she was concerned about her own image. She wanted people to believe she was a good mother, which is not the same as being one. It quickly seems like Nina's the one on trial, but she's not here to defend herself.

During recess one of the local newscasters says to me, "They're never going to convict him. That girl was a freak." The newscaster is well known, at least on this side of the bridge, and dresses in tailored beige suits for his reports on the morning news. He's built like a quarterback, with a square, rugged face. I imagine doing a little research, finding out what he's into, how many times he's cheated on his wife, and posting pictures with his statistics. It wouldn't take much.

I wake before court at six and pop my pill before typing my notes. I like going to court every day. I like the structure. A parade of schoolteachers take the stand. They recall Nina volunteering, escorting the children on field trips, bringing home and washing the class towels. Ron Zeno, the executive director of Safe Exchange, says every time Nina walked through the door she would get down on one knee, spread her hands, and the children would rush into her arms. Hans told Ron, "You'd be surprised if you knew what she was into. If you knew what her boyfriend was into."

According to witnesses Hans, the opposite of Nina, was openly hostile toward them. A parent from the school remembers a party during which Hans stated that his family was a burden to him and that he'd be better off financially if he didn't have to take care of them. An instructor recalls Hans interrupting her class to force Cori to write cursive for an hour, and the principal recalls having to talk to Hans about his disruptive behavior. He was irresponsible with the kids' documents, always late, incapable of even cleaning up after himself. He treated his mother like a servant. Some Monday mornings, after his weekend with the children, Hans' mother would have to call Nina and ask if she could come help get the children to school.

Paul LaRosa from *48 Hours* tells me Hans is the least sympathetic defendant he's ever seen.

After Nina left Hans, he sent her notes, one of which said, "*I think you are evil because you cannot help it.*" He made threats, like "*Those that are slow to anger are slow to cool.*" He became defined by a hatred of his wife so pure and radiant it obliterated everything in its path. "*It is June 1941*," he wrote, "*and you are the Nazis and you think we will not suffer the necessary amount to defeat you. We will.*"

When Hans met Nina he was like all clients of bride services: he was searching for a good deal, a woman who was smarter, prettier, and kinder than the women willing to spend time with him back home. He paid $20 for Nina's contact information. He didn't think that maybe she was looking for something too. Nina had her own ambitions. Hans told Nina he was a famous scientist, and he might have been. The only thing holding back wider acceptance of his innovations was his personality. He thought if he brought Nina to America she would be so grateful she would love him forever, ignore his narcissism, his months away, his bitter ugly view of the world. Hans thought he could convince her to love him without becoming loveable. He was wrong about that. No relationship can survive contempt. Every con is based on the mark's own greed.

"You're transferring," my friend Kay says. "You think Nina is your mother and Hans is your father." Several times a week I call Kay to talk about the trial. Because her mother is a psychologist she often sees the world through subconscious motivations.

"That's ridiculous," I say. But I do find myself pulled toward Nina, understanding the fierce attractions in orbit around her. Who doesn't want a mother who volunteers at the school, won't accept a job that won't give her time with her children, and keeps a dry erase board with a meal schedule on the fridge so you always know what to expect?

Hans was convinced that Nina had Munchausen syndrome by proxy, a rare disorder in which the affected create illnesses for their children to draw attention to themselves. He reported her to the child abuse hotline, explaining for over half an hour how his estranged wife was forcing their son into unnecessary medical procedures because she wanted the boy to be weak, because she hated him. The decision was made not to investigate.

The children's doctor remembers Cori, three years old, throwing a tantrum, and Nina on her hands and knees, whispering to him until he calmed down. The pediatrician ended treatment after receiving a threatening phone call from Hans. Cori was suffering hearing loss and sharp pains and needed his adenoids removed, a routine procedure similar to removing tonsils. Hans said he would sue the doctor if she went forward with the operation. He had been reading up on the subject. The problem, he thought, was probably allergies related to Nina's cat.

I close my eyes when the doctor recounts the call. I have a collection of correspondence between the local hospital and my father. My mother is dying of multiple sclerosis and they're refusing to offer treatment. In his letters to Swedish Covenant, he wrote it was too much of a burden to drive his sick wife to another hospital farther away, but they wouldn't relent. He was too disruptive, too threatening. When he sent me the letters along with his clippings and his unpublished memoir he must have thought I would see his side of the story. He kept the letters twenty years, evidence of the wrong done to him. But I know exactly why that hospital refused treatment to my mother. My father strongly distrusted doctors. Like Hans, he thought people were stupid, especially experts. What was the point of a college degree when it was so easy to lie on a résumé? My father was fond of books full of predictions made by specialists that turned out to be false. He was accustomed to people backing down and wasn't aware of the effect his temper had on others. In his memoir he writes about my mother's friends failing her, not coming around to keep her company after she fell ill. He doesn't remember slamming the door so hard it seemed the frames would splinter, and screaming, "Get the fuck out of my house!"

"I'll leave him," my mother told me once, struggling to hold her chin high. "I'll get better and I'll go back to England. You'll see." I was ten or eleven years old, sitting on the couch with her, the end of her blanket across my knees. We'd turned the television off and the house was stunned silent. I don't know if my father had just gone into the bedroom, or his basement office, or left again to meet one of his other women somewhere in the city. But there had been yelling, the kind you never get used to. It came from nowhere, or a place I was too young to understand. The noise was so loud, the violence reaching toward us until our ears threatened to pop. There was name calling; I was a cocksucker, motherfucker. There were accusations: "When we got married we had a bargain. I make the money and you take care of the children. You're not living up to your end of the bargain." We sat in the hum that always followed, a silence you could feel creeping across your skin like gel.

I was just starting to use drugs, opening the window near my bed at night, dropping softly onto the lawn. Running with Roger, Javier, and Justin to the park two blocks away. My mother was crying and angry, exhausted, trying and failing to keep her head steady, to sit forward. She wanted me to believe she could stand up for herself. But she couldn't. And I couldn't stand up for her. Or I could have, but I didn't. She should have gone, the day of her diagnosis, home to her parents and sisters in the small hill town outside of Sheffield, England. But it was too late now. Instead she was stuck in the North Side of Chicago. Her body became her prison. Her head shook violently and she leaned back against the pillow.*

As I got older and my mother got sicker she stopped confiding in me. I avoided her, or badgered her for money, with the result that my father stopped leaving money with her. She didn't complain anymore when she smelled cigarette smoke on my clothes or noticed the streaks

*My mother's type of MS is much less common today following the advent of drug treatments in the mid-nineties.

on my face that were left from inhaling spraypaint out of a plastic bag halfway down the alley. A year before she died, recognizing something in my look, she told me if I ran away, it would kill her. I didn't want the responsibility so I waited. I came home as little as possible, just long enough to do my chores: empty the bucket of urine next to the couch, wash the dishes, take out the trash, maybe make her a cup of instant coffee with lots of milk, maybe open myself a can of something to eat. Like her friends, I was chased away by my father's rage. Transformed by it, perhaps. That's what the caseworkers could never understand. It wasn't the handcuffs or the beatings or his shaving my head. That was nothing. It was the terror. I stayed away. I grew my hair out, skipped school, wore tattered rock T-shirts held together with safety pins. While the chemo glowed across my mother's atrophied frame I sat in the metal pumpkin at Indian Boundary Park, slid another hit of sunshine below my tongue, and waited for the gang to arrive. My mother cried frequently and I have a distinct impression toward the end she didn't care for me too much. I hadn't given her reason to. If she had gone into remission she might have left me behind as well. People tell me it's not true but I don't see how they would know.

Hans' mother, Beverly Palmer, wears a cobalt blue skirt that runs to her ankles and a matching jacket with a neck collar. She's almost seventy years old, with defenseless, wide-open eyes. Her bright copper hair, streaked with gold and white, rises in dry curls like an electric storm.

She takes the stand for two days but can hardly remember anything. She remembers Hans telling her he was sleeping in his car in the period between when Nina went missing and when he was arrested and charged with murder five weeks later. She wants to believe her only child isn't a killer and that Nina is hiding somewhere. She doesn't recall saying Nina was extremely conscientious and that leaving the children would be atypical of her, totally out of character, but she doesn't dispute it's her voice on the recording. She remembers being concerned about Nina's disappearance but she doesn't remember telling the police Nina was a lovely person. "I think people are a mixture of things."

When Palmer came back from Nevada Tuesday night, September 5, Hans met her at her friend's house. They were unpacking their things after a trip to the Burning Man Festival. Hans got a call while he was waiting. It was Nina's friend Ellen and a police officer. "Nina has been missing for two days," Ellen said. "You were the last to see her. Do you know where she might be?"

"You'll have to talk to my lawyer about that," Hans said, and hung up the phone.

When his mother was ready to go it was almost ten o'clock. Hans said he had something to tell her but it would upset her so he would tell her in the morning. She thought he wanted to borrow money again. He already owed her $40,000. But what he wanted to tell her was that the mother of her grandchildren was gone.

The next day Palmer found out that Hans had bought all new towels and stolen her car. She has two cars, a Honda Hybrid and a CRX that Hans often used. He wouldn't give her back the Hybrid. She asked where the CRX was and he wouldn't say. Up in the hills, without a car, you're stranded. Hora asks why she didn't call the police.

"I'm his mother," she says.

"So if he wants he can just take both cars?" Hora asks.

"I guess that's what it comes to, doesn't it?" she replies. She rented a car instead.

Everything that happened then is just a blur, or she's covering for her son. She remembers the new towels, but can't remember if the old towels were gone. She says the beam in the middle of the living room, where police found a smear of Nina's blood, hadn't been cleaned in twenty years. "I kept meaning to refinish it," she says. "But I never did." When the police found the smear, eleven days after Nina disappeared, the blood was still a bright red. The iron in the blood hadn't rusted into brown like all blood does eventually, and there was no dust or debris on top of the stain.*

*Blood cannot be dated through DNA testing.

Under cross-examination, Du Bois asks about her husband, the man she married after leaving Hans' father, who died seven years ago. "Is it fair to say he was the love of your life?"

"He was," she agrees.

"And since he died you have a hard time remembering things. Maybe you no longer care to remember things?"

"That's true. But I've never had a very good memory to begin with."

"Were you taking medication at the time?"

"No."

"Are you taking medication now?"

"Yes."

Hora plays a tape of a call from Hans after the police had tapped Beverly's phone, made September 23, at 9:06 PM:

HANS: *I had wanted to go to a mediator. I guess Nina decided that wouldn't be enough fun. It was more than that. She really had Munchausen by proxy disorder. She came up with these illnesses for Cori because she hated me and he was her proxy for me so by discovering he was borderline autistic that was her way of degrading me...Cori said he wanted to live only with me. That's because he understands his mother wants him to be sick and doesn't really like him on some deep conflicted level...She stole money. And you know, at the time I was asking people to take pay cuts she was spending money like crazy... She did things like kick me and then call the police...Being decent is a mistake. A mistake I paid for heavily...She didn't just abuse me, she looked for every possible way she could screw me and did it. The fact that I'd been a good husband just seemed like weakness to her.*

PALMER: *As awful as these things are, it's still sad whatever happened to Nina. Don't you think?*

HANS: *I think my children shouldn't be endangered by her. All I ever wanted was to be nice to her and give her an opportunity to come to the United States.*

PALMER: *But she didn't deserve what happened to her.*

HANS: *Yeah, and neither did I. Neither did my son. The whole court system made it so much worse than it had to be. These lawyers systematically drained us of everything we had...It may be hard to reach me for a while...Bye mom. I love you a lot.*

BEVERLY: *Ha. Good. Bye bye.*

"You remember that call?"

"Yes. Vaguely."

"Why did you sound so surprised at the end when he said he loved you?"

"I was nervous."

"You were nervous?"

"How could one not be nervous about this?"

"You mean when he calls you up and tells you how much he hates Nina twenty days after she disappeared. That made you nervous?"

On September 18, 2006, two weeks after Nina disappeared, Hans met Artem Mishim at a custody hearing for Hans' children. The county had taken the children. Hans knew Artem from the judo academy where he took classes and Artem had agreed to be a character witness.

"How's it going, Scott?" Artem said. He was making a joke, referring to Scott Peterson. After court they left together, driving a strange path through Berkeley, avoiding the highway and major streets, then stopping for dinner on Solano Avenue. Following dinner they looked beneath the car, as if they were worried someone had placed a tracking device. At the end of the evening Artem dropped Hans in Berkeley and Hans walked four blocks to the Honda CRX, which he'd left hidden on a side street. It took him thirty minutes to walk to the car, even though it was five minutes away. He walked around the block, past the car, then doubled back before climbing inside. He drove to the bottom of Shepherd's Canyon, parked the car near the highway where his mother or the police were unlikely to find it, and sprinted up the hill toward his home.

The police had been following Hans the entire day, using at least a dozen vehicles and a fixed-wing plane with glass sides and gyroscope-mounted binoculars. They wanted the CRX, which they thought held the key to unlocking the mystery behind Nina's disappearance. But the car posed more questions than it answered. The CRX had been thoroughly scrubbed, the floors soaked, the compartments holding an inch of standing water. The passenger seat was missing along with whatever it did or didn't contain. Hans was hiding something, but they were moving farther away from finding it.

"Where did he put the seat?" I ask Du Bois during recess.

"He threw it in a dumpster," Du Bois says.

"That doesn't make any sense," I say. "It's one thing to remove a seat, it's another to throw it away. It wasn't even his car."

I ask him about a drawing Cori drew of his father coming down the stairs to the basement where the two children are sleeping, carrying Nina in his arms.

"That's ridiculous," Du Bois says. "Why would Hans carry his dead wife into his children's room?"

"You want us to accept that he's rational when it comes to carrying his dead wife down the stairs, but irrational when he throws away a perfectly good car seat?"

Du Bois barely acknowledges my comment. "All of that will come out in the trial." This is a hallmark of the case, Du Bois promising some exciting new detail in the coming days that will prove his client's innocence, and then failing to deliver. A TV producer asks Judge Goodman if the case is likely to stretch into a fourth month and he says no. "I don't think the defense has much of a case." He means the defense isn't going to call many witnesses, but the subtext is obvious.

I ask Du Bois why the children haven't seen or heard from their mother. "If she wants to carry this charade out she has to stay away from her children for now." It occurs to me that Du Bois must know what he's saying isn't true. Nina's dead and he's aware of that. She's certainly not in Russia, where her disappearance is front-page news. Why would she work so hard to get American citizenship only to frame Hans with a murder, abandon her children, and go into permanent hiding? She wouldn't even know Hans was going to be charged with murder. I point this out to some friends. "He's lying," I say. "He's just doing his job," they reply. Du Bois continues to say everything will be explained in the trial, but I doubt it. I can see how he communicates. The strategy of the defense is to confuse situations. He's not going to answer questions; he's going to propose possibilities. The point is not truth. The point of the defense is that there is no truth.

LAX

Rafael Campo

"Don't talk to me, I'm driving," Palm trees sway
beneath a sky of airplanes, sky of blue.
I think we're lost, but don't know what to say.

Beneath a sky of airplanes, sky of blue
an enemy descended. Something frayed.
We pass another parking lot, asphalt gloom.

Don't talk to me—I'm praying as they sway,
reliving those twin towers, love and doom.
I'm sure we're lost. I hope my flight's delayed.

O sky of blue, beneath you we are few:
An endless movie set, an endless day,
Black, Muslim, homosexual, and Jew—

are they lost, those Mexicans who we say
must be illegal? We pass them by, dimmed in the blue-
gray haze of the car's exhaust. Palm trees sway,

reminding us to witness beauty's truth,
that place where minds end, where the longest day
begins again. We're lost, beneath the blue

and freeway exit signs that point the way
toward God. Airplanes roar, saying nothing new.
Don't waste this time, I think, while palm trees sway.
I know we're lost, but can't think what to say.

POINT LOBOS OUTLOOK

Jim Powell

PERSISTENT at the brink, the cypresses
lean away backward to receive the winds
prevailing on this spot, balancing
resistance and compensation in the open-weave
basketwork of their limbs:

weight braced facing a single way
against an invisible pressure from ahead
in veering weather and when the air falls quiet
steadfast in the same stance, a posture of defense
by success, then habit,

decides the limits of a life—but Susan, look,
we are not rooted in one place,
we are not stuck
in the identical configuration
always:

we can
step across our shadows

we can turn
and face the light.

WATTS TOWERS—A SOARING, BAFFLING MONUMENT

Robin Rauzi

WATTS IS NOT MONTREAL. The latter is where I thought I would be about now, squeezing a week of Euro-esque travel out of my handful of vacation days and Euro-unfriendly budget. Those plans, however, were derailed by the onset of an acute bout of joblessness. And so my unplanned summer stay-cation began with a midday trip down the Harbor Freeway.

An Angeleno who has never toured Watts Towers is the urban equivalent of a New Yorker who has never bothered with the Statue of Liberty. You think it will always be there, that you'll get to it someday, maybe when you have out-of-town visitors. And then 14 years later, you find yourself staring at a job posting in Ohio or Oregon and realize you might leave L.A. without having made the trip.

On a smoggy Friday, I exited at Century Boulevard prepared to be underwhelmed. The website said the towers were "scaffolded." When I called, I was warned that I could see them only "through the fence." Tours had been restricted since May 2008, when FEMA coughed up $569,000 to repair damage from torrential winter rains three years previous. The scheduled March 2009 re-opening had been delayed to at least late September; three workmen had been laid off because of the city's budget crisis.

Still, there were plenty of undeterred visitors. I joined half a dozen in the adjacent Watts Towers Arts Center for the 12-minute documentary, "The Towers." The 1957 film—made before Watts Towers was laden with cultural and political symbolism—has an odd, noir feel. A narrator's gravelly voice sets the scene over an eerie "Twilight Zone"-ish flute: "The little city of Watts clings to the outer edge of the city of Los Angeles, a scattered collection of shacks, trailers and weather-beaten bungalows. Flat and impoverished, it is the last place on Earth to look for the extraordinary."

More stucco, fewer trailers, but otherwise the assessment of Watts holds up. I stepped outside with a guide to see what I could. As it turned out, the scaffolding was gone and plenty can be seen through the fence.

My guide laid out the story of Sabato ("Simon" or "Sam") Rodia, the 4-foot-11 immigrant from southern Italy who'd started out in Pennsylvania's coal mines before heading west. Multiple wives and many unaccounted for years later, he arrived in Southern California, bought a wedge of land right up against the Red Car tracks, and in 1921 began building a landmark during evenings and weekends. He was 42.

In 1954, when he was about 75, Rodia left, handing the deed to a neighbor. Many narratives paint his departure as mysteriously abrupt, but my tour guide said he'd fallen and broken a hip and went to live with his sister.

Writers have offered many poetic and erudite descriptions of Rodia's creation, and it's hopeless to try to match them. Suffice it to say that the towers are a folk art marvel on the micro and macro levels. Thousands of small bits of tile, pottery, colored bottle glass, shells and even ceramic figurines adorn the walls, fountains, basins and mortar-encased towers—17 structures in all. And yet for all that detail, parts soar nearly 100 feet. If the Statue of Liberty stepped off her pedestal and strolled over to Watts, Rodia's tallest spires would reach past her chin.

If Watts Towers, like Lady Liberty at the mouth of the Hudson River, was positioned in a prominent locale (say next to the intersection of the 10 and the 405), more Angelenos might demand it get sufficient attention and care from the tangle of government agencies it's been entrusted to. The skinny pie-slice of a lot and adjacent park are owned by the California State Parks but administered by Los Angeles' Department of Cultural Affairs, under a lease that lasts another 20 years. Since 1990, the site also has been on the National Register of Historic Landmarks, but that means it's worthy of protection, not that there's cash set aside to do it.

Just last month, two city commissions—Cultural Affairs and Cultural Heritage—met at City Hall to face dogged complaints of inadequate maintenance and poor conservation at the towers. There's talk of asking for help from the Getty Conservation Institute or from the Los Angeles County Museum of Art, and of soliciting private donations. It'll take an estimated $5 million to get them back in prime condition, and probably lots of years of scaffolding and looking through the fence.

It's a funny thing about monuments. They're designed to immortalize a specific person or idea. But meanings, like concrete exposed to the elements, can be unexpectedly fragile. The Statue of Liberty, a gift from France marking our nations' shared history of revolution, soon represented the U.S. as an immigrant nation, as new arrivals sailed past on their way to Ellis Island. It wasn't until 1903, 17 years after the statue was installed, that Emma Lazarus' poem ("Give me your tired, your poor...") was engraved on a plaque there. For me, its proximity to lower Manhattan has refocused its symbolism on other aspects of liberty since 9/11.

Symbolism and interpretations have accumulated on Rodia's magnificent piece of "outsider art," so much so that Italy's University of Genoa hosted an international conference about it in April. Ordinary visitors like me stand looking at the filigree and make of it what they will. Maybe they stand across 107th Street and trace the towers' ship-like profile and see the Italian immigrant as another new-world explorer. That the towers emerged unscathed from the 1965 Watts riots transformed them into a symbol of the African American neighborhood and black pride. Others see in the mosaic of broken tiles, Asian dishes, glass and shells a beautiful metaphor for diverse Los Angeles, or in their decay, government's inability to do anything right. Some reflect on Rodia's lost years of drifting and alcoholism and read spiritual redemption. Others chalk it all up to the work of an obsessed madman.

On that smoggy jobless Friday, when I looked at Watts Towers, here's the message it gave to me: Halfway through life, you can start again and build something new.

THIS AIN'T SAN FRANCISCO

Cheryl Klein

ANNA LISA: LILAC MINES, 1965

There were no direct buses from Fresno to San Francisco within Anna Lisa's price range. This one curves up the arched spine of the state into towns with names like Angels Camp and Lilac Mines. At each stop they pick up a few more people until, by Lilac Mines, Anna Lisa feels like an old timer. The girl next to her—who got on in Modesto—bounces a red-faced baby on her lap. She sings songs and plays pat-a-cake, but the child keeps crying. A few people grumble, but most shoot mother and child looks of tired sympathy. Anna Lisa doesn't feel sorry for them. *The world loves you*, she thinks. The woman is doing what women are supposed to do. In Lilac Mines, a barely-there town at the foot of a mountain, she steps out to give her ears a break.

She's scared to leave her suitcase—the one that sat, packed, in her closet for three weeks while she worked up the courage to leave, saved her money, composed a note that explained as much as she could without explaining too much—in the bus, so she lugs it to the drugstore, where she scans the menu for cherry cola. It's not there, so she settles for regular. Her throat and stomach welcome the icy sweetness. Even though she's wearing her thinnest dress, blue-flowered and nearly transparent, the heat is sinister in its persistence. At the other end of the soda fountain, a young man takes his own soda from the shopkeeper. When he sits down next to Anna Lisa, she sees that there's a cherry in his.

"I thought they didn't have cherry cola," she says. "It wasn't on the menu."

"Just gotta ask," he says, smiling. She recognizes him from the bus. He has thick hair that grows in several different directions, or maybe that's just the legacy of napping on the road. There's a gap in his smile. "I'm John."

What a horribly dull name, Anna Lisa thinks. Boys so frequently have dull names. She likes the way girls' names sound like flowers, even names that aren't Rose or Daisy. Even names like Christine and Delia and Phoebe.

"Anna Lisa," she says.

"Nice to meet you, Anna Lisa. Can I buy you cherry cola?"

"Oh, no, thank you," she says quickly. She's only gone on one date before. She didn't know what to do with her hands or where to look, afraid of what each gesture might mean to this creature who opened doors and twisted his class ring on his finger. She's not sure if John is trying to turn their bus break into a date, but she doesn't want to take any chances. She lifts her glass. "I'm almost done with this one anyway."

John is unfazed. The world is full of girls thirsty for cherry cola. "So why are you going to Eureka?" he asks.

"I'm not, I'm going to San Francisco." She didn't pay attention to where the bus went after that. She hopes he won't ask why she's going to San Francisco.

John frowns. "Not on this bus, I hope. This bus goes through a few more small towns and then on up to Eureka. I'm going to get a logging job."

"No, it goes to San Francisco first." Her voice is thin, existing only in her mouth, as if her lungs have deserted her.

Now John smiles with half his mouth. The look is part pity, part righteousness. "You can check at the bus station if you want."

Anna Lisa leaves her soda in its ring of condensation and runs out of the drugstore, slamming her suitcase into a rack of magazines that she doesn't bother to pick up. It's late Saturday afternoon; the sign on the single window of the tiny bus station informs her that it closed an hour ago and will not re-open until Monday morning. But a yellowed schedule confirms that John is right: the bus she's on will snake through the Sacramento Valley and stop in Eureka, skipping San Francisco. The next bus to San Francisco departs Wednesday. She has enough money for a ticket, but not if she spends four nights in a hotel. The next bus back to Fresno costs less and leaves Tuesday, which she can manage if she doesn't eat over the weekend. She reaches into her purse and touches the stack of bills curled like a snail in hopes of divining an answer. She can't believe her own stupidity. She replays her original ticket purchase over and over—her question whispered so low that the woman at the window made her repeat it three times.

Maybe, Anna Lisa concludes, she is not meant to go to San Francisco. Maybe San Francisco is for girls like the girls of 3-B, girls who smoke and wear black stockings. Destiny is laughing at her for thinking she could have a big, wild life. She should call her parents now. She can hear her mother's voice: *I don't know what got into you.* Anna Lisa will repeat it back: *I don't know what got into me*, affirming her mother in herself, her promise to live a life more like her mother's from now on.

But for the moment there's no leaving Lilac Mines. She checks into the first hotel she finds, the Lilac Mines Hotel, quite possibly the only one. As soon as she rattles open the door to her room with a skeleton key, she flings herself on the bed. Her sweat-drenched dress clings to her torso and legs, and the comforter is itchy, but her lungs have returned to her. A giant sigh leaves her body. She relaxes into the secure sleep of a decision made for her, if just for tonight.

When she wakes up, the room is dark. For a minute she's not sure where she is. Her hands grope for something familiar. They land on her watch. It's 10:15. Outside her window the moon is a copper penny demanding to be spent. This may be her only night away. She can't imagine sleeping through till morning.

Downstairs the restaurant-and-bar is sparsely populated, but somehow it glows enticingly. She thinks of saloons in Westerns, swinging doors, girls in ruffles and garters. This must be what those bars look like in color, when you're *in* one and not just watching. She has changed from her wilted dress to a pair of slacks. Now her thighs don't stick together; she feels vaguely like a cowboy. She sits at a small round table in the corner, hoping the waiter won't see her for a while, since she can't order anything. She touches the round slump of her belly, wondering how long she can go without food. Already she is hungry, but maybe her body will give up hope of being fed if she waits long enough.

Anna Lisa finds herself gazing at the broad back of a man at the bar. He's wearing a work shirt, his hand rests on a bottle of beer the same light amber as his hair. Mushrooming over the barstool, his hips are large for a man's. There are so many things Anna Lisa doesn't know how to do: talk to boys, order a drink, buy a bus ticket apparently. Are these skills a matter of time or destiny? What would happen if she transformed herself into a person like Suzy? If she walked up to the man at the bar and said something friendly? She reminds herself that nothing will come of it—she's returning to Fresno in a few days—and this emboldens her.

She slides onto a stool near the man with the beer, leaving a stool between them. The bartender is on the other side of the square bar, twirling a rag on his finger with a blend of boredom and intense concentration. The man glances up at her, then back down. Anna Lisa wills herself to look at him. She takes in his profile: small straight nose, soft chin, freckles a shade lighter than her own. Blonde eyebrows that fade out at the edges. And somewhere in these details lies a revelation. The man is a woman.

"Hi," she says, which is what she'd planned to say to a man, too. She did not know a woman could look like this. She did not know that girl hips could find a home in straight brown trousers. As alien as the ensemble is, she's the right alien for it; on her planet, this must be what women look like.

"Hey," she says. Her voice is dark ale.

"Do you live here?" Anna Lisa needs to know where this planet is.

"What's it to you?"

"I just wondered..." Anna Lisa stutters. "I was going to San Francisco," she adds, as if this explains her presence in Lilac Mines.

The woman makes a face not unlike John's, but it's just a stopping point on her way to a full smile. "Well, this ain't San Francisco. But sure, I live here. It's not so bad."

"I'm Anna Lisa."

The woman laughs. "Seriously? You sure don't look like an Anna Lisa."

Anna Lisa has never thought about what she looked like, name wise. It's just something she was born into. Now she has a burning desire to know what she *does* look like, but she can't ask; it would seem flirtatious.

"Name's Jody." Indeed, Jody looks like a Jody: Irish, tough, friendly, boyish. "Hey, what're you drinking?"

"Um, I'm not. I'm too young, and besides—"

"Gotta start sometime, right?" Jody waves to the bartender. "A Pabst for my friend, *Anna Lisa.*" She says it in that inside-joke way, and in this faraway bar with a woman who looks like a man, Anna Lisa feels like one of the girls. The warmth in her chest is so strong and rare that she can't send back the bottle that lands in front of her, an uncapped twin to Jody's.

Is it possible that Jody is buying the beer *for* her? She's not sure if she wants this to be the case or not, but when the bartender—his fingers tickling the rag at his side, promising to return to it—says, "Sixty-five cents," Jody doesn't reach for the wallet that bulges from her back pocket.

So Anna Lisa extracts her coin purse, which she suddenly wishes were a real wallet. She touches the coins it would take to pay for the beer. She touches the sleeping bills next to them. Blood races past her ears. "Can I also get a ham and cheese sandwich?" she hears herself saying. The words make her hunger rear up, stomp its feet. "And a side of mashed potatoes?" she says. "And a strawberry shake?"

"All right," Jody says. "That's what I call a real man's appetite." If Anna Lisa's mother said she was eating like a man, she'd be telling her daughter to slow down, chew 20 times before swallowing. But from Jody it sounds like a compliment.

Jody washes dishes at "this bar down on Calla Boulevard" four nights a week and is helping a man fix his barn. What Jody really wants is a job at the sawmill, she says. That's where the good jobs are. Jody shakes her head and runs her fingers through her short, fuzzy hair. Jody says there are ghosts in the mines above town if you're stupid enough to believe in that stuff. Jody smells vaguely like wood. Jody is intimate but guarded. Jody seems to be inviting Anna Lisa somewhere, but she's not about to give away the directions.

When Anna Lisa's shake is half gone and there is only an inch of bitter-tasting beer left in the bottle, a Negro woman walks into the restaurant. She wears a red dress that matches her lipstick and clutches her purse with both hands. When she spots Jody, she lets her purse slide down her arm and swing on her elbow.

"That's my girl," Jody says to Anna Lisa without taking her eyes off the woman.

Can a girl have a girl? Can a white girl have a black girl? The possibilities make Anna Lisa's head throb. Could she have a girl?

Jody makes introductions: Imogen, Anna Lisa. Anna Lisa, Imogen. There were three Negroes at Lincoln High School. Anna Lisa knew each of their names and never had occasion to talk to any of them. Imogen is standing so close Anna Lisa can see the clumps of mascara on her eyelashes. And she's Jody's girl. Anna Lisa feels slightly dizzy. Maybe it's the beer.

"We're going over to Lilac's," Jody says. "It's the bar where I work, 'cept I'm off tonight. Wanna come?"

Imogen looks at Jody, alarmed. "Is she cool?"

Jody smiles. "I've got a hunch."

Imogen has not touched Jody, but from the way she rolls her eyes beneath her mascara and her night-blue eyeshadow, Anna Lisa knows they have been together a long time and that they are in love. "*Your* hunches are always getting *us* in trouble. But I'm not one to be rude. Anna Lisa, you said your name was? Come on with us."

They leave Main Street behind and begin climbing Calla Boulevard, a steep street with older buildings and shorter streetlights. Anna Lisa studies the figures in front of her on the narrow sidewalk. Jody's love handles, her echoing work boots that hint at hollows beneath the pavement, her hair that might be called strawberry blonde if the title didn't seem somehow undignified. Imogen clicks along next to her. Thin waist and unashamed breasts wrapped in rose print. Her black hair is curled in a controlled and intricate pattern. Her arm swings next to Jody's, occasionally brushing it. As if this were all perfectly natural.

Anna Lisa's breath quickens as they climb. And we're going to a *bar*, she thinks.

Jody stops abruptly in front of a squat, wood-sided building. There's no sign over the closed door, but a rectangular halo of light surrounds it. The night has turned chilly, and Anna Lisa imagines it's warm inside. When Jody halts, Anna Lisa bumps into her.

"Okay, here's the rules," Jody says. "No putting the moves on somebody else's girl, but I don't think you're dumb enough to do that. No nursing one beer all night—you're in a bar, you drink. And if Caleb flashes the light, it means stop dancing or switch to a guy, 'cause the cops are coming."

Imogen puts a hand on Anna Lisa's shoulder. It's warm and heavy. "We don't have cops. We have one sheriff who bothers with us maybe once every two months. Just breathe, honey."

Anna Lisa doesn't know what the insides of regular bars look like. She doesn't know the names of beers. She thinks 90 cents sounds expensive, but she can't be sure. She's never danced with anyone besides her own relatives at weddings.

The first beer has already rendered the night twirly, but she follows Jody's lead and orders a Rheingold. Her voice is so quiet that Caleb, a thin man with dark, center-parted hair and a blue turtleneck sweater—what Anna Lisa imagines a poet might look like—makes her repeat it twice. She hands him her money and silently says goodbye to her trip home.

"You gotta tip, honey," Imogen whispers.

The bar is dark with low ceilings. But the people: Anna Lisa's entire body tingles like a sleeping limb awakening. There are more women like Jody. They prop elbows on the bar, extend booted feet into walkways, emit low whistles at pretty girls. Upon seeing these women who act like men, Anna Lisa is startled by just how differently the sexes carry themselves. The women who look like Imogen—except white—slide into the gazes of the Jodies. They figure-eight around tables and pull their limbs inward in a way that somehow exposes as it conceals: crossed legs revealing a sliver of thigh, crossed arms summoning cleavage. None of them look like the girls of 3-B, but Anna Lisa realizes this bar is nevertheless her book. The black ink has lifted; she's been invited to look and look.

FRIENDLY FIRE

Ruth Nolan

THE ATTIC DOOR opened easily
that pearl smooth August night
after a day hitchhiking in dusty wind,
no real labor, no hard breathing.

One push, we climbed on the roof,
two sunburned, runaway teenage girls,
a backpack full of cheese and fruit
stolen from the market that day.

We'd broken into a desert cabin.
I shot a window with my father's gun.
No one had been there for so long
the refrigerator was propped open.

We crawled through splintered glass.
You worried that there might be
a dead baby or rattlesnake inside.
I found an unopened bottle of wine.

I held the buck knife, and you held
the fruit. I sliced the salami and
licked my sticky fingers, then you
twisted the corkscrew and laughed.

We sifted through the box of jewels
stolen from our moms. You clasped
a silver necklace on my burnt neck
and I slipped an old ring onto you.

We shared an old wool army blanket
and a man's extra-large flannel shirt,
talked about all the guys we shared,
cock and breast size, abortion cramps.

You wanted to know what it was like
to fight fires; I told you I had no sisters.
I popped the cork, you passed the bottle.
I thought I could taste your tongue,

delivered like the silent rise of moon,
punctuating spaces between stars.
I watched Venus, Orion's Belt fade
while you spread oysters onto rye.

NORMA'S LINES

Tim Z. Hernandez

CONCERNING THE INHERITANCE OF SOLTERIA

SHE COMES FROM a long line of believers. All the way back to her great-great abuela, Rosa Constante de Felix, or as everyone referred to her, La Morena. Her mother never lets her forget that behind those quick cumbia steps she's mastered since the age of four, her hips, alma, y corazón run thick with sangre pura desde Matanzas, Cuba. It's true. She's seen the photographs herself.

Once, when Norma was barely nine, her mother threw herself a pity party after being denied (for the third time) a green card. Present were a few neighbors, tías and their kids, and a dozen stray dogs. After everyone had crashed out and nothing but spilled bottles were left dancing on the empty floor, Norma's mother lugged out the ragged suitcase from beneath her bed and filed through the old photographs with her.

"See here," she said, pointing to a sepia photo of a teenage girl. "This is your great abuela, Norma Hilda Gonzalez. This picture was taken around 1900. She's pretty, no?"

Even though she clearly had a moustache that rivaled any man's, Norma nods politely and says, "Sí, 'amá, guapísima."

Next, her mother lifts out a warped black-and-white shot of an old woman and a young girl. "Who's this?" Norma asks.

"You don't recognize the girl?" her mother says, grinning sloppily from ear to ear. Her breath reeks of rum, but Norma doesn't mind because she rarely sees her smile these days and she'll take what she can get. She shakes her head. "Quién es?"

"That's me. When I was a little girl. And that's your abuela, when she was much younger too."

Her mother gets a faraway look in her eyes, and is nothing but a statue with her cold arm around Norma. She bends over and shuffles her fingers through the leaves of paper until she comes across a funny-looking woman dressed in tights and made up like a French ballerina. The photo itself looks as if it was snapped by a photographer on his first day of sobriety.

"Who's this?" she asks her mother.

Her mother snatches it from her hand and gazes into it, then shakes her head and laughs. "La Morena."

Here is where for the first time Norma is made aware that her great-great abuela, Rosa Constante de Felix, was a circus freak. Behind La Morena stands a deformed kid with fins for hands. A seal boy, just like the ones she's seen on PBS documentaries, whose legs were also attached mermaid-like at birth, and the only place anyone like that can turn to is a caravan of like-limbed bizarros who make a living and travel the world off their deformities. A massive beefy arm hangs over La Morena's shoulder and it belongs to the brick-headed muscle man who towers over the entire group of carnies. To the far left, squinting at La Morena with a fierce scowl, is a short woman with skin black as an orisha's kink, and an enormous bone pierced in one cheek and out the other. The whites of her eyes are haunting, and the pupils look as if they'll jump out of her skull and attack La Morena any second. She is clearly giving Norma's great-great abuela mal de ojo. But La Morena is poised. Because her only abnormalities are her gargantuan legs, muscular from years of tightrope walking, and her supple facial features. If she wasn't so dark, her mother once said, she'd look like one of those Russian matryoshka dolls. Norma has no idea what that is, but trusts that she is dead on.

"Why is that lady staring at her like that?" she asks.

Her mother doesn't tell her in that moment. Only mentions that it's way past her bedtime and shoos her off to her room. Norma stays up that night with the image of that bruja's eyes burned into her nine-year-old thoughts. And every time the house creaks on its own she swears it is her spirit coming to possess her. To distract herself, she thinks about the other photographs. Except for a few male cousins who were caught in the background doing some crazy shit like pinching their weenies, most of the people who populate her mother's old suitcase are women. Single women. She closes her eyes, content in knowing that her mother does not belong to this group, and for the time being, neither does she

As a child Norma has spent time observing her mother and father, and how they aren't afraid of public displays of affection. The way he grabs her mother's face with both hands every time they kiss, or the way her voice changes and sounds light and airy when she replies to him in a loving manner. Sometimes, when the moment feels right, she wedges herself between their embrace like sandwich meat, and relishes their sloppy love. These moments are especially memorable, and she'll hang on to them dearly for the rest of her life.

But when her mom gets to arguing with her grandmother over the phone about just how much love a woman can give a man before she loses herself completely and becomes nothing more than his esclava, Norma sees it in her mother's eyes, a hiccup of hesitation. As if for a nanosecond she considers her abuela's words. But then, thankfully, her mother recalls the three generations of uncommitted, loveless, and sexless women trapped in her suitcase. God forbid they try and put up a smile, or some hint of contentment long enough for a photograph to be taken. In the background, yards sunken and cluttered with dead things, flattened basketballs, car batteries, crow carcasses. Porches are nothing more than piles of sulking lumber infested with nails and splinters. In the kitchens, peeled linoleum and leaky faucets. In the living room, a warped velvet painting of La Virgen de Guadalupe, with the tiny cherub looking stepped on and defeated. All of this, evidence that whatever man once inhabited each of their lives, if only long enough to plant their seeds, was now nothing more than a memory. A bad one at that. Her mother thinks about all this. Norma thinks about all this. And early the next morning, while soaking in the bathtub before school, she clasps her small hands and thanks the sweet Lord for her mother and father, and all the shit they put up with in the name of love—in her name.

Right out of high school Norma and Lupe decide to move in together, and of course no one approves. Especially her mother.

"Hija, what are people gonna think when they see you two?" she says, packing on the guilt. Norma ignores her. "Catela is a small town," her mother continues. "Remember, people talk." But how could she ever forget. She's reminded every time her and Lupe hold hands in public.

Each morning she wakes up with her lover's warm breath spilling over her like a bucket of lechera. There is a sweet milkiness about it that she can't get enough of. Like clockwork, Lupe cooks breakfast for the two of them while she takes out the trash, and then they talk about what the day has in store. She complains to Lupe about how she can't stand working at the fruit packing plant with all the macho assholes cat-calling her non-stop, and how the shift manager just looks away and pretends to be deaf. And then Lupe tells her to quit and go back to school like she's always wanted, and for the hundredth time she has to explain why college isn't a good idea right now.

And then one day, as quickly as it started, it all comes to an end. Not like in *Love Story* where the love is intense and then one gets sick and dies and the other is there devoted until the last breath. Nothing like that.

Lupe is gone. Left Catela for good—according to the short note. Norma is alone. And in that loneliness she pulls out the suitcase that once belonged to her mother and father. One by one the pictures begin to make sense.

She glances over at a photo of her and Lupe that sits atop the television. Lupe is wearing a tank top and her supple shoulders shine from the hot lights of a flea market vendor. Norma is smiling, but Lupe's lips are barely lifted and her dark beautiful eyes seem to be saying something that only now, in the presence of all these photos of uncommitted, loveless, and sexless women, Norma is able to read. And in that moment, like a train wreck, it hits her. La Morena's blood isn't the only thing she has inherited.

HOW TO DATE A WHITE GUY

Naira Kuzmich

FIRST OF ALL, don't complicate things. You only need one card. If you're a Persian Jew, be Persian. If you're a poor Arab, that's great, that's quite sad, but also a bit redundant. Just say which country, which village you're from. If you're mixed, pick the one with the most syllables or better, the one currently being bombed. If you're American-born anything, remember: you are not American enough and you never will be. Pick a card and embrace it.

This is how it'll go down. You'll be at a lounge with your friends. You'll be wearing a dress that is two sizes too small for your chest and barely manages to get around your hips. But don't worry. This isn't your fault. You're not the target audience or the ideal customer. No one makes clothes for you but your grandmother, who still knits those unattractive blue and pink blouses that you wear from time-to-time to make her happy. Your friends think the shirts are *kitschy* and *cute*. They'll be wearing designer jeans with holes in them, sporting cool and ironic tees that say things like "Talk Nerdy to Me" or "Save a Horse: Ride a Cowboy." They like shopping at thrift stores, like walking down the streets of Silver Lake and Echo Park and feeling one with the people. They pay five dollars for two-dollar tacos from the Korean lady manning the truck ever since the Mexican was sent back. They say, *Keep the change*.

It'll be hot and packed inside the lounge and the dress fabric will cling to your skin. You'll be uncomfortable; you knew you should've worn pants but you don't go out often and you wanted to make this night count. Of course, though you don't want to admit this to yourself, by now you know "making it count" means making men want you.

This comes easy for you. It's in your blood.

The dress will do its job. Men will guide their hands to your stomach, piloting your waist as they make their way towards the crowded bar. They'll drop their phones impossibly close to your feet. They will bend and rise slowly. You'll smile meekly, sometimes meeting their eyes, more often not. Your parents raised you better, though not well enough. You're here, aren't you?

A faint blush will attack your cheeks, something warm filling your insides. You move your legs slightly closer together. Your thighs are strong and firm, like your mother's. You're a woman of the land. No explorer would leave your hearth for the dangerous seas. You are a find. Someone should say things like this to you. In this light, you are stunning.

You begin moving to the music, your neck rolling from left to right, dipping into a bare shoulder as your friend rants about that *asshole* in HR. You'll cringe imperceptibly. She uses such ugly words. You don't like to curse. Your mother poured chili pepper on your tongue when you were nine, when she heard you call your friend a "slut." Two years later, when she asked you what a virgin was, she smacked you for knowing.

Your hips are your best weapon and they'll rock and ripple in pleasure once the music picks up. You can't control yourself. It just does something to you. It's that beat, that rhythmic pounding, a reminder of distant drums and clashing cymbals; it awakens something in you—a secret throbbing, a fire. Your hands spin in shapes of delicate flowers and birds, of feathered creatures finding flight after periods caged. Remove that clip in your hair. Shake that dark mane of yours wild and free. Let it flood over the valleys of your shoulders. Let it relieve the yearning of your hard terrain. You'll be an explosion of light.

You'll see him. He won't be like all the others. You can tell he's an artist, someone who's sensitive. Maybe a writer, maybe a singer of sad songs. He wears a scarf. You'll try to catch his eye and when he finally notices, you won't look away. There's something in his gaze. There's something there.

Your friends will notice, will push you playfully towards him. "Go to him, girl," they'll say. "You deserve a little fun."

But they don't understand. You're not looking for fun. You're looking for meaning. You're looking for someone to save you.

Besides, you're a little old-fashioned, aren't you? A classy woman—a real throwback to those silent film stars, the beautiful damsels tied to railroad tracks. They don't make them like you anymore. You'll wait for him to come to you.

He'll approach you confidently. He'll have a beer in his hand and he'll take a long sip from it when he finally stops in front of you. "You make me nervous," he'll say and you'll be charmed.

Your friends will disappear. Good. They understand this game.

You'll exchange names. His will be something like John or Jack or Jim—something with a J, something typical and boring. If he's smart, he'll make a joke about this. Not like your name. So beautiful. He'll ask for its meaning. Give it to him. Land of the Canyons. Bringer of Hope. Gazelle Returning From Water. Your people have such a way with words. It'll excite him. He'll tell you (you were right!) he's a writer. You'll be impressed. He'll say you're prettier than anything he'd write. When he goes outside for a smoke, go with him.

He'll lean against the wall, cigarette in his mouth, and you will stand in front of him, between his feet. You're tall but he'll be taller, bigger. He'll make you feel small and safe. A few bystanders will whistle appreciatively; one or two will say something about your backside. He will throw down his cigarette in disgust and grab your hand, whisper *fucking assholes* against your skin. He'll want to defend your honor but you won't let him. You've had enough with all of the fighting.

Lean over and kiss him. You'll never have done this before but you can tell he's an amazing kisser. You'll worry if you're doing okay—don't. You're a natural. When you part for air, he'll growl against your neck. He'll say, "What have you done to me?"

He'll call you the next day and this is where things get difficult, but trust him, trust this—it'll help you get through the tough times. Lie to your parents about where you're going and who you're meeting. Tell them it's Zainah from Bio 310. Remember? They met her last year.

They let you go to that engineering conference in Houston once they saw that she was a sensible girl. She has her head on straight, they said. Her hair covered. You'll skip lab once or twice a week to squeeze in more time with him. Your grades will falter but if this all goes well, it won't matter. He'll take care of you. Stop going to those MCAT prep courses. Free your weeknights.

You two will talk and talk and he'll hang on to your every single word. He'll remember everything. He'll ask a lot of questions. Did you guys have power at night? Did your parents ever protest the regime? What's it like? He'll want to know everything about you. You'll find yourself telling him about some of your outdated traditions, about mother-in-laws waving bloodied bed-sheets like flags of honor or new fathers sacrificing lambs to ensure the survival of their sons. You'll say some phrases you learned as a kid, sing a few lullabies, and they'll roll off your tongue like stones thrown from Heaven, sounding lovelier than ever. He will lap them up like honey. Tell me more, he'll insist. Say it again. But slower. Slower.

He'll take you places. He'll know his city like the back of his hand. He'll love to travel. This'll be yet another thing you'll have in common. You come from a nomadic people and he is the son of conquistadors. You will kiss his eyes as he struggles to remember a poem in bed. You will hold his hand inside a tapas bar as he cries about his dead grandfather. He'll talk and talk and you'll listen. He'll have an incredible speaking voice and though his life won't be as exciting as yours, his stories will captivate you. You will never have imagined such intimacies. You were a product of an arranged marriage. Your mother's wide hips sealed the deal. Your parents never really liked each other. But you—you have found love. Consider yourself blessed.

Your parents will find out about him. It won't be your fault, or his—he just couldn't help himself. He was being thoughtful. He will have sent you a Valentine's Day bouquet in the mail. You won't hold it against him when your father calls you a whore, throwing the flowers in your face, the thorns scratching your cheeks and giving them a nice, red glow. Was it worth it, he'll ask. Did he make you feel special? Look your father in the eye and tell him yes. He'll call you a fool. He'll spit at your feet.

Pack your stuff while your mother weeps in the bathroom. Don't forget to take your grandmother's handmade quilt, the one collecting dust underneath your bed. Now you've found a use for it. Imagine making love to him on its rough surface.

Leave before they shut you out of the house. Because they will—you're sure of it. You won't look back.

When he comes to pick you up, he'll say that he loves you, that he's going to marry you, that he can't wait to see you round with his kid.

But promise, he'll say. Promise at the wedding we'll slaughter a cow like your people do.

LOVE POEM FOR LOS ANGELES

Sandra Beasley

TWO HUNDRED YEARS AGO, we set out west one
oath at a time, a long game of Telephone: You

are our strangest echo, the promise of Great American
Self-Storage. Los Angeles, I love your red-and-white

strip joints, your car dealerships, your Bob Hope Hall
of Patriotism. I love the graze of your fingernails,

your slow sparklers of palm trees, your buildings silver
and inscrutable, this constant haze as if a battle just

ended and your bloodied asking *Did we win? Did we win?*
Los Angeles, take off your sunglasses, roll your window

down; I like it when you let your hair whip into knots.
Los Angeles, even your salads glisten with fish and

though I know you dream of living forever, cancer
looks good on you. Los Angeles, I love the ways

you misunderstand me: *Jew* for *blue*, *erosion* for *ocean*.
I am rushing your Russians, I am cold for your gold.

When I tell you I'm married, all you say is *I do*.
When I say *Don't get hurt* you hear *Flirt harder*.

SONG FOR EL CERRITO

Tess Taylor

I USED TO HATE its working-class bungalows, grid planning,
power-lines sawing hillsides. It shamed me

the way my parents did for not making more money.
Now it looks like a Diebenkorn.

Now I want even the bad wood siding
in our living room, my mother's aging

books on modern Indian thought. Her tanpura
in sunlight. I want fox-weed in railroad trestles,

the endangered frogs in our gully.
I want a lemon tree.

On San Pablo, polyester collectibles, a folk-song store,
the "*All-Button Emporium: Open 10–4 Saturday's.*"

How did love lodge in these?
It might be how marigold light

forgives even the traffic islands.
December only yellows the gingkoes and reddens the maples.

A stream smells rich under our house.
For Christmas, my sister and I steal

persimmons from neighbors' yards.
Ten years on, I discover

how I keep falling in love here
among pickups and blackberry brambles.

Tonight it happened again:
We drove a bad car to the beach.

At dusk, a lone scrub pine—
clear, like a Japanese print. In the real sky, the moon

slid through clouds that were cinder-colored.

LAKEWOOD, CA

D. J. Waldie

1.

THE STREETS OF Lakewood occupy parts of three pages of the *Thomas Guide* to Los Angeles County. Lakewood is spread over so many pages as if to emphasize how uncentral to anything the city is or, perhaps, to show how marginal most of LA is.

Seen from one of the four freeways that frame Lakewood—from which you look down and off to one side at the city at seventy miles an hour—Lakewood is a generalization, part of the pattern between the points where you started and where you end.

In between, you are on *Thomas Guide* pages 765, 766, and 767.

2.

The truth is obvious when it rains. Lakewood is flat. So flat that the difference in elevation from the northwestern edge of the city's 9.5 square miles to the opposite southern edge is less than four feet.

When it rains—or even when an inattentive gardener runs a hose too long—dark water pools in gutters where the roots of the trees the city planted decades ago have bulged under the asphalt.

If geography is destiny, then Lakewood was destined for flatness. That isn't to say that flat is characterless. Flat is one of the reasons why it was possible to build 17,500 houses in less than thirty-three months beginning in 1950 and sell them for less than $12,000 each to regular Joes and their wives anxious to do what was expected of them, even when the expectations were not altogether clear. The new owners in 1950 typically had a high-school education. They were white. The husbands riveted planes together at the Douglas plant in Long Beach or monitored the cracking towers at the refineries in Carson and Wilmington, next to the Los Angeles harbor.

Flat put all of them, literally, on the same footing. If you plan to look down on your neighbors, you have to get a ladder.

3.

A lot goes on under Lakewood. Water flows in slow rivers through aquifers beneath the city, compressed between layers of rock and clay. Uplifts fold some of these layers into underground hills, although almost nothing mars the surface. Some of these hidden folds are broken, as if cut through by an immense knife. Offshoots of the biggest of these—the Newport-Inglewood Fault—run under central Lakewood, with at least some risk of a significant earthquake.

In the northeast corner of the city, where the uppermost aquifer can be only five or six feet from the surface, enough shaking will lead to liquefaction. The soil will become so water-saturated in an earthquake that the ground will go from a solid to a semi-liquid. In a prolonged yet only moderate earthquake, the foundations of some larger buildings will sink into the soupy ground. The houses probably won't. Built of stucco-over-chicken-wire nailed up to a sketchy wood frame, these houses will deform and crack, but they're so light. They will float on the liquefied soil, shelter even then.

4.

The thousands of houses of Lakewood were built quickly and cheaply because the land was flat. It was flat because all of it had been, over the preceding geologic era, a temporary bed of the Los Angeles and San Gabriel rivers. They were called "tramp" rivers in the 19th century. In a heavy rain, the rivers might shift their beds by as much as a mile. Or one river would braid a new course, loop it out to capture the flow of the other river, and take the combined flow of both to a new mouth at some indeterminate point on the coast until another season of rain rearranged the landscape.

Very little restrained these rivers from reclaiming their ghost beds until the mid-1960s, when the Army Corps of Engineers completed a system of storm drains, levees, and concrete walls across the center of Los Angeles County and through the flood-prone neighborhoods of Lakewood.

Our streets still flood, but they're supposed to. To prevent storm water from topping levees and spilling into the adjacent neighborhoods, the flood control system uses gates that close off the feeder channels whenever the main channel threatens to overflow. When the flap gates close, the storm runoff has to be temporarily stored somewhere. To do that, the flood control system exploits the memory of all the former riverbeds. The flood control system stores the threatening water on the streets of Lakewood.

Understandably, drivers complain. As a city official, I have to explain to them that the system floods the street around their marooned car to prevent the system's catastrophic failure in more distant, downstream neighborhoods, the home of someone you've never met.

5.

In 1961, the federal Office of Civil and Defense Mobilization published "The Family Fallout Shelter"—a homeowner's guide to atomic survival, printed on flimsy newsprint and costing 10 cents. The OCDM advised that a contractor-built shelter would cost about $1,500. That was 10 percent of the cost of a house in my suburb. If that was too much, dad could build a less adequate shelter in the basement, using plans in the OCDM guide, for about $500. Only no southern California tract house has a basement.

A pre-fab shelter dealer in Downey, across the street from the Rockwell Aviation plant on Lakewood Boulevard, sold fiberglass pods for burial in backyards. My parents never considered buying one, nor did any of our neighbors. Our mission, if the Cold War flashed into atomic brilliance, was to die with a minimum of fuss. Our lives were about other forms of survival, not the kind procured with a deer rifle behind the federally recommended 16 inches of cinder block and dirt.

6.

Fifty-five years have passed in a place that was supposed to be "as new as tomorrow" when it was thrown up on the lunar gray soil of 3,500 acres of former lima bean fields in a nondescript corner of Los Angeles County prone to flooding.

The tomorrows that arrived weren't exactly what the residents of "tomorrow's city" had been told to expect. By 1954, the experts all agreed what the future would look like. It would be sleek, edged in shining chrome, protectively enclosing, and traveling at supersonic speed. How a simple grid of streets, blue-collar lives, and boxy houses like mine fit into that picture was never made clear.

Some progressive city planners presumed Lakewood's streets of single-family homes would be replaced by rows of multi-story apartment buildings by 2000. Or Lakewood would be the sunlit slum that others predicted. Or Lakewood would be a treacherous no-man's-land revealing all the hollowness of suburbia. Or Lakewood would symbolize everything that was unearned about our lives. Some came to believe that all the mass-produced suburbs built since 1950 are, as one bitter critic put it in 1999, "the place where evil dwells."

7.

There are serious crimes in Lakewood, though less than you might think in a working-class city of 83,000 residents trying to make their way in a post-industrial economy. Hopeful, imperfect people live here. Their hope has sometimes led them to acts of courage and generosity. Their imperfections lead them sometimes to abuse and violence.

In the nightly news versions of our lives—in the stories that are only either heartwarming or horrific—their crimes are the final proof that no place is safe and every comfort is an illusion.

8.

A sense of place is Lakewood's essential quality.

Some of us think we have a sense of place at certain points of our lives, perhaps as a child running in the park; perhaps later in life in the company of neighbors. And then, for some of us, that feeling evaporates into disappointment. After all, we're well-trained consumers, TV remote control in hand and ready to switch channels or affections or hometowns whenever we're distracted. We run the risk, of course, of becoming so distracted that the connections between inner and outer landscapes break down entirely. In frustration and sorrow, some are ready to abandon the intimacy that had seemed so important. They turn away.

9.

We yearn for home—at least some of us do.

I live in the 957-square-foot house my parents bought on the edge of the "great flat" of the Los Angeles plain between the Los Angeles and San Gabriel rivers and not far from oil refineries and next to an aerospace plant, and I actually imagine that the place I live in is the sort of place that might inspire hope and loyalty.

My older brother was born into my house. My mother died from it. My father died in it.

10.

In 1950, everything in Lakewood was new and everything was incomplete.

Unfinished Lakewood was sold with a superb sales pitch. When you bought a little house you were supposed to be buying a piece of the big newness that the 20th century was going to deliver to everyone's doorstep, even yours in Lakewood. A van would pull up, and tomorrow would be rolled into your living room.

Some in Lakewood were hoodwinked by the pitch. Some were infuriated by it. Some followed it out of Lakewood and into one new paradise of the ordinary after another until one day they just stopped in Montana or Nevada or in internal exile behind the gates of a guarded subdivision and a lawn sign promising "immediate armed response."

Most of my neighbors, while accepting the optimistic premise of tomorrow's city, understood that some assembly of the future was still required.

11.

The grid of streets hasn't changed after fifty years. The small houses on small lots haven't changed in ways that matter. The flat landscape hasn't changed. What is different? Lakewood today is about as diverse as all of southern California is, meaning Lakewood is one of the more ethnically and racially diverse places in the nation.

Where once the demographic profile bulged at the bottom with so many young husbands and wives and tens of thousands of children under age 18, Lakewood residents today range from the very young to the very, very old. It's harder for community institutions to provide services across so wide a demographic—from single parent families to the frail, lonely elderly.

The demands on the social capital of the community have changed. Making up everything Lakewood lacks takes even more effort than it did in the 1950s. Today, it takes two jobs to make the mortgage payment, feed and clothe a family, and keep intact a sixty-year-old tract house. In Lakewood, those jobs are often held by immigrant families—like my anxious Latino, Filipino, Chinese, Lao, Korean, and Vietnamese neighbors. The experiences of my 1950s childhood can't be recreated for them, even if the landscape of my childhood hasn't changed all that much. But nostalgia isn't the subject of Lakewood. It's about falling in love.

12.

We all live on land we've wounded, land we've improved to our dissatisfaction. Yet we must be here or be nowhere and have nothing with which to make our lives together. How should one act knowing that making a home requires this? How should I regard my neighbors?

It's possible to answer with fury or neglect. It's possible to be so assured of privilege that contempt for a place like Lakewood is an answer. It's possible to be so rootless that the questions are merely ironic. It's possible to forget.

I don't think there is anything that I could erase from the story that I tell myself, including my failures, despite the appeal of amnesia. Everything I think of as ordinary and sacred is here.

PERMISSIONS

"Om" from *Sanctificum* by Chris Abani, 2008. © 2008 by Chris Abani. Reprinted with the permission of Copper Canyon Press, www.coppercanyonpress.org.

"The Motherhood Poems" by Beth Alvarado from *Necessary Fiction*, June 2009. © 2009 by Beth Alvarado. Reprinted by permission of the author.

Excerpt from "The Last Valley" from *West of the West* by Mark Arax, PublicAffairs, 2009. © 2009 by Mark Arax. Reprinted by permission of PublicAffairs, a member of Perseus Books Group.

"Love Poem for Los Angeles" from *I Was the Jukebox: Poems* by Sandra Beasley. © 2010 by Sandra Beasley. Used by permission of W. W. Norton & Company, Inc.

"The Guttering Promise of Public Education" by Gray Brechin. © 2009 by Gray Brechin. Reprinted by permission of the author.

Excerpt from *Blood Strangers* by Katherine A. Briccetti, Heyday, 2009. © 2009 by Katherine A. Briccetti. Reprinted by permission of Heyday.

"Fire, Storm, Oath, Apocalypse: The Writing of George Stewart" is an excerpt from "Natural Affinities" by Kenneth Brower from *California*, Summer 2010. © 2010 by Kenneth Brower. Reprinted by permission of the author.

"LAX" by Rafael Campo from *The Threepenny Review*, Fall 2009. © 2009 by Rafael Campo. Reprinted by permission of the author.

"Normal Time" from *Manhood for Amateurs* by Michael Chabon, Harper, 2009. © 2009 by Michael Chabon. Reprinted by permission of HarperCollins Publishers.

"The Architecture of Pelicans" by Carolyn Cooke from *The Redwood Coast Review*, Spring 2010. © 2010 by Carolyn Cooke. Reprinted by permission of the author.

"Labor War in the Mojave" by Mike Davis from *The Nation*, 29 March 2010. © 2010 by Mike Davis. Reprinted by permission of the author.

"Ask Me If I Care" from *A Visit from the Goon Squad* by Jennifer Egan, Knopf, 2010. © 2010 by Jennifer Egan. Used by permission of Alfred A. Knopf, a division of Random House, Inc.

Excerpt (chapter 7) from *The Adderall Diaries* by Stephen Elliott, Graywolf Press, 2009. © 2009 by Stephen Elliott. Reprinted with permission of Graywolf Press, Minneapolis, Minnesota, www.graywolfpress.org.

"Front Yard Fruit" by Ellen Estilai from *Alimentum—The Literature of Food*, Winter 2010. © 2010 by Ellen Estilai. Reprinted by permission of the author.

"California" (revised version) by Jennifer Elise Foerster from *Parthenon West Review*, 2010. © 2010 by Jennifer Elise Foerster. Reprinted by permission of the author.

"Boy Cleaning Trout" by Albert Garcia from *Cutthroat*, 2009. © 2009 by Albert Garcia. Reprinted by permission of the author.

"Father Close, Father Far" by Dagoberto Gilb from *The Threepenny Review*, Summer 2009. © 2009 by Dagoberto Gilb. Reprinted by permission of the author.

"Norma's Lines" from *Breathing, In Dust* by Tim Z. Hernandez, Texas Tech University Press, 2010. © 2010 by Tim Z. Hernandez. Reprinted by permission of Texas Tech University Press.

"Return to Devil's Gulch" by Darla Hillard from *Bay Nature*, July–September 2009. © 2009 by Darla Hillard. Reprinted by permission of the author.

"The Mere Mortal" by Louis B. Jones from *The Sun*, May 2010. © 2010 by Louis B. Jones. Reprinted by permission of the author.

"This Ain't San Francisco" from *Lilac Mines* by Cheryl Klein, Manic D Press, 2009. © 2009 by Cheryl Klein. Reprinted by permission of Manic D Press.

"How to Date a White Guy" by Naira Kuzmich from *Necessary Fiction*, May 2010. © 2010 by Naira Kuzmich. Reprinted by permission of the author.

"Afghanistan Can't Wash Away Vietnam" by Andrew Lam from *New America Media*, 2 December 2009. © 2009 by Andrew Lam. Reprinted by permission of the author.

"Virginia Lowry Aguilar" by Judith Lowry from *News from Native California*, Summer 2010. © 2010 by Judith Lowry. Reprinted by permission of the author.

"How to Choose a Soundtrack for a Bank Robbery Getaway" by Joe Loya from *McSweeney's, No. 33; The San Francisco Panorama*, 13 December 2009. © 2009 by Joe Loya. Reprinted by permission of the author.

"San Clemente" by Carol Muske-Dukes from *Alehouse*, 2010. © 2010 by Carol Muske-Dukes. Reprinted by permission of the author.

"Friendly Fire" (revised version) by Ruth Nolan from *Poemeleon*, Summer/Fall 2009. © 2009 by Ruth Nolan. Reprinted by permission of the author.

"Peregrine Beginnings" and "To Tame a Peregrine" from *Lift* by Rebecca K. O'Connor, Red Hen Press, 2009. © 2009 by Rebecca K. O'Connor. Reprinted by permission of Red Hen Press.

"The Tao of the Cow" from *4 Mules Blog Thoughts* (weblog) by Bruce Patterson, 22 February 2010. © 2010 by Bruce Patterson. Reprinted by permission of the author.

"John Wayne Loves Grandma Dot" from *Drift: Stories* by Victoria Patterson, Mariner, 2009. © 2009 by Victoria Patterson. Reprinted by permission of Houghton Mifflin Company. All rights reserved.

"Point Lobos Outlook" (revised version) by Jim Powell from *The Threepenny Review*, Winter 2010. © 2010 by Jim Powell. Reprinted by permission of the author.

"Watts Towers—a Soaring, Baffling Monument" by Robin Rauzi from the *Los Angeles Times*, 25 August 2009. © 2009 by Robin Rauzi. Reprinted by permission of the author.

"My Kitsch Is Their Cool" by Sandip Roy from ColorLines and *New America Media*, 1 August 2009 (a longer version was originally commissioned by The San Francisco Foundation and Grants for the Arts/San Francisco Hotel Tax Fund through support from The Wallace Foundation). © 2009 by Sandip Roy. Reprinted by permission of the author.

"George Blanda Ate My Homework" by Brad Schreiber from *Black Clock*, Spring/Summer 2010. © 2010 by Brad Schreiber. Reprinted by permission of the author.

"Our Golden State" (revised version) by Fred Setterberg from *Solstice Literary Magazine*, Summer 2010 (the piece is also an excerpt from the forthcoming *Lunch Bucket Paradise*, Heyday, 2011). © 2010 by Fred Setterberg. Reprinted by permission of Heyday.

"Bluebelly Lizard, or Western Fence Lizard" from *A California Bestiary* by Rebecca Solnit and Mona Caron, Heyday/Oakland Zoo, 2010. Text © 2010 by Rebecca Solnit. Reprinted by permission of the author.

"Dear Mr. Atende" by Susan Straight from *The Normal School*, Spring 2010. © 2010 by Susan Straight. Reprinted by permission of the author.

"A Flood Story" by Emily Taylor from *Crate*, Spring 2010. © 2010 by Emily Taylor. Reprinted by permission of the author.

"Song for El Cerrito" by Tess Taylor from *Swink*, 2008–2010. © 2008 by Tess Taylor. Reprinted by permission of the author.

"Jundee Ameriki" from *Phantom Noise* by Brian Turner, Alice James Books, 2010. © 2010 by Brian Turner. Reprinted with permission of Alice James Books, www.alicejamesbooks.org.

"Polaroids of Tom" (revised version) by Burlee Vang from *The Massachusetts Review*, 2010. © 2010 by Burlee Vang. Reprinted by permission of the author.

"Definitions of Imperial" from *Imperial* by William T. Vollmann, Viking, 2009. © 2009 by William T. Vollmann. Used by permission of Viking, a division of Penguin Group (USA), Inc.

"Lakewood, CA" (revised version) from *Where We Are* (weblog) by D. J. Waldie, 28 July 2010. © 2010 by D. J. Waldie. Reprinted by permission of the author.

"Turtle Island" from *I Hotel: A Novel* by Karen Tei Yamashita, Coffee House Press, 2010. © 2010 by Karen Tei Yamashita. Reprinted with permission of Coffee House Press, Minneapolis, Minnesota, www.coffeehousepress.org.

AUTHOR BIOGRAPHIES

CHRIS ABANI'S latest works include the novella *Song for Night* (Akashic, 2007) and poetry collections *Sanctificum* (Copper Canyon Press, 2010), *There Are No Names for Red* (Red Hen Press, 2010), and *Feed Me the Sun* (Peepal Tree Press, 2010). His website is www.chrisabani.com.

BETH ALVARADO is the author of *Not a Matter of Love* (New Rivers Press, 2006) and the fiction editor of *CUTTHROAT: A Journal of the Arts*. Her website is www.bethalvarado.com.

MARK ARAX, a journalist and writer, is author of *In My Father's Name* (Simon & Schuster, 1997), *The King of California* (PublicAffairs, 2003), and *West of the West* (PublicAffairs, 2009).

SANDRA BEASLEY is the author of the poetry collections *I Was the Jukebox* (W. W. Norton & Co., 2010) and *Theories of Falling* (New Issues Press, 2008). Her website is www.sandrabeasley.com.

GRAY BRECHIN is an historical geographer, founder and project scholar of California's Living New Deal Project, and author of *Imperial San Francisco* (University of California Press, 1999). His website is graybrechin.net.

KATHERINE A. BRICCETTI writes and edits fiction and nonfiction and is the author of the memoir *Blood Strangers* (Heyday, 2010). Her website is www.kathybriccetti.com.

KENNETH BROWER is a biographer and environmental writer, author of *Yosemite: An American Treasure* (National Geographic Society, 1990) and *The Starship and the Canoe* (Holt, Rinehart and Winston, 1978).

RAFAEL CAMPO teaches and practices medicine at Harvard Medical School and Beth Israel Deaconess Medical Center in Boston. His fifth book of poems is *The Enemy* (Duke University Press, 2007), and his website is www.rafaelcampo.com.

MICHAEL CHABON is a Pulitzer Prize–winning author whose novels include *The Amazing Adventures of Kavalier and Clay* (Random House, 2000) and *The Yiddish Policemen's Union* (HarperCollins, 2007). His website is www.michaelchabon.com.

CAROLYN COOKE is the author of *The Bostons* (Mariner, 2001) and the forthcoming *Daughters of the Revolution* (Knopf, 2011) and *Amor & Psycho* (Knopf, 2012).

MIKE DAVIS is an urban studies historian and prolific writer best known for *City of Quartz* (Verso, 1990) and *Ecology of Fear* (Metropolitan, 1998).

JENNIFER EGAN is the author of the National Book Award finalist *Look at Me* (Anchor, 2002), *The Keep* (Knopf, 2006) and most recently *A Visit from the Goon Squad* (Knopf, 2010). Her short stories have appeared in *The New Yorker, Harper's, Granta,* and *McSweeney's*. Her website is jennifer egan.com.

STEPHEN ELLIOTT is the author of the memoir *The Adderall Diaries* (Graywolf, 2009). Editor-in-chief of the online magazine *The Rumpus*, he hosts his own website at www.stephenelliott.com.

ELLEN ESTILAI is the former executive director of both the Riverside and the San Bernardino Arts Councils.

JENNIFER ELISE FOERSTER's writing has appeared in *Ploughshares*, *Passages North*, *Many Mountains Moving*, and *Drunken Boat*. She was a Wallace Stegner Fellow in poetry at Stanford University and is a member of the Muscogee (Creek) Nation of Oklahoma.

ALBERT GARCIA has published two books of poems, *Rainshadow* (Copper Beech Press, 1996) and *Skunk Talk* (Bear Star Press, 2005).

DAGOBERTO GILB's most recent book is the novel *The Flowers* (Grove Press, 2008). His website is at www.dagobertogilb.com.

TIM Z. HERNANDEZ, a poet, novelist, and performer, is author of *Breathing, In Dust* (Texas Tech University Press, 2010) and *Skin Tax* (Heyday, 2004).

DARLA HILLARD has written pieces for *National Geographic*, *Highlights for Children*, and *Summit*. She is the codirector of the Snow Leopard Conservancy in Sonoma.

LOUIS B. JONES's new novel, *Radiance,* will be published by Counterpoint in 2011. He is also the author of *Ordinary Money* (Viking, 1990), *Particles and Luck* (Pantheon, 1993), and *California's Over* (Pantheon, 1997). His website is www.louisbjones.com.

CHERYL KLEIN is the author of the novels *The Commuters* (San Diego City Works Press, 2006) and *Lilac Mines* (Manic D Press, 2009). Her website is www.cheryl-klein.com.

NAIRA KUZMICH is a graduate student of creative writing at Arizona State University.

ANDREW LAM is the author of *Perfume Dreams* (Heyday, 2005) and *East Eats West* (Heyday, 2010). He is also cofounder of *New America Media* and a commentator on NPR's *All Things Considered.*

JUDITH LOWRY is an artist, writer, and educator. *Home to Medicine Mountain* (Children's Book Press, 1998) features her illustrations, and her artwork was recently purchased for the permanent collection of the Smithsonian Institution's National Museum of the American Indian.

JOE LOYA is an essayist, playwright, and the author of the memoir *The Man Who Outgrew His Prison Cell: Confessions of a Bank Robber* (Rayo, 2004). His website is www.joeloya.com.

CAROL MUSKE-DUKES is the author of four novels—most recently *Channeling Mark Twain* (Random House, 2007)—and seven books of poetry, including the National Book Award finalist *Sparrow* (Random House, 2003). She is currently California's Poet Laureate. Her website is www.carolmuskedukes.com.

RUTH NOLAN's poetry has appeared in the *Pacific Review, Mosaic, Women's Studies Quarterly, San Diego Poetry Annual, Poemeleon,* and *Phantom Seed*. She is editor of *No Place for a Puritan: The Literature of California's Deserts* (Heyday, 2009). She blogs about life in the California desert at ruthnolan.blogspot.com.

REBECCA K. O'CONNOR is a writer, animal trainer, and conservationist. Her most recent publication is the memoir *Lift* (Red Hen Press, 2009). Her website is rebeccakoconnor.com.

BRUCE PATTERSON is the author of *Walking Tractor* (Heyday, 2008) and *Turned Round in My Boots* (Heyday, 2010). His website is 4mules.com.

VICTORIA PATTERSON's most recent book is the novel *This Vacant Paradise* (Counterpoint, 2011). She is also the author of *Drift* (Mariner, 2009), and her website is www.victoriapatterson.net.

JIM POWELL's latest book of poetry is *Substrate* (Pantheon, 2009). His translation of Sappho's poems was published by Oxford University Press in 2007.

ROBIN RAUZI is a writer, editor, and journalist and the founder of Get Rauzi Editorial Services, www.getrauzi.com.

SANDIP ROY is an editor with *New America Media* and host of "New America Now" on KALW 91.7 FM San Francisco.

BRAD SCHREIBER's books include a history of the L.A. Coroner, *Death in Paradise* (Running Press, 2001), the humor how-to *What Are You Laughing At?* (Michael Wiese Productions, 2003), a compendium of theatrical disasters,

Stop the Show! (Da Capo, 2006), and the biography *Becoming Jimi Hendrix* (Da Capo, 2010). His website is www.BradSchreiber.com.

FRED SETTERBERG is the author of *The Roads Taken* (University of Georgia Press, 1993) and coauthor of *Toxic Nation* (John Wiley & Sons, 1993), *Under the Dragon* (Heyday, 2007), and *Grassroots Philanthropy* (Heyday, 2008). His work has been featured in *The New York Times*, *The Nation*, *Utne Reader*, and *Columbia Journalism Review*. His *Lunch Bucket Paradise* will be published by Heyday in late 2011.

REBECCA SOLNIT is a writer and scholar whose most recent publications include *Infinite City* (University of California Press, 2010), *A California Bestiary* (Heyday, 2010), and *A Paradise Built in Hell* (Viking, 2009).

SUSAN STRAIGHT's seventh novel is *Take One Candle Light a Room* (Pantheon, 2010). *Highwire Moon* (Houghton Mifflin, 2001) was a National Book Award finalist.

EMILY TAYLOR's short stories have appeared in the *Green Mountains Review*, *The Baltimore Review*, *Inkwell*, and *Ecotone*. Her website is www.emilytaylor.org.

TESS TAYLOR is the author of *The Misremembered World* (Poetry Society of America, 2003). Her work has appeared in *Atlantic Monthly,* the *Boston Review, The Times Literary Supplement, Memorious,* and *The New Yorker.* Her website is www.tess-taylor.com.

BRIAN TURNER is the author of the poetry collections *Here, Bullet* (Alice James Books, 2005) and *Phantom Noise* (Alice James Books, 2010).

BURLEE VANG was the winner of Swan Scythe Press's 2010 poetry chapbook contest for *The Dead I Know* (2010), his first publication. His writing has appeared in *Ploughshares*, *North American Review*, *Alaska Quarterly Review*, and *Massachusetts Review*. His website is burleevang.com.

WILLIAM T. VOLLMANN's National Book Award–winning novel is *Europe Central* (Viking, 2005). *Kissing the Mask* (Ecco, 2010), his most recent work, is a nonfiction exploration of Japanese Noh theater.

D. J. WALDIE is the author of *Holy Land* (W. W. Norton & Co., 1996) and *Where We Are Now* (Angel City Press, 2004). His blog about Los Angeles and its suburbs is housed at www.kcet.org/socal/voices/where-we-are.

KAREN TEI YAMASHITA is a novelist whose *I Hotel* (Coffee House Press, 2010) was a finalist for the 2010 National Book Award.

ABOUT THE EDITOR

GAYLE WATTAWA, thoroughly addicted to contemporary literature, always carries with her a well-worn public library card and a relentless weakness for book reviews, literary journals, and lit news blogs. She is the editor of *Inlandia: A Literary Journey through California's Inland Empire*, and she has supervised the assemblage of a half-dozen other literary anthologies as Heyday's acquisitions editor.

ABOUT THE SERIES

"NEW CALIFORNIA WRITING" is an annual literary anthology that collects fresh and thought-provoking writing about California that has been published in the previous year, with a special emphasis on Californian writers, publications, and publishers.

Heyday welcomes and encourages your suggestions. For more information about what we are looking for and how to submit material, please visit http://www.heydaybooks.com/newcaliforniawriting.html.

HEYDAY

into California

About Heyday

Heyday is an independent, nonprofit publisher and unique cultural institution. We promote widespread awareness and celebration of California's many cultures, landscapes, and boundary-breaking ideas. Through our well-crafted books, public events, and innovative outreach programs we are building a vibrant community of readers, writers, and thinkers.

Thank You

It takes the collective effort of many to create a thriving literary culture. We are thankful to all the thoughtful people we have the privilege to engage with. Cheers to our writers, artists, editors, storytellers, designers, printers, bookstores, critics, cultural organizations, readers, and book lovers everywhere!

We are especially grateful for the generous funding we've received for our publications and programs during the past year from foundations and hundreds of individual donors. Major supporters include:

Anonymous; James Baechle; Bay Tree Fund; B.C.W. Trust III; S. D. Bechtel, Jr. Foundation; Barbara Jean and Fred Berensmeier; Berkeley Civic Arts Program and Civic Arts Commission; Joan Berman; Peter and Mimi Buckley; Lewis and Sheana Butler; California Council for the Humanities; California Indian Heritage Center Foundation; California State Library; California Wildlife Foundation/California Oak Foundation; Keith Campbell Foundation; Candelaria Foundation; John and Nancy Cassidy Family Foundation, through Silicon Valley Community Foundation; The Christensen Fund; Compton Foundation; Lawrence Crooks; Nik Dehejia; George and Kathleen Diskant; Donald and Janice Elliott, in honor of David Elliott, through Silicon Valley Community Foundation; Federated Indians of Graton Rancheria; Mark and Tracy Ferron; Furthur Foundation; The Fred Gellert Family Foundation; Wallace Alexander Gerbode Foundation; Wanda Lee Graves and Stephen Duscha; Walter & Elise Haas Fund; Coke and James Hallowell; Carla Hills; Sandra and Chuck Hobson; James Irvine Foundation; JiJi Foundation; Marty and Pamela Krasney; Guy Lampard and Suzanne Badenhoop; LEF Foundation; Judy McAfee; Michael McCone; Joyce Milligan; Moore Family Foundation; National Endowment for the Arts; National Park Service; Theresa Park; Pease Family Fund, in honor of Bruce Kelley; The Philanthropic Collaborative; PhotoWings; Resources Legacy Fund; Alan Rosenus; Rosie the Riveter/WWII Home Front NHP; The San Francisco Foundation; San Manuel Band of Mission Indians; Savory Thymes; Hans Schoepflin; Contee and Maggie Seely; Stanley Smith Horticultural Trust; William Somerville; Stone Soup Fresno; James B. Swinerton; Swinerton Family Fund; Thendara Foundation; Tides Foundation; TomKat Charitable Trust; Lisa Van Cleef and Mark Gunson; Whole Systems Foundation; John Wiley & Sons; Peter Booth Wiley and Valerie Barth; Dean Witter Foundation; and Yocha Dehe Wintun Nation.

Getting Involved

To learn more about our publications, events, membership club, and other ways you can participate, please visit www.heydaybooks.com.